Devils in the Details

Devils in the Details

embracing modern Devil's Advocacy to help
reduce risk and manage uncertainty

By Robert Koshinskie

Copyright © 2020 by Robert Koshinskie
All rights reserved.

ISBN 9798623851925
Library of Congress Control Number: 2020910357

Publisher's Cataloging-in-Publication Data

Names: Koshinskie, Robert, author.
Title: Devils in the Details : embracing modern devil's advocacy to help reduce risk and manage uncertainty / Robert Koshinskie.
Description: Burlington, NC : Ringbolt Press, 2020.
Identifiers: LCCN 2020910357 (print) | ISBN 9798623851925 (paperback)
Subjects: LCSH: Risk management. | Project management. | Business. | Perception. | Thought and thinking. | BISAC: BUSINESS & ECONOMICS / General.
Classification: LCC HD61 .K67 2020 (print) | LCC HD61 (ebook) | DDC 658.15/5--dc23.

Image of playing cards in Chapter 3 by Kati, Niedersachsen Deutschland. Photograph of the businesswoman in Chapter 2 by Igor Link, Offenbach am Main, Germany. Other photographs and backgrounds by Pexels, Pixabay.com. All other diagrams, tables, and images are copyright by the author, including the trademarked devil's advocate in a tug of war icon on the front cover.

Dedication

To Ann,
mother to me and my two brothers,
who hoped for
a physician, a lawyer, and a priest,
but who loves us just the same.

TABLE OF CONTENTS

INTRODUCTION 1

CHAPTER 1: DO YOU THINK THAT'S AIR YOU'RE BREATHING? 23
    THE THINKING SKILLS GAP 25
    OUR MENTAL MODELS AND THE REAL WORLD 31

CHAPTER 2: ARE YOU CONTROLLING WHAT YOU CAN? 50
    TYPES OF THINKING 51
    REAL ARGUMENTS 57
    NOTABLE BIASES AND FALLACIES 65

CHAPTER 3: ARE YOU RECOGNIZING WHAT'S BEYOND YOUR CONTROL? 87
    BLACK SWAN EVENTS 88
    THE IMPACT OF LUCK 91
    RISK AND UNCERTAINTY 97

CHAPTER 4: ARE YOU SURE THAT'S THE RIGHT TOOL? 100
    SKETCHES AND GRAPHS 101
    WEIGHTED LISTS 104
    FINANCIAL RETURNS 123
    CAUSAL LOOP DIAGRAMS 132
    STOCK AND FLOW SIMULATIONS 138
    MONTE CARLO SIMULATION 143
    GROUP DECISION-MAKING 166

CHAPTER 5: WELCOME TO WONDERLAND 177
    SUGGESTED GUIDANCE 178
    CLOSING THOUGHTS 186

SUGGESTED READING & RESOURCES 188

APPENDIX A: GENERIC DECISION-MAKING PROCESS 191

APPENDIX B: VERDE VS. THÉRÈSE 195

APPENDIX C: THE TOO FLEET-FOOTED MERCURY 198

APPENDIX D: THE CREATION OF MODERN MYTHOLOGY 201

APPENDIX E: LITTLE GREEN ARMY WO(MEN) 203

ABOUT THE AUTHOR 206

ENDNOTES 207

Acknowledgments

I would not have written this book were it not for a decision-making course that I created, and I would not have created that course if it were not for Holly Sullenger, Ph.D. In the preface of this book, I tell the story of my chance meeting with Holly. Thanks also go to the following individuals who graciously gave their time to read evolving drafts of the book and to offer their frank critique and suggestions.

David Johnson and Linda Hurwitz. David is the former president of and current senior advisor to Laerdal Medical Corporation, and Linda is an entrepreneur, advisor, and coach to CEOs and business owners. Both David and Linda offered thoughtful comments from the perspective of the C Suite. Their critiques helped me identify what content would matter to readers in executive roles and to their reports – insight which also led to the subtitle for this book.

Gene Bellinger, an organizational theorist known for his work in systems thinking and knowledge management. Gene was an early mentor in my Systems Thinking education and I appreciate his support and feedback which helped confirm that my approach was on solid ground.

Thomas Dyar and Tracie Coletto. Tom is a specialist in machine learning and artificial intelligence and former Manager for External Innovation & Data Science at Becton Dickinson, and Tracie is a former Senior Field Marketing Manager for Philips Healthcare. Tom and Tracie represent those very experienced managers of teams for whom I hope this book will be particularly useful.

Thomas Hogan, entrepreneur, former Chief Financial Officer, and General Manager. Tom is also a long-time friend and confidant who patiently listened to my challenges during the writing of this book and provided me a valuable sounding board.

Kristan Wheaton who kindly provided the Foreword. An attorney and educator who trains intelligence analysts and strategists, Kristan in many ways embodies the ideal modern Devil's Advocate. I'm confident that educators like Kristan and their students will extend the long line of Devil's Advocates well into the future.

Last and certainly not least, special thanks to my wife, Diane. A former critical care nurse and current clinical research nurse coordinator, Diane has a special ability to balance encouragement and frank critique. I thank her for her unwavering support over our many years together as I pursued my various projects - and for calling *codswallop* on me when I needed it most!

Foreword

I first met Bob Koshinskie when I was a Professor of Intelligence Studies at Mercyhurst University. I was seeking assistance with a project that my students were conducting, and Bob was quick to offer his help. Since that initial contact, we've kept in touch, sharing information and thoughts on a variety of topics related to critical thinking and analysis. So, when Bob asked me to comment on a few items in a draft of this book, I was happy to do so. Although I tried to stick to Bob's specific questions, his draft was so well-written and accessible that I just kept reading. The comments that I share below are my own and are not an endorsement by the United States Government or of the US Army War College where I am currently Professor of Strategic Futures.

A core issue that this book addresses is the power of conformity and the willingness of our minds to adopt the majority view despite clear evidence to the contrary. One of the best-known examples of this troubling behavior was demonstrated in the 1950s by social psychologist, Solomon Asch. Asch's experiments revealed how subjects easily and accurately matched a series of simple lines by their length when tested individually but were swayed when tested in groups where Asch's accomplices intentionally gave wrong answers. On average, the test subjects conformed to the group and gave wrong answers as well 32% of the time with 5% of the test subjects adopting the majority view on every instance!

Conformity is just one of several hundred biases that scientists have identified in the soft tissue between our ears. These biases are the result of evolutionary pressure and may well have been helpful in the savannas of eastern Africa at the dawn of mankind. In today's complex world, however, our cognitive biases can often cause systematic errors in judgment and poor outcomes. This book is a laudable effort to correct sloppy thinking, and it starts with an age-old solution, Devil's Advocacy.

The original Devil's Advocates were individuals skilled in legal methodology who were tasked by the Catholic Church to argue against the canonization of popular candidates. The Church leadership intended their Devil's Advocates to ensure that someone who everybody believed was worthy of sainthood truly met the standards for sainthood. Bob's core premise is that the widespread practice of modern secular Devil's Advocacy can offer significant benefits in our personal and business lives. Indeed, Bob makes a strong case in the early chapters that, if we are ever to overcome our deep-seated biases, then we must collect additional and disconfirming evidence, form and evaluate alternative hypotheses, and regularly look at our problems from diverse and new viewpoints.

More than just making a case for better thinking, Bob has also given us tools to do so, including methods and techniques from a variety of disciplines that have served him well over a career of addressing real-world problems. It was this methods section that first caught my eye because I have spent the better part of a lifetime as an instructor, advisor, author, and speaker studying and communicating about how to think. I was surprised, then, to see so many new or less familiar methods described in the book. Moreover, each section was clearly highlighted with a variety of helpful icons, warnings, and illustrations.

In both clarity and concision, *Devils in the Details* is a worthwhile addition to the library of anyone who is responsible for crucial decision-making. You will find, as I did, an accessible and almost conversational book that is filled with useful anecdotes, methods, and deep insights.

Kristan J. Wheaton, JD
Professor of Strategic Futures, US Army War College
Author of *The Warning Solution: Intelligent Analysis in the Age of Information Overload* and recipient of the CIA Seal Medallion

Preface

The book you hold is the result of a chance meeting I had in September of 2018 while attending a networking event at the North Carolina State University (NCSU) McKimmon Center in Raleigh, NC. It was there that I met Dr. Holly Sullenger, a well-known corporate trainer, and speaker who at the time was the Assistant Director for NCSU Technology Training Solutions.

Holly and I talked about our backgrounds and our mutual interests in education and training, including the widely acknowledged need for improved critical thinking skills. We agreed that businesses regularly lament the lack of critical thinking skills in their hiring candidates and employees who are tasked to make reasoned decisions in an increasingly complex world. We also agreed that adult learners could benefit from an introduction to basic critical-thinking and decision-making.

I told Holly about my collection of critical-thinking resources that I had gathered up over the years, from textbooks and training certificates to software simulation tools. I had used these materials for presentations at events like the local chapter of the International Institute of Business Analysis (IIBA), the annual ProductCamp RTP conference, and addressing graduate-level students at The Joint School of Nanoscience and Nanoengineering (JSNN). These events, however, provided only enough time for me to lightly cover just one or two concepts.

As our conversation grew to a close, Holly offered me the opportunity to conduct a "practice teach" for her and her staff – a short PowerPoint presentation in which I would outline the topics for a critical thinking class. I returned a couple of weeks later and delivered my presentation after which Holly asked if I would create and teach the class that I had just proposed. I accepted Holly's challenge and in January 2019 *Improve Your Decision-Making Skills* went live.

As I was developing the class, I followed author James Thurber's advice, "It is better to know some of the questions than all of the answers." Rather than presenting a list of prescriptive processes and dubious ironclad solutions, I wanted the course to be an informal discussion that would encourage open, thoughtful debate and reflect the uncertainty of real-world decision-making.

Recognizing that the attendees would have a wide range of experience and training, I designed the course to build upon simple ideas and analogies to more advanced concepts. I've written this book as a primer that is intended to convey the casual tone and open exploration of the live course.

I've provided references in the endnotes and suggested resources so you can explore more deeply those topics that catch your interest. Although this book is intended for business professionals from the CEO to the newly minted manager, it will also be of interest to anyone with a natural curiosity from college-level students to adult learners.

In search of a title for this book, I reflected on Devil's Advocates of long ago. Tasked to build and present a case in opposition to a candidate for sainthood, Devil's Advocates were placed into battle against popular opinion - and often at odds with powerful people who could simply ignore the Advocate's findings and recommendations. Nonetheless, these original Devil's Advocates conscientiously pressed ahead to help ensure that claims were being properly vetted before important decisions were made.

This book calls for the rise of the modern secular Devil's Advocate who will help better assess judgments and decisions and thereby reduce risk and manage uncertainty. Modern Devil's Advocates can challenge not only business cases but the dubious assertions of our politicians, misleading charlatan claims, and the minions of malicious misinformation. Modern Devil's Advocacy can also help us thoughtfully question our own assumptions, beliefs, and judgments.

Robert Koshinskie

INTRODUCTION

The goal of this book is to encourage more people to embrace the role of a modern Devil's Advocate and thereby involve more of these particular "*devils* in the details" of important daily decision-making. I hope to convince you that the practice of modern Devil's Advocacy can help reduce risk and manage uncertainty in our businesses, communities, and personal lives. My proposition is based on various perspectives that I explore in this book, including two key points. First, that thinking skills and informed skepticism contribute to better performance and outcomes. Second, that thinking skills and informed skepticism can be developed and effectively applied through the practice of Devil's Advocacy.

Devil's Advocacy is typically associated with an individual who challenges the majority view, but the practice also offers a means to critically assess our own beliefs and judgments and to work with other Devil's Advocates. Modern Devil's Advocacy provides an open-ended and flexible form of inquiry and analysis that can be useful in the business setting. Further, practically anyone from the CEO to the new hire can become a modern Devil's Advocate if they have the desire to do so.

Devil's Advocacy helps ensure that beliefs, assumptions, and claims are reasonably challenged and substantiated. We'll see how such challenges are neither cynical nor pessimistic, but intentionally counterbalancing – moderating both unfounded enthusiasm and pointless gloominess. Modern Devil's Advocates are tasked to bridge the simplified and ideal world that exists in our minds and the complex physical world in which we live and work.

The perspectives I offer throughout this book include my decades-long career, mostly in the regulated medical device industry. Over those years I have founded and worked in startups and have held senior management positions in international market leaders. Along the way I have been trained as a PRINCE2 Practitioner and in other proprietary processes,

INTRODUCTION

some of which I helped develop and manage.[1] I currently provide business consulting services, mentor participants in the National Science Foundation (NSF) I-Corps Program, and teach a class that I created on decision-making.[2] These and other experiences afford me a unique and broad view of how people and companies struggle with daily decision-making and execution of plans, and a perspective about how Devil's Advocacy can be beneficial to those activities.

This book introduces foundational concepts and methods that a modern Devil's Advocate can use in daily practice. As you read the material ahead you may begin to feel unsure about the validity of your own strongly held beliefs, and that doubt would be a good sign. Hesitation to respond automatically to questions with simple and widely accepted answers is a beneficial and useful behavior for a modern Devil's Advocate.

The concepts discussed in this book require little to no background in business, science, or any other domain of expertise. Written with the adult learner in mind, this book is primarily intended for business professionals who are responsible for decision-making and execution. However, this book will also be of interest to any inquisitive reader, including college-aged adults who are about to venture into the waiting world and its many thorny problems. I've organized this book into chapters as follows.

- **Chapter 1:** We will look at the thinking skills gap and how that gap is impacting our personal and work lives. We will consider the difference between how we believe that things work and how we attempt to use those beliefs in the real world through formal processes. We will examine different kinds of processes and why even so-called best practices should not be shielded from thoughtful challenges.
- **Chapter 2:** We will explore several areas over which we have control, including the different kinds of thinking that we can apply to Devil's Advocacy. We will see how real arguments can be used to express our assumptions and conclusions and to examine the assumptions and conclusions that others make. We will also look at examples of key bias and fallacy that we need to acknowledge and manage so they do not cloud our thinking.
- **Chapter 3**: We will examine conditions over which we may have little or no control, including unexpected disruption, uncertainty, and luck.

We will consider how to integrate these conditions into our thinking and analyses.
- **Chapter 4:** We will explore a variety of tools that can be helpful, including how to capture and document what we believe are cause-and-effect relationships, and how to test those relationships in dynamic simulations. We will also examine methods for group decision-making and how teams can make decisions in a timely fashion even in the absence of unanimous agreement.
- **Chapter 5**: We put the prior chapters into perspective and conclude with some guidance on how to proceed on the path of a modern Devil's Advocate and final thoughts based on my experience.

> ⏱ A stopwatch symbol identifies comments that are outside of but related to the main discussion.

> 💡 A lightbulb symbol offers a pause to think critically about the material just presented and consider if and how it may be put to practical use.

▶ DETOUR ▶

Banners like the ones above and below indicate the beginning and end of more detailed discussions. If you find these discussions particularly challenging, then you can bypass these areas and still benefit from this book. I'm confident, however, that you will glean useful information between these banners even if you need to proceed a bit more slowly or read several times.

END DETOUR

> ⏱ Throughout the book I use gender-based pronouns (he, she, his, hers) randomly so the content is inclusive – no other meaning should be attributed to the use of these pronouns.

Introduction

A Very Brief History of Devil's Advocacy

Given the theme of this book, I want to provide some background on the origin of Devil's Advocacy, a very old idea that serves as a model for the modern Devil's Advocacy discussed in this book.

The concept of Devil's Advocacy originated in the Roman Catholic Church around 1381 AD and was institutionalized as a Church practice a couple of hundred years later.[3] The purpose of this function was to investigate popular candidates for whom sainthood was proposed. The men who were tasked to conduct these investigations were officially designated *Promotor of the Faith*. Working **against** a person's sainthood, however, they were commonly referred to as the *Devil's Advocate*.

The role of the original Devil's Advocate emerged from a decision by the Church leadership to have more uniform standards for sainthood. Through such standards, all candidates would be judged by the same set of examination rules rather than by the whims of individual parish leaders. This move toward a laws-based approach to saint-making was likewise reflected in the creation of the Courts of the Inquisition and is why both endeavors shared the structure of a trial (i.e. witnesses, depositions, evidence).[4] An incentive for the Church's decision to take a more critical review of saint-making in the 1630s may have also been due, in part, to disparagements by Protestant reformers.[5]

By the 20th Century, the duties of the Devil's Advocate included the prevention of any "rash decisions concerning miracles or virtues of the candidates" and "to suggest natural explanations for alleged miracles, and even to bring forward human and selfish motives for deeds that have been accounted heroic virtues".[6] Similarly, the modern Devil's Advocate contribution is to challenge the veracity of claims, identify the influence of bias and fallacy on decisions, and thereby help arrive at better decisions (absent the need for miraculous claims).

You may find it interesting that the Church has essentially eliminated the role of the Devil's Advocate, a decision that has opened the floodgates to modern saint-making. According to *US Catholic Magazine*,

"Revisions to the canonization process in 1983 ensured we will see more saints in the future...John Paul II canonized more saints than the popes from the previous 500 years combined."[7]

Shifting from the original, religious intent of Devil's Advocacy to the modern secular form discussed in this book, we can look to a concise definition provided by former CIA intelligence analysts Richards Heuer and Randolph Pherson in their book, *Structured Analytic Techniques for Intelligence Analysis*,

"A process for critiquing a proposed analytic judgement, plan, or decision, usually by a single analyst not previously involved in the deliberations that led to the proposed judgment, plan or decision...The Devil's Advocate is charged with challenging the proposed judgment by building the strongest possible case against it. There is no prescribed procedure."[8]

The practice of Devil's Advocacy serves as the foundation for both *Red Hat Analysis* and *Red Team Analysis*.[9] In the intelligence community, practitioners of these forms of Devil's Advocacy attempt to get inside the mind of an adversary (i.e. the Blue Team). By adopting the mindset of their opponents, intelligence analysts hope to understand their adversaries' view of the world and thereby avoid the natural human inclination to assume that everyone sees the world in the same way. Devil's Advocacy practice can provide insight that uncovers underlying weaknesses in assumptions and judgments that underpin a widely held position.

The Devil's Advocacy method is one of over forty-five analytic techniques that Heuer and Pherson include in their book. Certainly, the modern Devil's Advocate should explore, learn, and apply a variety of techniques that are appropriate and useful for different situations. I've decided to focus on Devil's Advocacy in this book rather than the many other methods for two main reasons.

First, Devil's Advocacy requires thinking skills and an inquisitive perspective, both of which are foundational behaviors in all analytic techniques. Second, Devil's Advocacy typically involves a single analyst who can make a difference through their actions rather than assuming that others will take responsibility and act. This "inhibiting influence" that others have on our inclination to act (i.e. the *Bystander Effect*) is a common phenomenon that can be particularly troubling in the business setting as we'll discuss further ahead.[10,11]

Devil's Advocacy embodies the habits of a good analytic thinker as itemized by Heuer and Pherson,

1. Know when to challenge key assumptions – usually far more often than you think, according to Heuer and Pherson

2. Consider alternative explanations or hypotheses for all events (see Bias and Fallacy in Chapter 2)

3. Look for inconsistent data that provides sufficient justification to quickly discard a candidate hypothesis

4. Focus on the key drivers that best explain what has occurred or what is about to happen (see Causal Loop Diagrams in Chapter 4)

5. Anticipate the customers' needs and understand the overarching context within which the analysis is being done (see Chapter 5 guidance)

I propose that through the promotion of modern Devil's Advocacy we can create more individuals who are better prepared and willing to participate in many forms of analytic techniques, thereby reducing risk and managing uncertainty.

INTRODUCTION

Why Devil's Advocacy Matters Today

No doubt you've noticed how a majority opinion can lead to very impressive, although sometimes perplexing, outcomes. Popularity can propel an otherwise unremarkable person into a high office or turn a social network blogger into a wealthy and influential celebrity. Such majority support can lead to unwanted and negative outcomes, but Life goes on.[12,13] Perhaps the popular majority opinion is generally a good thing that ought to be protected from examination by Devil's Advocacy? Perhaps not.

Consider the case of the Theranos company whose youthful founder, Elizabeth Holmes, attracted broad support for her venture with a baritone-voiced visionary persona that she created. Holmes successfully gained initial supporters and raised funding for Theranos, reinforcing a foundation of credibility that engaged high-profile supporters and more funding.

Holmes' roster of investors contained many highly regarded individuals, including "Oracle founder Larry Ellison, venture capital firm Draper Fisher Jurvetson, now Secretary of Education Betsy DeVos and media mogul Rupert Murdoch."[14] The din from the growing number of fervent Holmes' supporters and the escalating valuation of Theranos seemed to drown out reasoned dissent offered by several notable parties, including[15]

- Dr. Phyllis Gardner, a Stanford Medical School professor who expressed skepticism about Holmes concept on technical grounds
- Theranos Chief Financial Officer Henry Mosley who "was fired after questioning the reliability of its technology and the honesty of the company"
- The chief medical officer of Safeway who questioned "discrepancies in the test results" which didn't dissuade Safeway's CEO
- Lieutenant Colonel David Shoemaker who "raised concerns about Theranos' regulatory strategy to the FDA" and reportedly revised his position after "battling James Mattis, who was on the Theranos board"[16]

The arc of the Theranos journey peaked at a $9 billion valuation and collapsed under the weight of criminal investigations and indictments of Holmes and her co-founder. If we were seeking an example of a case where

INTRODUCTION

dissenting voices should have been heeded, then Theranos is such an example.

Similar consolidation of decision-making is going on today, the results of which won't be known for some time. For example, the *Wall Street Journal*[17] has noted that Facebook CEO, Mark Zuckerberg, tends to create an environment that discounts dissent and *The New York Times* reported that Zuckerberg has built a board of directors that favors his decisions,

> "The board isn't exactly a check on his power. Last year, Kenneth Chenault, the former chief executive of American Express, suggested creating an independent committee to scrutinize the company's challenges and pose the sort of probing questions the board wasn't used to being asked…Other board disagreements, specifically around political advertising and the spread of misinformation, always ended with Mr. Zuckerberg's point of view winning out."[18]

I'm not comparing Zuckerberg's intentions and actions to those of Holmes, but perhaps there is good reason to be concerned about the consolidation of decision-making, lack of transparency, and absence of strong dissent?

Modern Devil's Advocacy may also offer benefits outside of the business domain, particularly as a *tonic* against widely believed misinformation. For example, as I was writing this book, unfounded claims about COVID-19 were spreading as quickly as the pandemic. The following are the more popular allegations that were circulating on the internet.[19]

- It is a **bioweapon** that was inadvertently or intentionally unleashed – this claim has reportedly been linked to "former Iranian president Mahmoud Ahmadinejad, Chinese Foreign Ministry spokesman Lijian Zhao, and US Sen. Tom Cotton of Arkansas"[20]
- A **patented virus** as part of a plot involving Microsoft® founder, Bill Gates – reportedly advanced by conspiracy theorists who also believe that the United States military put Donald Trump into the White House to save the country from pedophilic Satanists[21]

- **Corona® brand of beer** has something to do with the virus – reportedly "16% of beer drinking Americans were confused about whether Corona beer is related to the coronavirus"[22,23]
- Certain **"colloidal silver solutions"** are effective cures for the virus, including a tonic promoted by the disgraced televangelist, Jim Bakker,[24] and a "nanosilver toothpaste" promoted by the infamous conspiracy theorist, Alex Jones[25]

Such bizarre beliefs aren't uncommon and can be difficult to rectify, especially in highly charged situations. During the 2015 and 2016 Zika epidemic in Brazil, even the best efforts to correct misinformation led to counterintuitive results as investigators reported,

> "…efforts to counter misperceptions about diseases during epidemics and outbreaks may not always be effective. We find that corrective information not only fails to reduce targeted Zika misperceptions but also reduces the accuracy of other beliefs about the disease."[26]

The suggestion that active attempts to correct erroneous information may fail is particularly troubling when you consider that little to no such corrective action is taken to confirm the countless claims made daily on social networks. One recent survey conducted by Harris Poll,[27] for example, revealed how easily misinformation can be spread through social networks, noting that,

- 86% of people don't fact check the news they read on social media
- 79% of Americans on social media said they trust at least some of the content shared by friends
- When Americans read a news article shared by a friend on social media, the most common action they took was to then share it themselves (32%). That's an important point because it highlights just how easily news that may be erroneous, misleading, inaccurate, or entirely made up can spread.

Even more troubling, it appears as though when fact-checking **is** provided it may do little to change the opinion of those who are misinformed and might harden their strongly held beliefs. Researchers at *The Brookings*

INTRODUCTION

Institution[28] looked at the "political informedness" of participants in four categories,

1. **Informed**: those who know a fact and are confident in their knowledge
2. **Uninformed**: those who know that they don't know a fact
3. **Misinformed**: those who believe they know a fact but are mistaken
4. **Ambiguously Informed**: those who acknowledge that they are just guessing

After being asked a series of questions, the participants were shown the related fact checks. The fact checks confirmed for the Informed what they already knew and benefitted the Uninformed, Misinformed, and Ambiguously Informed. However, the Misinformed benefitted least from the fact check and were more likely to continue to choose the wrong answer even after reading the fact check. Further, although a story clearly labeled as a fact check helped readers get the facts right, the fact check label also led people "to become more likely to report that the fact-check was biased."

As examples like those above indicate, it seems that people may be content or predisposed to simply accept and share information that is misleading or false, even when we have good reason to believe that the information is misleading or false. This counterintuitive behavior opens wide a door for those who wish to spread misleading and false information as a kind of prank or to advance an agenda. Imagine, however, if more individuals embraced the behaviors of a modern Devil's Advocate and took the initiative to employ informed skepticism and a little critical thinking.

I'm hopeful that a larger presence of modern Devil's Advocates in society can help serve as an effective barrier against the flood of misinformation that spills out of our connected devices every day. Perhaps the behaviors of individual modern Devil's Advocates can also influence others to rely upon evidence-based claims and to refute divisive drivel?[29]

Don't Crowds Make Better Decisions?

You may be familiar with the claim that estimates made by a large group of people offer results that are more accurate than those of experts? This view, made popular by the book *The Wisdom of Crowds*,[30] traces back to an article by statistician Francis Galton in the March 1907 publication of *Nature*. Galton's article was entitled *Vox Populi* which is Latin for the "voice of the people" - a term that is commonly used to mean "the opinion of the majority of the people".

In his article, Galton describes a "weight-judging competition" held at an annual stock and poultry exhibition. Participants secretly marked on ballots their guess for the actual "dressed" weight of a (presumably) live ox – the weight after the "hide, head, feet, and gut are removed".[31] Galton noted that,

> "The competitors included butchers and farmers, some of whom were highly expert in judging the weight of cattle; others were probably guided by such information as they might pick up, and by their own fancies. The average competitor was probably as well fitted for making a just estimate of the dressed weight of the ox, as an average voter is of judging the merits of most political issues on which he votes, and the variety among the voters to judge justly was probably much the same in either case."[32]

If Galton's, subjective estimate of the crowd composition was correct, then you might reasonably expect that the weight estimates for the ox were not particularly influenced by expertise as would be the case if the crowd was made up solely of butchers, farmers, and others with some experience and skill in estimating the weight of livestock.[33] So how well did the crowd do in estimating the dressed weight of the ox?

After plotting out the weight guesses from 787 ballots, Galton determined that the "middlemost estimate" (i.e. the median) was 1,207 pounds versus the actual weight of the ox at 1,198 pounds (a bit high by 9 lb., or 0.8 percent the actual weight). Galton noted that the result was "more creditable to the trustworthiness of a democratic judgment than might have been expected."

INTRODUCTION

As with many popular *memes*, certain claims based on the Galton article are stated as fact, however, the truth is more nuanced. For example, some have suggested that "Galton found evidence that the median estimate of a group can be more accurate than estimates of experts."[34] In fact, Galton did not compare a subset of livestock expert estimates against the estimates of the other participants, did not report if the winners of the competition were experts, and did not make the specific assertion that any group estimate can beat any expert estimate.

Galton's very brief article has been revisited by researchers and evidence has been offered to support the idea that group estimations can result in remarkably accurate results. There appears, however, to be a set of four required conditions to achieve accurate crowd estimates.

1. Diversity of expertise (not everyone in the group is a butcher, physician, psychiatrist, etc.)
2. Diversity of opinion (not everyone holds the same perspective)
3. Estimates are not influenced by the group (individual estimates are not shared with other group members)
4. Information is aggregated (all of the estimates are collected and examined in a *centralized* way)

You can imagine that ensuring the conditions above would be quite a challenge in many settings, including the typical business. For one thing, teams generally do not include hundreds of members. Members of small project teams likely have similar expertise (e.g. marketing, engineering), commonly held opinions about their projects, and freely share their estimates of the current and future metrics. As science writer Philip Ball observed, such conditions may lead to unwise group decisions,

> "…researchers found that, as the amount of information participants were given about each other's guesses increased, the range of their guesses got narrower, and the centre of this range could drift further from the true value. In other words, the groups were tending towards a consensus, to the detriment of accuracy. This finding challenges a common view in management and politics that it is best to seek consensus in group decision making. What you can

end up with instead is herding towards a relatively arbitrary position."[35]

You may also wonder about the usefulness of group estimates the further one travels from simple questions like the dressed weight of an unfortunate ox? As one reviewer of *The Wisdom of the Crowds* pondered (referring to the four conditions stated above, bold is mine),

> "...can we trust the crowd to make wise decisions in moral matters? Are the historical examples of crowds choosing to follow leaders in destructive acts representative of the impaired wisdom of crowds? We may also ask if indeed the four conditions are necessary for crowds to make wise decisions, then **why are crowds not wise enough to create such conditions?**"[36]

These same kinds of questions would certainly apply to the real-world issues that businesses face when estimating beyond relatively simple questions like market size and price sensitivity (e.g. what should be done about the misinformation that is promulgated via popular social networks). Here, too, I propose that Devil's Advocacy offers useful opposition that can encourage more thoughtful consideration of important, complex issues.

In the opening sentence of his article, Galton makes a succinct observation about popular judgments that is more poignant and important today than Galton could have known when he wrote it,

> "In these democratic days, any investigation into the trustworthiness and peculiarities of popular judgments is of interest. The material about to be discussed refers to a small matter, but is much to the point."[37]

> If you like *wonky* statistical analysis discussions, then you may want to check out "Revisiting Francis Galton's Forecasting Competition"[38] at https://projecteuclid.org/euclid.ss/1411437521

Introduction

Is Devil's Advocacy Effective?

Devil's Advocacy has certainly had its critics from its early inception to today. Undoubtedly, Devil's Advocacy has not always achieved its intended goals over its centuries of use by the Catholic Church.

More recently, the secular community has also questioned the effectiveness of Devil's Advocacy. Of the various criticisms raised against Devil's Advocacy today, perhaps the most common one is that it is a form of *inauthentic* dissent that can be more harmful than useful. For example, Heuer and Pherson note that,

> "If group members see the Devil's Advocacy as an analytic exercise they have to put with…this exercise may actually enhance the majority's original belief." [39]

Likewise, psychologist Dr. Charlan Nemeth, who has researched and written about the value of dissent, has stated that,

> "Role-playing may actually thwart serious consideration of new alternatives. Armed with the possibly incorrect belief that other options have been considered, thoughts may corroborate one's initial belief and confidence may be inflated." [40,41]

Such criticism of inauthenticity is reinforced when Devil's Advocacy is framed as a form of *role-playing* (see Framing Bias in Chapter 2). Of course, declaring that *playing* Devil's Advocate is inauthentic dissent is a bit like saying that *playing* doctor is inauthentic medicine. Someone simply going through the motions of Devil's Advocacy without investing any effort in thinking and analysis, is like a physician who nods her head as you relay your symptoms while she's preoccupied with what she's going to have for lunch. The Devil's Advocacy discussed in this book has nothing to do with role-playing, so other than this paragraph we won't again mention *"playing* Devil's Advocate" (except when quoting others' comments).

Psychology defines *authenticity* as, "…the extent to which people act coherently with themselves,"[42] but how can we know whether or not dissent is authentic? I don't know of any instrument that reliably and objectively reveals authentic dissent like a digital thermometer reveals body temperature – although that would be a really neat gadget!

Even when a person's authenticity isn't known, effective dissent can still be provided. Defense lawyers, for example, typically don't know the actual guilt of their clients when they argue their clients' cases.[43,44] When successful, these lawyers create reasonable doubt in a judge or jury that has no way of knowing the lawyer's authenticity regarding his case relative to his internal beliefs about his client's guilt.[45]

You may view the creation of a counter position based on premises that you promote but doubt as unseemly and cynical. However, our adversarial legal system requires staunch counter positions to enable a vital critical examination of facts and claims before a judgment is rendered. This same kind of useful opposition outside of a courtroom is what Devil's Advocacy can provide.

Just as a lawyer requires experience and knowledge to practice law, a modern Devil's Advocate may require specific domain expertise, depending upon the position that they will challenge. For example, in a company that is developing a new drug, experience and knowledge in pharmaceutical science is necessary if the position that will be challenged is scientific. Likewise, issues related to marketing and selling the new drug would need those who are familiar with the marketing rules of the regulated drug industry. In some instances, challenges can be made by teams that are composed of members who possess specific subject matter aptitude (e.g. marketing, sales, operations) – a Red Team approach. In other instances, a lone Devil's Advocate without specific expertise can quickly create a useful counter position.[46,47]

Devil's Advocacy has been suggested for various policy decisions while acknowledging the challenges that modern Devil's Advocates will encounter. An article in *Foreign Policy* about the government response to a pandemic observed that (bold is mine),

> "Governments and companies knew about the risk of a pandemic, but they did too little. To prevent the next one, they need designated devil's advocates on the state payroll… The problem is: Who's going to point out that the

> seemingly sensible strategy won't work? In most organizations, that person is a self-appointed **devil's advocate, whom everybody dislikes because he or she sees the gaps in everyone else's ideas or decisions.**"[48]

Of course, the fact that Devil's Advocacy may face stiff opposition does not mean that the practice should be avoided. It's also important to know that even thought-leaders who question the value of Devil's Advocacy acknowledge that "...compared to groups with no counterpositions, it [devil's advocacy] can provide benefit."[49] Further, there are real-world examples of Devil's Advocacy, including several that were identified in an article about anecdotes to groupthink,

> "Numerous organizations use some form of devil's advocacy. For example, Royal Dutch Petroleum regularly uses a devil's advocacy approach. Before making a major decision, such as entering a market or building a plant, Anheuser-Busch assigns some group the role of critic with the purpose of uncovering all possible problems with a particular proposal and making a case for each side of the question. IBM has a system that encourages employees to disagree with their bosses. The thinking is that a devil's advocate who challenges the CEO and top management team can help sustain the vitality and performance of the upper echelon of the organization. All of these companies have the same goal: improve organizational performance by institutionalizing dissent." [50]

There are some signs that more people are accepting the power of dissent a trend that could accelerate the rise of modern Devil's Advocates. Recent research, for example, refers to "constructive confrontation" that encourages a regular practice of dissent, noting that,

> "...as a group people need to be able to challenge internal agreements. Often this is more about personal relationships in the group than the issue itself. Groups that are used to disagreeing openly generally handle changes better than groups that focus on agreement."[51]

The researchers suggest that as little as a half-hour per week practice can help improve group communications by enabling dissent and offer the following guide for such weekly practice, which may sound easier than it likely is to conduct, but aren't the potential benefits worth the effort?

1. Ask for the behaviour you want more of, not less of, from others. Practise: Challenge the person next to you for behaviour you want more of.
2. When you get criticized – listen and don't defend yourself. Show that you are grateful. Practise: Receive feedback, including unpleasant feedback, with a thank you.
3. Make decisions and acknowledge others people's decisions. Practise: Take turns being in the leader role. For example, let the person who normally speaks least lead a meeting.
4. Appoint a person who challenges decisions (devil's advocate). Practise: Dedicate roles to play devil's advocate. Take turns in this role. The main task is to challenge decisions and come up with alternative views. The group is obliged to take these seriously.
5. Challenge routines and habits. Practise: Try something new, like changing the meeting room you always sit in. Bring in outsiders. Practise working on increasing curiosity, not uncertainty.
6. Dare to challenge the expert. Practise: Avoid expert roles, where one person owns certain areas of knowledge – even if the team consists of experts. Everyone should be able to challenge. Practise daring to challenge the expert. Experts can practise letting themselves and their knowledge be challenged by those who are not experts.
7. Ask why, ask for an explanation. Practise: Work on doing this so that it is perceived as constructive.
8. Practise arguing for the views of others. Practise: Change roles and positions.
9. Be honest and clear. Don't sugarcoat messages. But be constructive. Practise: Be concrete and straightforward about your own views, avoid packaging them.
10. "Step on toes". Practise: Challenge others in areas that may seem personal. Work on not taking things personally. The boundary is when suggestions do not contribute constructively to solving or performing the team's task. Speak up immediately if something seems unreasonable, and avoid bringing up old annoyances.

The guidelines above may understandably create concern for executives and managers who fear that open challenges could lead to outright war across the enterprise. However, there are examples of firms that encourage respectful dissent. Rand Fishkin, co-founder and former CEO of the inbound marketing analytics software company MOZ, has referred to the benefits of *psychological safety*[52] among employees, noting (bold is mine),

> "It's this ability to have creative, transparent, **healthy conflict that drives better plans** and better sentiment...When everyone on the team has that same positive excitement and hopefulness, and when they know **it's okay to be openly skeptical or critical**, and that they don't have to hide those feelings or risk their standing with their peers or managers by expressing them, the plans and the quality of work both improve."[53]

Aren't Devil's Advocates Just Disagreeable Cynics?

You may have the impression that Devil's Advocates are by nature disagreeable *cynics* - faultfinding critics who have an ill-natured inclination to point to insignificant shortcomings and raise annoying objections.[54] Devil's Advocacy, however, isn't about questioning plain facts or proposing far-out *conspiracy theories*. For example, claiming that 2 + 2 doesn't equal 4 or asserting that alien lizards rule us are not positions that modern Devil's Advocacy is intended to challenge.[55]

Unlike cynics and conspiracy theorists, modern Devil's Advocates seek practical and useful alternative perspectives to widely held positions. This contrarian posture places modern Devil's Advocates squarely into the camp of *skeptics* - adherents or advocates of doubt who question the truthfulness of claims.[56] There are many forms of skeptics ranging from those who believe that nothing can ever be known or believed to those who view skeptical inquiry as an essential, positive, and constructive tool in all facets of our lives. The modern Devil's Advocate rejects the former pessimistic view in favor of the latter constructive stance.

The late philosopher, Paul Kurtz, specifically noted that "Skeptical inquirers are not negative skeptics, naysayers, debunkers, or nihilists" and he offered a set of principles for what has been called *exuberant skepticism*.[57] Following are elements of Kurtz's principles which I've distilled to the behaviors of a modern Devil's Advocate,

- Applies skepticism to all areas of human endeavor, including everyday life, to achieve positive ends
- Recognizes that critical thinking is an inherent component of skeptical inquiry
- Seeks "clarity rather than obfuscation, lucid meaning in place of confusion"
- Acknowledges the benefits of the theoretical but seeks to objectively test claims with "facts, not suppositions…logical inference and deduction, not faith or intuition"
- Questions absolute dogmas and creeds and believes in "inquiry rather than authority, reason in the place of custom"

The benefits of skeptical inquiry are not simply the opinions of philosophers like Kurtz but can be seen at work in the real world. The field of financial auditing, for example, relies on *professional skepticism* which has been described as,

> "… an attitude that includes a questioning mind and a critical assessment of audit evidence…regardless of any past experience with the entity and regardless of the auditor's belief about management's honesty and integrity."[58]

Note that the statement above does **not** presume intentional fraud, rather professional skepticism is neutral and "…relates to the integrity and good faith of the auditor who **does not assume honesty or dishonesty** on the part of the audit client".[59] Professional skepticism can be further categorized as either *evidence skepticism* or *judgment skepticism*. As the names indicate, the first type questions the facts while the second type questions decision-making. Financial auditors provided the following two examples that may be similar to your own experiences.[60]

Evidence Skepticism	**Judgment Skepticism**
"During my first busy season, I took the word of the HR dept regarding headcounts of one of my client's subsidiaries and it turned out to be wrong."	"Upon taking on a job that was new to me as a manager I placed more reliance than I should have on the prior team's work. I should have spent more time challenging some of the conclusions and understanding them such that I could own them throughout the audit process."

Of course, the benefits of professional skepticism are also found outside of financial accounting; for example, Dharmesh Shah, Founder, and CTO at HubSpot has noted that,[61]

- Skeptics can be extremely useful members of a team. They don't just accept ideas, proposals, opinions, or even 'facts' as offered – they need to be convinced.

- Skeptics like to look at data. They like to analyze. They like to assess. Skeptics like to weigh and measure and draw their own conclusions.

- Skeptics don't wear rose-colored glasses. Skeptics temper the enthusiasm – often in a good way – of the instantly enthusiastic and in the process often apply a level of analysis and rigor that transforms a good idea into a great idea — and just as important, help recognize bad ideas.

By creating an opposing view, the modern Devil's Advocate can challenge not only the "instantly enthusiastic" to which Shah refers but also the chronically gloomy. This means that the Devil's Advocate can help expose weaknesses of a popular pet project **and** they can propose strengths of a project that the majority believes is doomed to fail. The modern Devil's Advocate is not invested in a particular perspective and so is open to creating a counter position to whatever the majority view happens to be.

INTRODUCTION

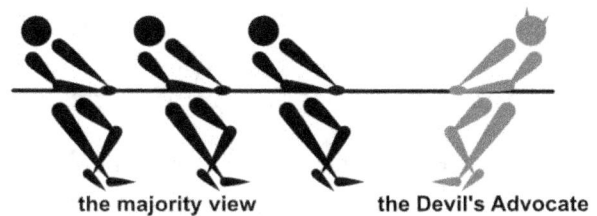

The Devil's Advocate role is intended to help ensure that assumptions, judgments, and decisions are more fully examined

We will be referring to "the" modern Devil's Advocate because it is generally the case that an individual is serving in the role. This reference is certainly not meant to imply that only one or a few parties can or should embrace a thoughtfully skeptical posture in an organization. It could be immensely helpful to an enterprise if everyone from the CEO to the new hire has a common understanding of modern Devil's Advocacy. In any setting, there may be individuals who are more strongly predisposed to the practice of modern Devil's Advocacy, but many team members can make useful contributions to the efforts of individual Devil's Advocates.

If you are a CEO or senior manager, then you may worry that Devil's Advocates could create a serious logjam as they endlessly debate the pros and cons of an issue, effectively bringing progress to a halt. However, if more individuals within an enterprise understand the purpose, benefits, and practice of Devil's Advocacy, then the likelihood of reaching better decisions in a more timely fashion may be improved (we will discuss this point later in Group Decision-Making).

Finally, you may believe that Devil's Advocacy isn't necessary because executives and professional managers are already making good assumptions, judgments, and decisions. As we saw above and will explore further in the next section, evidence suggests that this presumption is unfounded.

> What are popular examples or personal experiences where a dissenting opinion may have been beneficial to you, your workplace, or community? What popular opinion do you now hold that may benefit from a more thoughtfully skeptical perspective?

Introduction

In this Introduction, we explored how modern Devil's Advocacy evolved from an ancient practice of intentional doubt to a practice of professional skepticism that can provide thoughtful, useful dissent.

Let's move into the first chapter of this book where we'll consider the current thinking skills gap that is contributing to poor judgments and outcomes, how our mental models differ from the real world, and why it's important to regularly challenge our mental models, processes, and practices.

> In the book, *Conspiracy Theories and the People Who Believe Them*,[62] conspiracy researcher, Joseph Uscinski, notes that Conspiracy Theories offer some benefits such as encouraging transparency and fostering a healthy skepticism. Uscinski asks, "If conspiracy theorists do not test establishment truths, who will do it?" My answer to Uscinski's question is, modern Devil's Advocates!

Chapter 1: Do You Think That's Air You're Breathing?

There's a scene in the movie, *The Matrix*, where Morpheus is trying to explain the illusion of the Matrix to Neo as they engage in some friendly, simulated combat. After easily knocking an exhausted, heavy-breathing Neo to the mat, Morpheus asks, "You think that's air you're breathing now?"

A story about a man coming to grips with the illusion he's been living, *The Matrix* also provides an analogy to the kind of illusions that we create in our minds versus living in the real world. Sometimes the way that we imagine things working is reasonably close to the way that things do work in the physical world. Sometimes, however, the reality is so different from our imagined expectations that we experience discomfort known as *cognitive dissonance*.[63] To reduce the discomfort we may change our existing belief, add new beliefs, or discount the importance of our existing belief. In *the Matrix* movie, Neo changed his beliefs, but changing our beliefs is hard.

To be effective in their role, modern Devil's Advocates will need to build their thinking skills through daily practice, including reflection on their own beliefs and actions. The investigatory nature of Devil's Advocacy is neither routine nor prescribed but more creative and fluid so it may focus on the unique features of a given situation and avoid cookie-cutter solutions.

Modern Devil's Advocates will often find themselves criticized for challenging rote procedures that are widely accepted the way that people in *The Matrix* believed in their illusive world. These kinds of challenges, however, are intended to be as enlightening to those who the modern Devil's Advocate serves as was Morpheus' challenge to Neo.

CHAPTER 1

In this chapter of the book, we will first look at the current gap in thinking skills, see how wide and deep that gap is and why filling that breach is so important to ourselves, businesses, and communities. We will focus on how the way we imagine the world operates (our *mental models*) directly influences our attempts to drive results in the real world (our *formal processes*).

We will consider how a valued process can lead us to unexpected and unwanted outcomes, while different processes can end up at the same desired outcome. We will look at two different process types (*trailing* and *trailblazing*), so-called *best practices*, and why even widely accepted processes and practices should not be shielded from challenges by modern Devil's Advocates.

A departing reference to *The Matrix* movie before we continue. At a pivotal moment early in the movie, Morpheus extends his hands to reveal a red pill in one palm and a blue pill in the other. Morpheus then offers Neo a choice,

> "You take the blue pill, the story ends. you wake up in your bed and believe whatever you want to believe. You take the red pill; you stay in Wonderland and I'll show you how deep the rabbit-hole goes. Remember, all I'm offering you it's the truth, nothing more."

Spoiler alert... Neo takes the red pill. Wonderland, however, isn't so wonderful. Neo didn't escape the illusion of *The Matrix* and arrive in a beautiful, trouble-free world. Rather, Neo found that many of the ills of his sham world also existed in the grimy real world. Likewise, modern Devil's Advocates and those they serve should expect that Devil's Advocacy practice may lead to more questions and new challenges. By finding previously unraised questions and challenges, however, the modern Devi's Advocate helps to ensure that we're not comfortably nestled in our beds, blithely believing whatever we want to believe.

The Thinking Skills Gap

To actively probe an issue requires intentional thinking rather than reflexive responses. This need for dynamic thinking is particularly true if the intention is to look at a widely held position and create an opposing view. Unfortunately, our world is experiencing a thinking skills gap today that is leading to questionable judgments and poor outcomes.

A quick Google search on the subject of thinking skills will lead you to a host of articles regarding the need for better critical thinking skills in our schools and workplaces. The search will also reveal various initiatives where schools, government, and private organizations have attempted to close the thinking skills gap. There has been so much activity related to critical thinking that you may wonder how a critical thinking skills gap could exist. Is it possible that no critical thinking skills gap exists? Perhaps the thinking skills gap problem is so *thorny* that the many prescriptive processes intended to improve critical thinking skills simply aren't working?

In *The Future of Jobs Report 2018,* The World Economic Forum[64] cautioned that trouble around the globe lies ahead due in part to poor skills like critical thinking and problem-solving (bold below is mine).[65]

- By 2022, no less than 54% of all employees will require significant reskilling and upskilling.
- Skills continuing to grow in prominence by 2022 include **analytical thinking** and innovation as well as **active learning** and learning strategies.
- Proficiency in new technologies is only one part of the 2022 skills equation, however, as 'human' skills such as creativity, originality and initiative, **critical thinking**, persuasion, and negotiation will likewise retain or increase their value, as will attention to detail, resilience, flexibility and **complex problem-solving**.
- Emotional intelligence, leadership, and social influence, as well as service orientation, also see an outsized increase in demand relative to their current prominence.

CHAPTER 1

The Report observes that industries appear to limit their skills training for employees to today's roles rather than to future skills needs, and advises that industries should actively address future skills and close the gap, to become "learning organizations".[66]

The Forum Report also advises workers to "take personal responsibility" for their "lifelong learning and career development" adding that "many individuals will need to be supported through periods of job transition and phases of retraining and upskilling by governments and employers". The Report suggests that a combination of personal responsibility and worker support could lead to voluntary skills upgrade under some form of a "universal lifelong learning fund" for individuals to use as needed. These kinds of personal development initiatives could create fertile ground to promote and expand the availability of modern Devil's Advocates.

Another perspective on the importance of thinking skills was offered in *Good Data Won't Guarantee Good Decisions*.[67] The authors of the article reported their findings from an evaluation that included 5,000 employees at 22 global companies and how those employees made sense of data that was available to them. The evaluation sorted employees into three distinct groups:

1. **Unquestioning Empiricists** who trust analysis over judgment

2. **Visceral Decision Makers** who go exclusively with their gut

3. **Informed Skeptics** who the authors identified as those "employees best equipped to make good decisions - effectively balance judgment and analysis, possess strong analytic skills, and listen to others' opinions but are willing to dissent"

The authors concluded that the *Informed Skeptics* were "the kind of data-savvy workers every company should try to cultivate" because these workers had higher performance. The authors noted, however, that "only 38% of employees, and 50% of senior managers, fall into this group." This finding complements the Forum Report view that industries and workers are facing a significant gap in skills and behaviors that can hinder productivity.

The problems created by poor thinking skills and weak analysis are recognized at the highest levels of business organizations. In *The Case for Behavioral Strategy*, the authors recount a survey that was conducted with 2,207 executives which revealed that,[68]

- Only 28% of respondents said that the quality of strategic decisions in their companies was generally good
- 60% thought that bad decisions were about as frequent as good ones
- 12% thought good decisions were altogether infrequent
- Cognitive biases affect the most important strategic decisions made by the smartest managers in the best companies
- Mergers routinely fail to deliver the expected synergies and strategic plans often ignore competitive responses
- Large investment projects are over budget and over time—over and over again

The observations above indicate some kind of inability or inaction on the part of business leadership to correct problems of which they are well aware. Could moves by business executives to cultivate and distribute modern Devil's Advocates throughout their enterprise help correct these known problems? This is a particularly important question to consider because our learning institutions may not be adequately addressing the skills gap. Failure of businesses to address this gap may lead to significant short-term and long-term effects on their businesses.

In 2019, *The Global Learner Survey*[69] was completed by over eleven-thousand people between sixteen and seventy years of age who were located around the world. Findings from the survey included the following insights:

- Almost half of those in the US, UK, Australia, Canada, and Europe don't think that higher education prepared them for their career
- Workers everywhere want skills that machines and Artificial Intelligence (AI) can't yet compete with — critical thinking, problem-solving, and creativity. Educational institutions aren't yet meeting this need.
- 70% of people agree that colleges and universities care more about their reputation than educating students.

- 74% of respondents agree that colleges and universities focus too much on young students and should offer better options for working adults.

A similar perspective on the need for soft skills is provided in the 2019 IBM Institute for Business Value report entitled, *The Enterprise Guide to Closing the Skills Gap*,[70] that included the following findings,

- Digital skills remain vital; however, executives tell us soft skills have surpassed them in importance.
- Executives recognize the skills gap. They know it's both real and problematic. But most of their organizations don't appear to be actively or effectively tackling the issue.
- Not surprisingly, different management styles are required as well – ones that encourage an agile work environment that includes autonomous decision making, work product iteration, experimentation, peer-to-peer coaching, and flexible team structures.
- IBM Chairman Ginni Rometty coined the term *new collar* – "jobs [that] emphasize academic and technical skills, along with professional competencies such as critical thinking, collaboration, and communication."

Beyond the benefits to business, improved thinking skills may offer personal benefits. According to *Predicting Real-world Outcomes*, for example, critical thinking ability is a better predictor of life events than intelligence.[71] In their conclusion the authors noted,

> "There is ample evidence that critical thinking can be taught, so there is hope that teaching critical thinking skills might prevent the occurrence of negative life events. We advocate for critical thinking instruction as a way to create a better future for everyone."[72]

The kinds of skills development discussed above can be viewed in a useful *metacognition* learning perspective that includes,

> "…thinking about one's thinking. More precisely, it refers to the processes used to plan, monitor, and assess one's understanding and performance. Metacognition includes a

critical awareness of a) one's thinking and learning and b) oneself as a thinker and learner."[73]

Metacognitive skills may be organized in a framework that includes the following,[74]

- task orientation – determining what is to be done
- goal setting – establishing what is to be achieved
- systematic planning – the planned steps to reach the goal
- self-monitoring – confirming that the plan is being followed
- outcome evaluation – showing if the goal was achieved
- reflection – thinking about what was learned from the experience and the outcome

Of course, skills development requires moving from theory to daily practice as noted in *Teaching Critical Thinking: Some Lessons from Cognitive Science*, where the author observed,

> "For students to improve, they must engage in critical thinking itself. It is not enough to learn about critical thinking. Many college professors seem unaware of this point: they teach a course on the theory of critical thinking and assume that their students will end up better critical thinkers. Other teachers make a dissimilar mistake: They expose their students to examples of good critical thinking (for example, having them read articles by professional philosophers), hoping that students will learn by imitation. These strategies are about as effective as working on your tennis by watching Wimbledon. Unless the students are actively doing the thinking themselves, they will never improve."[75]

Likewise, there is a need to regularly reinforce critical thinking across **all** learning activities as noted in *What Our Students Have Taught Us About Critical Thinking*,

> "Critical thinking is not a process used only occasionally, but a complete way of thinking. Making it a basis of every course could facilitate more questioning attitudes, logical

thinking, and clearer communication by students and teachers alike."[76]

Certainly, these kinds of regular and active practices to reinforce critical thinking skills would be beneficial to businesses that strive to be learning organizations. As expressed in the book, *The Fifth Discipline: The Art & Practice of The Learning Organization*, a learning organization is one

> "...where people continually expand their capacity to create the results they truly desire, where new and expansive patterns of thinking are nurtured, where collective aspiration is set free, and where people are continually learning to see the whole together."[77]

The modern Devil's Advocate is not only ideally suited for a learning organization but also a useful participant in the creation and maintenance of learning organizations.

Obviously, there are opportunities to significantly improve the way that we operate in the world by strengthening our critical thinking and decision-making skills. We will explore later how gaps in such soft skills can lead us to blindly accept a majority view, especially if it fits our beliefs and biases.

First, let's take a look at the way that we imagine the world (our mental models) and how we attempt to apply our idealized imaginations in the physical world (our formalized processes). In particular, we will explore the need to seek out discrepancies between our mental models and formal processes, and the benefits of challenging even those models and processes in which we may have unwavering faith.

Our Mental Models and The Real World

Throughout this book, we will be speaking about *mental models* although we won't always be referring to them as such. Mental models are those simplified representations of concepts that we hold in our minds and use continuously (often unconsciously) to explain to ourselves how the world works.

An historical example of a mental model is the idea of the atom that was proposed around 1900 by physicist William Thomson (aka Lord Kelvin).[78] Thomson's model envisioned atoms as "uniform spheres of positively charged matter in which electrons are embedded" – a description that led to a comparison to plum pudding. While this analogy is useful to quickly convey the general idea that Thomson had, we understand that's where the usefulness ends - we shouldn't further imagine other pudding-like characteristics of the atom such as taste and texture.

Models like Thomson's are abandoned when they are found lacking and are replaced by other models that offer a better explanation. A similarly simplified mental model today is of very tiny vibrating *strings* proposed by physicists to explain gravity. While the string model may be useful for its intended purpose, it shouldn't be confused with a string from your shirt or socks.[79]

We also use mental models to interpret actions that we and others take, assessing possible causes and effects of those actions. Our mental models may or may not accurately reflect the actual situation at any given time because our interpretations include personal beliefs, cognitive biases, and fallacies that can (and do) effectively mislead us.

You may believe that you will retire with millions – as many people reportedly believe, even though an estimated 15% of Americans have no retirement savings at all.[80,81] You may believe that you would do well as an NFL defensive lineman even though you have never played football and weigh one hundred and twenty pounds straight out of the shower. You may believe that you deserve being in a physically abusive relationship which somehow will change if you just give it a little more time. These examples of dubious mental models can lead to the poorhouse, a visit to an emergency room, or worse. We will do well to remember two popular cautions about mental models (bold is mine).

> "A map is not the territory it represents, but, if correct, it has a similar structure to the territory, which accounts for its **usefulness**."
> - *Alfred Korzybski, scientist, and philosopher*[82]

> "All models are wrong, but some are **useful**."
> - *George E.P. Box, statistician*[83]

Note that both warnings refer to the *usefulness* of models not because they are absolutely "right" but because they may reasonably represent the world and therefore provide us with valuable insight and understanding. Upon his death, the New York Times noted Korzybski's view that "men did not properly evaluate the world they talked about ... spoke before observing and then reacted to their own remarks as if they were fact itself."[84] The modern Devil's Advocate certainly should avoid emulating those kinds of behaviors and help others to do the same.

To share our mental models with others, we can express them as formal, written, or diagrammed processes - "a series of actions or operations conducing to an end."[85] Processes for our mental models may be as simple as a map that you sketch to show someone how to get to your house to very specific steps to produce a product. Although there are particular processes within specialized fields, the diagram below is a very simple example of a Generic Decision-Making Process (see also Appendix A).

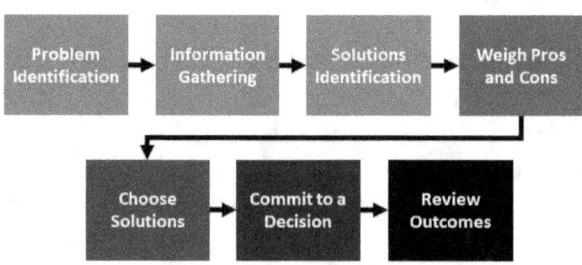

A generic decision-making process diagram

Many processes seem to just make "common sense" and this appearance can entice us to accept them at face value. By simply accepting a commonsense process, however, we can contribute to *groupthink* - "a pattern of thought characterized by self-deception, forced manufacture of consent, and conformity to group values and ethics."[86,87] Consider how the work of psychiatrist Elisabeth Kübler-Ross was widely interpreted after the publication of her seminal book, *On Death and Dying*.

Reportedly,[88] Kübler-Ross's goal was to start a conversation about how to improve care for terminally ill patients. In her book, Kübler-Ross described in detail five stages of emotion experienced by such patients: denial, anger, bargaining, depression, and acceptance. Apparently, "The five stages took on a life of their own. They were used to train doctors and therapists, passed on to patients and their families." However, there were never only five stages and everyone didn't go through the stages in a specific order, rather the model was intended to be a "loose framework". George Bonanno, professor of clinical psychology, observed that "People who don't go through these stages - and as far as I can tell that's most people - can be led to believe that they are grieving incorrectly." While we may find a linear, stepwise understanding of our world comforting, such a view can also obscure the fact that straightforward and certain paths are not necessarily (or reasonably) assured.[89]

Our formal processes emerge from our mental models which makes such processes ideal "targets" for Devil's Advocacy work. By examining our processes, we can better understand the underlying beliefs and challenge the reasonableness of the foundational mental models, premises, and judgments. **Because I propose that the examination and challenge of formal processes are fundamental in Devil's Advocacy practice, we will spend the balance of this chapter exploring some characteristics of formal processes and considering examples that I hope you will find both compelling and useful.**

> What are some examples of mental models that you use? What is an example of a mental model that you use automatically without much thought? Can you give examples of mental models that may have led you to undesirable outcomes?

CHAPTER 1

The Different Paths from Beginnings to Ends

It used to be said that "all roads lead to Rome" which was mostly true for ancient times in Italy when Rome was essentially at the center of that part of the world. Conversely, you could start in Rome and end up in a variety of other destinations. The same options of routes are true for our processes due to equifinality and multifinality.[90]

Simply stated, *equifinality* is when the same outcome occurs even when starting with different initial conditions and taking different actions (all roads lead to Rome). *Multifinality* is when a given set of initial conditions and actions may lead to different outcomes (starting from Rome you may end up at many different destinations).

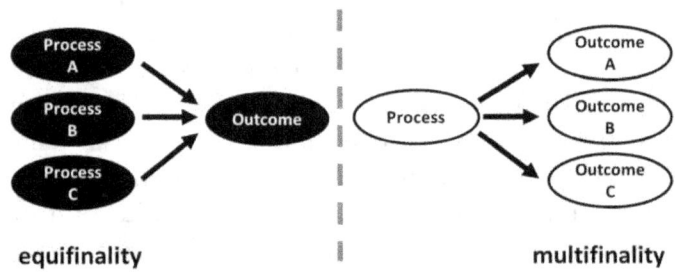

Left: *"all roads lead to Rome"* **Right**: *a traveler from Rome may end up in many places*

For example, different product development teams working at different companies with different resources and following different processes could all end up building a nearly identical product. We see examples of this kind of equifinality in common products like shoes and cell phones, and services like ride-sharing and online banking.

At the same time, different teams within the same company, presumably following the company processes, can experience very different outcomes. Team A launches a product that is successful while a product that Team B launches is a failure. We see examples of this kind of multifinality in the successes and failures of prominent companies (e.g. the successful Macintosh LC vs. the unsuccessful Macintosh Portable).[91]

There are two important takeaways from equifinality and multifinality. First, no one mental model or process is necessarily any better than another model or process to achieve a goal. Second, any model or process may lead us where we don't want to go.

The historical framework of process development may help explain certain questionable beliefs we may have in our processes. As noted in *Equifinality in Project Management Exploring Causal Complexity in Projects*,[92] (bold is mine),

> "The field of project management has been dominated since 1969 by a prescriptive paradigm that places an emphasis on process control and the **artificial separation of planning from execution**. This emphasis stems from an engineering closed-systems tradition, which **assumes that projects can be isolated from their environment, broken down into predictable parts, and manipulated like machines** to achieve the desired results, with certain specifications and under certain controlled initial conditions.
>
> **Goals are predetermined, objectives are clear, the sequence of activities is prescheduled**, and it is just a matter of the managers, who are accountable for any deviation or change, supervising the execution of plans. Advocates of the closed-systems paradigm apply operations management techniques, such as queuing, scheduling, and resource planning to project management.
>
> These techniques are very effective when they are applied to environments with predictable activities with clear goals, controllable sequences and predictable results like manufacturing, **but in the case of innovation projects which regularly involve fuzzy missions and goals, with objectives that are not clearly rooted in a fixed reality, and where solutions need time to emerge within complex and emergent social processes, these techniques have been found lacking.**

CHAPTER 1

> Given that the prescriptive paradigm provides universal predefined solutions, there is **the implicit assumption that it can predict project conditions accurately, which leads to overlooking the need to provide methods that allow for flexible management.**"

In a similar vein, *Causal Complexity of New Product Development Processes* discusses how the cause and effect of actions and outcomes becomes more difficult to ascertain as the complexity of a project increases,

> "The outcomes of new product development (NPD) processes are dependent on the interplay of several interdependent activities. One product development activity can be dependent on the presence or absence of other activities, different kinds of NDP processes may lead to the same outcome, and specific kinds of activities may have a positive effect in one process but no effect in other processes. However, we currently lack the means to examine and explain this causal complexity inherent in NPD processes."[93]

Having spent many years in process-driven environments, I have promoted various formal processes, urging my associates that if we remain true to the dogmatic and prescribed procedures and methods then we **will** achieve success. In these instances when a process is deemed sacrosanct and passionately defended by its practitioners, poor outcomes can easily be blamed on individuals' incompetence rather than a fault in the process.

An unfortunate result of faulting the practitioners of a process is that questionable processes and practices can be repeatedly used without anyone seriously challenging their reliability of achieving the desired outcome. In the worst case, practitioners may agree that the process isn't working but won't speak up for fear of challenging the majority view or attracting the ire of leadership. In such a situation, a fatalistic view of the environment may evolve where otherwise engaged and productive professionals resign themselves to just go through the motions day in and day out.

Equifinality and multifinality inform us that just because we believe in – and express in a formal process, some clear path to a certain end doesn't make it so. Of course, this is not to say that all processes are useless, but our belief in the value of a given process should be clearly and regularly confirmed to be useful.

The Usefulness of Trailing Processes

Certain processes prove their usefulness by demonstrating that they reliably lead to an intended goal. I refer to these process types as *trailing* because they are often documenting steps that many others have taken before us to successfully reach a goal. A trailing process analogy is a well-marked hiking path that will reliably lead anyone with a watchful eye through the woods and around obstacles to a beautiful vista spot.

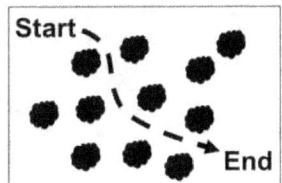

Trailing processes are like well-marked hiking trails

A bread recipe is another simple example of a trailing process type. Rather than struggling through trial and error to figure out how to make bread on your own, you can use a bread recipe that lists the ingredients and steps that many others followed to make a loaf of bread. You can proceed with reasonably high confidence that the recipe will work for you, too, provided you faithfully follow the steps.

The diagram below for bread-making states a linear path from **Start** to **End** through defined steps indicated by the right-pointing pentagonal blocks. The arrows chasing their tails beneath the blocks indicate that within each step you may have other activities like letting the dough rise a second time before baking. Each stage is arranged in a way where the activities in a prior step are intended to create a solid foundation on which the next steps will advance to the desired result.

CHAPTER 1

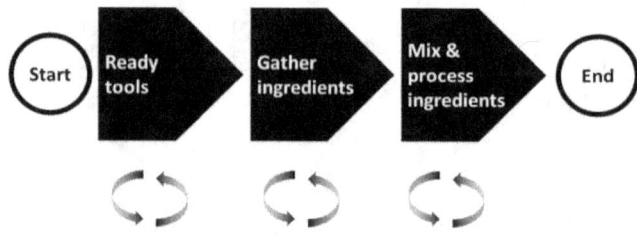

A simple bread recipe

Business operations like the customer order process diagram below are also examples of the trailing process type.

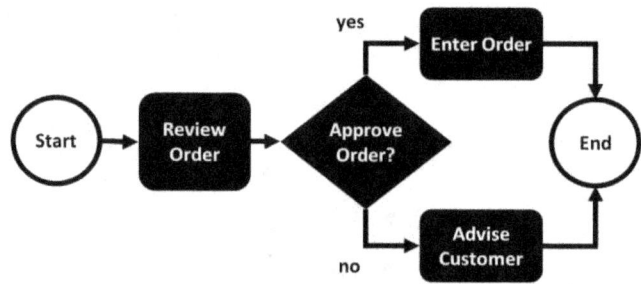

A simple order review and approval process

There are many other tasks like baking or order entry where stepwise trailing processes can be remarkably effective. Preflight checklists, for example, are used by pilots before takeoff to improve flight safety by helping to ensure that no critical preparation tasks are overlooked.[94] Similarly, pre-surgery checklists are used by healthcare professionals to avoid errors and reduce patient morbidity and mortality.[95]

In addition to the simple kinds of processes described above, more advanced frameworks of processes have proven to be very effective. Six Sigma,[96] for example, includes a variety of techniques and tools intended to greatly reduce the causes of defects and variability in manufacturing. So useful are trailing processes, however, that we may attempt to apply them even when the process would not reasonably be useful. For example, referring to one process within Six Sigma, DMAIC,[97] a certified Six Sigma Black Belt practitioner observed,

> "...in some situations, DMAIC is just the wrong approach to a business problem, and when that is the case proceeding with a project can worsen the situation rather than fixing it, or at best delay a proper solution." [98]

This same Black Belt offered several warning signs that DMAIC may not be appropriate for a project, including:

- The project sponsor or Six Sigma director cannot clearly state the problem that the project was chartered to solve
- There is no way to obtain sufficient data to evaluate process performance and/or customer satisfaction
- The solution to a problem is already clear, but leaders are hesitant to implement it for political or similar reasons - to essentially put the burden on someone else.
- The process or organization is undergoing such dramatic changes that a DMAIC project would not be effective

Of course, to be beneficial, any formal processes must exist in a form that is useful and consistently followed. Yes, this seems obvious, but I can attest that it is not always the case even in well-established firms.

For example, I had the experience of being asked to assess the documentation for a company's new product development process. The initial assumption presented to me was that there was insufficient process documentation. It turned out, however, that there was a lot of documentation, including many nearly identical documents for the same purpose (e.g. project benefits scoring). Further, none of the documents had any clear instructions for their use.

Individual managers would choose from a book of available documents the ones that they preferred and fill in the blanks, using their subjective judgment on how to answer specific questions. Consequently, there was no way to compare the documents among projects. The resolution effort that I led included a streamlining reduction of the number of documents available and the inclusion of specific, detailed instructions about how to use the documents (similar to tax forms that include instructions for each field). These changes also established the groundwork for a uniform project portfolio management approach.

Because our formal processes reflect our mental models, a modern Devil's Advocate challenge to formal processes can reveal the underlying assumptions, beliefs, and judgments of those who either created or who are following the processes. Understandably, challenging a person's mental models and favored processes can create a lot of tension and even anger. What can make challenges to our processes particularly difficult is when we believe a process to be a dependable *best practice*.

> Can you give examples of when a highly regarded, trailing process did not lead to a successful outcome? Can you give examples of when different trailing processes led to essentially the same successful outcome?

We're Trying Our Best Practices?

It's not uncommon for a process to be branded as a *best practice* – "a procedure that has been shown by research and experience to produce optimal results and that is established or proposed as a standard suitable for widespread adoption."[99] As we explored above, however, equifinality and multifinality may cast shadows on claims of optimal results and suitability for widespread adoption.

Many of us who have been tasked to "make things happen" have sought out practices that might provide a reliable path to success. It's not unusual for employers to require formal training in one or more popular processes, believing that the investment in time and money will achieve smoother operations and better outcomes. Having been trained in various processes, however, I have often felt that the promised benefits were oversold (unintentionally or deliberately). Further, such training is often unquestioningly accepted by companies and their employees as truly the "best" – after all, that's what they're called!

For all the time, energy, and money that has been and will be spent on training in best-practice processes you might wonder why there are still many instances of poor results and outright failures today? What's going on? Are many practitioners lazy, stupid, or just not implementing the processes properly? Are practitioners being forced to veer from the process by higher authorities in the organization to achieve mandated delivery dates?[100] Or is it possible that best practices can't be adequately researched and regularly tested and so may be no better than practices that some may consider subpar? I ask these questions, in part, due to my own experiences with best-practice processes.

For example, a former employer created a training manual for planning marketing activities. A compendium of marketing best practices that were designed to create successful programs, the manual was well made with thick paper and color-coded tabs, and oozed confidence. But the stated best practices seemed lacking to me for several reasons:

- The manual did not reference any actual successful marketing project that resulted from anyone following the best practices described in the manual
- There weren't any examples of project successes offered during the live classroom training that accompanied the manual
- I knew of no other manager who had achieved success by using the stated best practices – not one, although I did ask many other managers about their experiences

Perhaps there were well-documented successes attributable to the proposed best practices that were never revealed for some reason. It seems to me an odd omission to not share successes, but I also acknowledge that success stories are anecdotal and lack robust metrics and methods to objectively determine the effectiveness of a process.

On another occasion, at another firm, I spoke with a senior manager about discrepancies that I saw between processes that the company claimed to be following and how employees were actually operating daily. I felt that the inconsistency between claimed processes and actual practice could lead to poor outcomes because there was no reliable way to monitor and confirm the use and usefulness of the processes. The manager nodded in agreement and confided that he wouldn't drive over a bridge that the company built - fortunately, the company wasn't in the business of bridge-building! The manager's metaphorical comment, however, underscores the kind of *Kabuki theater* that I have repeatedly witnessed over many years where claimed process adherence was more style than substance. In the absence of rigorous objective testing and evidence, who's to say if proclaimed best practices are actually being practiced or "work" even if they are being faithfully followed?

CHAPTER 1

In *Metrics for Measuring Product Development Cycle Time*, researchers examined thirty-five projects for claims that a quality function deployment process (QFD) decreased both product development cycle time and cost found that (italics are the authors'),

> "In no instance was *inarguable* evidence that the QFD had measurably improved development cycle time or cost uncovered. The primary problem of evaluating QFD's impact that these firms was that no one had ever specifically measured how long product development took prior to implementing QFD."[101]

Likewise, the State Education Resource Center of Connecticut (SERC) make the point that best practices may not reliably lead to desired results (bold is mine),[102]

> "The term Best Practice has been used to describe what works in a particular situation or environment. As good consumers of information, **we must keep in mind that a particular practice that has worked for someone within a given set of variables may or may not yield the same results across educational environments.**"

> "Professional wisdom allows educators and family members to adapt to specific circumstances or environments in an area in which research evidence may be absent or incomplete. But **without at least some empirical evidence, education cannot resolve competing approaches, generate cumulative knowledge, and avoid fads and personal biases.**"

Adding another layer of doubt to the moniker of "best practices" is the fact that situational changes can occur quickly or so slowly as to hide in plain sight. A consequence of change is that even highly regarded best practices may not work as they once seemed to do. Determining when the limits of a best practice effectiveness are exceeded and are no longer useful can be as difficult as detecting the real-time growth of your fingernails.

Even if conditions are stable over time, all other things being equal, the effort required to objectively demonstrate that a practice is *the best* by some measure would be practically impossible. Practitioners would need to somehow apply different processes to numerous "identical" projects under the same conditions (e.g. staff, budget, market) to see if a significant difference in outcomes could be detected - like a clinical trial designed to show medication effectiveness.

Further, even if companies were able to rewind the clock and run a successful project with the same initial conditions but following a different process, what would be their incentive? Why would a company that is achieving acceptable revenues and profits want to tinker with their operations and possibly experience poorer outcomes (even though better outcomes may be achieved by a better, best practice)?

The point is that while processes can be helpful the designation of "best" is likely more an article of faith than a rigorously demonstrated fact. Consider, too, that adoption of a *best practice* may represent condoned, institutionalized groupthink that is resistant to dissenting voices. Consequently, even our "best practices" should not be shielded from critical challenges by Devil's Advocacy.

If challenges reveal that a process or best practice won't likely achieve the desired result, then Devil's Advocacy can assist in *trailblazing* alternate routes to the desired goal.

Are you currently following any best practices? Do you know how these practices were determined to be *best*? Have projects failed even though you faithfully followed the best practice guidelines? How often are your best practices tested to help ensure they are still useful? How do you test your best practices?

CHAPTER 1

Trailblazing Differs from Trailing

By *trailblazing* I mean activities that may **not** be "able to be definitely ascertained, calculated, or identified". Projects that are quite different from previous ventures do not have a clear and reliable "trail" to follow.

The diagram below suggests how using an established trailing process to a trailblazing problem may lead us headlong into new and unknown obstacles and distract us from new and more efficient paths.

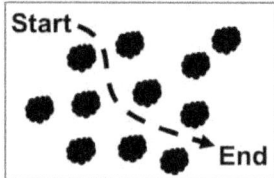 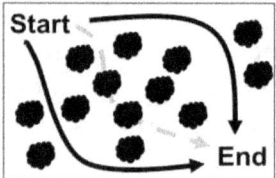

Left: *the trailing processes diagram from above.* **Right**: *applying a trailing process to a trailblazing situation*

Projects that require trailblazing may include innovation creation and the development of truly disruptive products and services. Unlike trailing processes that offer reliable paths to follow, trailblazing is more like parachuting into a wilderness and then trying to find your way out by "making or pointing a new way" in the absence of any marked trails.[103]

To be clear, I'm **not** stating that no process should be followed in trailblazing situations, rather that we need to understand what kind of situation we are facing. It may be that a trailing process is the only practical option available to us to start trailblazing projects. By recognizing the differences between trailing and trailblazing situations, however, we can help establish more reasonable expectations in stakeholders and manage uncertainty.

Consider the article, *What Your Innovation Process Should Look Like* that proposed a process for innovation.[104] The authors of the article make several observations regarding the current situation in companies, including:

- Organizations often pursued innovation without following a disciplined process

- In the absence of a disciplined process, decisions were often based on presentation skills and politics rather than on any requirement to obtain evidence (e.g. customer interviews and testing of minimally viable products).
- The valuation of proposed innovations is made by committees of "well-intentioned, smart people"

The authors concluded that a need exists for a "self-regulating, evidence-based innovation pipeline". They propose a "canonical Lean Innovation process" that is intended to better "curate and prioritize" proposed innovations, creating substantial evidence in support of developing an innovation before engineering resources are involved. The *chapters* of the authors' proposed *canon* are as follows:

- **Innovation sourcing** to generate a "list of problems, ideas, and technologies that might be worth investing in."
- **Curation** whereby those tasked with innovation "talk to colleagues and customers" to identify existing common issues, solutions, and the building of a minimally viable product (MVP) that expresses a possible solution to a problem.
- **Prioritization** of the proposed innovation for development. Note that at the time of the article the authors recommended using the McKinsey Three Horizons Model but a couple of years later questioned the merits of the model in certain disruptive environments.[105]
- **Solution exploration and hypothesis testing** that is conducted by the innovation team over a six to ten-week period. During this time, the team generates a model that defines typical business questions (e.g. the customer need, market, etc.). At this stage, the team may feel that they have a compelling case to move the innovation into an engineering phase or have concluded that the innovation lacks sufficient merit to proceed.
- **Incubation** during which time "teams championing the projects gather additional data about the application, further build the MVP, and get used to working together."
- **Integration and refactoring** which contemplates either assimilation of the innovation development into an existing organization (or as a separate division or business entity and stabilizing the MVP while adjusting the team to enable scaling the innovation in production.

CHAPTER 1

You may agree that this proposed innovation process seems reasonable on its face. Reflecting on the differences between trailing and trailblazing, you may ask yourself some questions about the process. Do the proposed steps define a trailing process in its compartmentalized and stepwise format? Do the proposed steps suggest certitude that the desired outcome will be achieved? Has the proposed cannon been robustly tested and proven likely to lead to the desired outcome? Is the outcome of the process, in other words, as reliable as a bread recipe?

Adopting a process like the one suggested above may be useful, but if by regular challenges to the process we realize that it isn't working as intended, then we may need to adopt a trailblazing perspective.

> Note the authors' choice above of the word *canonical*, one definition of which is "a regulation or dogma decreed by a church council".[106] Perhaps the issues facing the modern Devil's Advocate are not so different than those confronting the original Devil's Advocates!

Navigating in the Fuzzy Hemisphere

Trailblazing activities are *fuzzier* than the stepwise path of trailing processes due to the absence of a proven path to follow. The practice of modern Devil's Advocacy is a kind of trailblazing activity itself as the Advocate questions what many accept as "the" right course of action (i.e. a widely accepted mental model or formal process). Trailblazing activities, however, are not as clear cut as are trailing activities.

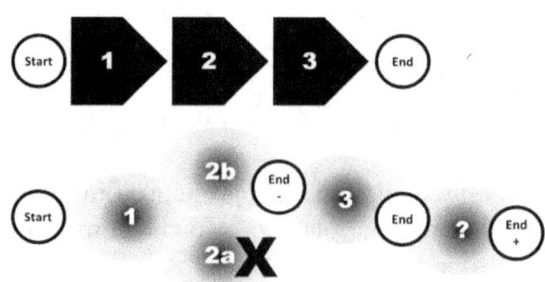

Top: *trailing process example.* ***Bottom:*** *trailblazing project example.*

At the top of the diagram above is our earlier bread-making example with fixed and well-defined steps. At the bottom of the diagram is an example of trailblazing activities where the stages are neither fixed nor well-defined. Rather, the exact number of stages is unclear, and the possible stages overlap like drifting, wispy clouds. The steps shown in the example indicate that initial exploration led to a dead-end (X in 2a) and the need to take another direction (2b) either by backtracking through our initial start (1) or *evolving* from (2a) into (2b). While the desired end is known in trailblazing activities (e.g. an innovation), the position of the endpoint on the fuzzy route is not exact (i.e. the innovation may occur before stage 3, after stage 3 or after some unknown number of stages).

Trailing and trailblazing processes exist in two connected hemispheres of the same world. The trailing hemisphere contains processes where relationships are *deterministic* - "phenomena are causally determined by preceding events or natural laws".[107] In the trailblazing hemisphere, causes and effects are uncertain (we'll look at uncertainty in Chapter 3).

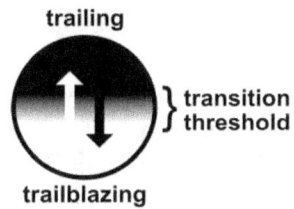

Trailing processes and trailblazing activities exist in two different but connected hemispheres

Trailing processes emerge from trial and error activities that are conducted in the trailblazing hemisphere and eventually migrate to the trailing processes hemisphere. Returning briefly to our bread-making process example, if you attempted to bake pumpernickel bread (for which you have no recipe) using your white bread recipe then your efforts would not likely produce pumpernickel bread. You could, of course, start trailblazing and through trial and error figure out the required change of ingredients, baking temperature, and time. By the end of your trailblazing efforts, you would have created a recipe for pumpernickel bread that you and others can reliably follow (i.e. a new trailing process).

CHAPTER 1

The threshold to cross from the trailblazing activities hemisphere to the trailing processes hemisphere is vague but hopefully, the transition will occur only if and when success is objectively demonstrated over many instances.[108] This expectation of objective and sufficient evidence of process effectiveness, however, is a serious challenge (an issue that we considered earlier under Best Practices). Likewise, trailing processes may fall back into the trailblazing hemisphere when they are no longer useful to achieve desired goals and require either modification or abandonment (like Thomson's plum pudding atomic model).

Trailblazing activities may begin on a trailing process path; however, we need to accept that the trailing process we select may require continuous modification or abandonment along the way. Recall the warning above that a "prescriptive paradigm" includes "the implicit assumption that it can predict project conditions accurately, which leads to overlooking the need to provide methods that allow for flexible management."[109] Failing to acknowledge a lack of predictive power in a process and the benefits of flexibility may lead us deeper in the woods rather than to our desired destination.

If you agree with the ideas expressed above, specifically, that we regularly, confidently, and inappropriately apply trailing processes then you may also wonder why this behavior is so? We touched on some of the possible factors above that included managers making an honest but mistaken judgment and cases when a process is intentionally misused to shift responsibility. Perhaps the strongest force on our preference for trailing processes is our human desire for simple answers and absolute certainty.

In their book, *Superforecasting: The Art and Science of Prediction*, the authors note differences between those who tend to rely upon a narrow view and who speak with confidence about future outcomes (the authors refer to these people as *hedgehogs*) and those who take a more diverse view that considers a range of likely future outcomes (the authors refer to these people as *foxes*). The authors found that the foxes do a better job forecasting than do the hedgehogs. However, even when popular hedgehog forecasters like those featured on television news and talk shows get it very wrong, they are still sought out for their opinion! The authors' explanation of hedgehog forecaster fame speaks to our human condition,

> "The simplicity and confidence of the hedgehog impairs foresight, but it calms nerves — which is good for the careers of hedgehogs."[110]

⏱ The discussion in this chapter is intended to offer a simple, flexible, and (hopefully) memorable view of process types, strengths, and weaknesses. More prescriptive models include the *Stacey matrix*[111], *the Cynefin framework*[112], and the *WHOW matrix.*[113] You may wish to explore these concepts further and consider if they may be useful references for Devil's Advocacy practice. See also *Little Green Army Wo(men)* in the appendices.

💡 What kinds of projects do you typically manage, trailing or trailblazing? How do you know if a project is trailing or trailblazing? Can you give examples where you may have applied a trailing process to a trailblazing project and what were the results?

In this chapter, we saw the breadth of the thinking skills gap and how that gap contributes to poor decision-making and outcomes. We also saw how informed skeptics can be beneficial to business operations and outcomes and that thinking skills can be taught and cultivated.

We considered how our mental models differ from the real world, and how gaps exist between the way we imagine the world and our formalized processes. We discussed the benefits and shortcomings of trailing processes, why best practices may not be demonstrably "the best", and why even best practices should not be spared from critical challenges. We also discussed the importance of knowing when we are operating in the deterministic hemisphere of trailing processes or the fuzzy hemisphere of trailblazing.

As noted in the Introduction, Devil's Advocacy does not follow a "prescribed procedure". The absence of a stepwise paradigm for Devil's Advocacy requires that the Devil's Advocate assumes an open-ended, flexible, and professionally skeptical attitude rather than to try imposing yet another process that is specific to the practice of Devil's Advocacy. In the next chapter, we'll consider how to think and act like a modern Devil's Advocate.

CHAPTER 2: ARE YOU CONTROLLING WHAT YOU CAN?

Epictetus, the noted Stoic philosopher observed, "Some things are in our control…opinion, pursuit, desire, aversion, and, in a word, whatever are our own actions."[114] This observation expresses the Stoic idea that we tend to act impulsively to our situation but can learn to avoid *false judgments* by monitoring our emotions and making rational choices.[115]

Today, we see this ancient idea reflected in mental health methods like Cognitive Behavioral Therapy (CBT) where patients monitor their feelings and how their emotions affect their actions.[116,117] Similarly, modern Devil's Advocacy calls on practitioners to be particularly attentive to any impulsive reaction and automatic judgments that they and those around them may be inclined to indulge.

A first step toward making rational choices is to understand a bit about different kinds of thinking. In this chapter, we'll briefly look at a few types of thinking that we can employ to monitor and manage our impulsive and misleading emotions. We will also see how *real* arguments can help us visualize the strengths and weaknesses of beliefs, assumptions, and conclusions. Finally, we will look at several important forms of bias and fallacy that can cloud our thinking and decision-making.

Of course, our efforts to ensure that we're making unbiased reasoned decisions will be influenced by our human nature. Our challenge is to use our daily practice of modern Devil's Advocacy to help us better control those things that we can.

Types of Thinking

We don't use just one kind of thinking but many types: abstract, analytical, creative, concrete, critical, convergent, divergent, reflective — the list goes on. We are going to be looking at five types of thinking: System 1, System 2, Analytical, Systems, and Critical. I've chosen these five types of thinking because they provide a simple model that can be useful to the work of a modern Devil's Advocate.

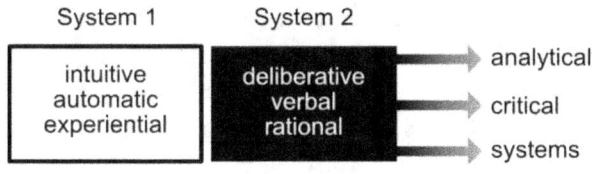

The diagram above shows how five types of thinking are delineated by System 1 and System 2 categories, and that analytical, systems and critical thinking fall within the System 2 category.

Dual Process Thinking Models

Cognitive research has proposed a *dual-process* theory[118] about thinking where one process is automatic while the other process is controlled. There are many models of dual-process,[119] but you may be familiar with the terms *Systems 1* and *Systems 2* (aka Type 1 and Type 2) thinking due to the work of psychologist and economist, Daniel Kahneman, and his popular book, *Thinking, Fast and Slow*.[120,121] According to Kahneman and others who have looked at dual processes in thinking, both types are constantly in play but we are generally in automatic mode.

System 1 thinking is the *fast* type that is associated with the "intuitive, automatic, natural, nonverbal, narrative, and experiential".[122] System 1 thinking is what happens when we follow our instincts or when we employ one of the many mental shortcuts known as *heuristics* that we deem good enough to address everyday questions. Heuristics, however, can lead us to false conclusions if we aren't attentive (bold is mine),

> "Examples of heuristics include the **representativeness heuristic**, in which people categorize objects (or other people) based on how similar they are to known entities—assuming someone described as "quiet" is more likely to be a librarian than a politician, for instance. The **availability heuristic** describes the mental shortcut in which someone estimates whether something is likely to occur based on how readily examples come to mind. **Satisficing**, another well-known heuristic, is a decision-making strategy in which the first option that satisfies certain criteria is selected, even if other, better options may exist." [123]

The impact of heuristics may be benign but can also lead to critical negative outcomes, including misdiagnosis and inappropriate medical treatment.[124,125]

An interesting example of automatic thinking was demonstrated by a study conducted within a group of associates in a university setting.[126] The associates had access to a shared coffee station that was funded by voluntary contributions. Researchers created a series of small cards that included the suggested contribution amount and an image of either flowers or of a person staring forward. Over ten weeks, the cards were changed weekly in revolving order – staring eyes, flowers, staring eyes – and no two images were the same.

The researchers found that "People paid nearly three times as much for their drinks when eyes were displayed rather than a control image." Regarding the increase in payment when the eyes image was displayed, the researchers surmised that it was "possible that the images exerted an automatic and unconscious effect on the participants' perception that they were being watched." The underlying motivation may have been "reputational concerns" and so subjects made an automatic decision to pay.

System 2 thinking is the *slow* type of thinking that is associated with the "analytical, deliberative, verbal, and rational". System 2 thinking is what happens when we consciously and methodically work our way through an issue. Note that the dual-process model may inadvertently lead us to view System 1 and System 2 thinking as two independent mechanisms that are separated by clear and sharp borders. These two types of thinking, however, appear to work in a more interactive (if not cooperative) way.

In one study, for example, researchers investigated the mental process among medical students.[127] The researchers used the Cognitive Reflection Test (CRT) which is designed to assess the "ability or disposition to reflect on a question and resist reporting the first response that comes to mind"[128] – to intentionally shift from System 1 to System 2 thinking. The first question of the original CRT is,[129]

> "A bat and a ball cost $1.10. The bat costs $1.00 more than the ball. How much does the ball cost?"

A typical intuitive (Type 1) answer is that the ball costs $0.10 which is incorrect (correct answer below). The researchers found that:

- 10% of subjects answered none of the CRT questions correctly
- 21% answered one question correctly
- 25% answered two correctly
- 44% answered all correctly

The researchers concluded that "…intuition is a dominant force in the minds of medical students. It has also shown that it is possible for this intuitive force to be put aside and for logic to prevail".

Knowing that we have two general types of thinking going on inside of our heads and that we can shift from intuition to logic may be beneficial particularly **if** we know **when** we are leaning toward System 1 or System 2 thinking. Kahneman, however, suggests that a high level of personal awareness regarding our thinking may be challenging if not practically impossible,

> "I would say that if one made a film on this [thinking types], type two would be a secondary character who thinks that he is the hero because that's who we think we are, but in fact, it's type one that does most of the work, and it's most of the work that is completely hidden from us." [130]

CHAPTER 2

> ⏱ **Answer to the ball cost question above: $0.05**
> A typical intuitive answer is that the ball costs $0.10. If the ball costs $0.10, however, then the bat must cost $1.10 ($0.10 ball + $1.00) and the total cost of bat and ball must then cost $1.20 ($1.10 bat + $0.10 ball) which is incorrect because that answer is larger than the total cost of $1.10. If the ball costs $0.05 then the bat must cost $1.05 ($0.05 + $1.00) and the total cost would then be $1.10 ($1.05 bat + $0.05 ball) which is correct. Working deliberately and analytically through the math above is Type 2 thinking.

Analytical and Systems Thinking

Recall from our diagram above that Systems Thinking is a form of System 2 thinking – don't confuse "Systems Thinking" with "System 2" thinking.

Analytical and Systems Thinking may be viewed as two sides of the same coin. **Analytical thinking** is the process of breaking down complex concepts into basic parts and principles. One of the purposes of analytical thinking is to gain an understanding of one component within a larger system of many components. A *system* may be defined as "a set of things working together as parts of a mechanism or an interconnecting network; a complex whole"[131] – like the organs within a human body or the departments within a company.

Systems thinking is the process of understanding how basic parts and principles influence one another within a larger structure or system. One of the purposes of systems thinking is to gain a more complete view of how components interact to achieve a larger purpose or goal.

Consider the image below which shows a fully assembled and functional automobile to the left and a few of the many parts that go into the finished car to the right. Suppose that the vehicle is yours and that something stops working properly – maybe you feel vibration when you brake.

ARE YOU CONTROLLING WHAT YOU CAN?

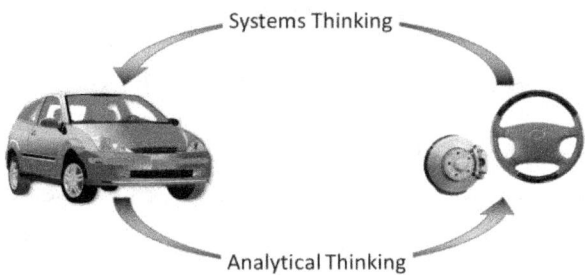

Analytical thinking focuses on parts of a complete system as if they were separate from the system. Systems thinking considers how all the parts of a system work to achieve the purpose of the system.

To determine the origin of the vibration and make a repair, you or your mechanic would focus on those parts that might be causing the problem. You may look closely at your brakes which could be worn or warped but you likely wouldn't start investigating the brake lights or the radio because those parts wouldn't cause the vibration problem that you are experiencing. This process of moving from the complex (complete car) to the simple (breaks) is an example of Analytical Thinking.

Now suppose that you are an engineer who is tasked to redesign an automobile to achieve higher performance characteristics, specifically, improved fuel efficiency and better safety during a front-end collision. In this case, you need to understand how your design changes might affect **both** the fuel efficiency and collision performance of the vehicle.

One way that you can achieve better fuel efficiency is to lower the overall weight of the car, so you may consider making the car smaller to reduce its weight. Making the car smaller and lighter, however, may reduce the effectiveness of the *crush zone* between the front bumper and the passenger compartment that helps protect passengers during front-end collisions. Your decision to make a smaller, lighter car may lower the safety of the vehicle. This process of moving from the simple and isolated question to the more intricate cause and effect relationships is an example of Systems Thinking.

Chapter 2

Critical Thinking

According to the Foundation for Critical Thinking, *critical thinking* is "the art of analyzing and evaluating thinking with a view to improving it."[132] Critical thinking applies to both our analytical and systems thinking activities. The Foundation notes that a critical thinker expresses the following behaviors:

- Raises vital questions and problems, formulating them clearly and precisely
- Gathers and assesses relevant information, using abstract ideas to interpret it effectively
- Comes to well-reasoned conclusions and solutions, testing them against relevant criteria and standards
- Thinks open-mindedly within alternative systems of thought, recognizing and assessing, as needs be, their assumptions, implications, and practical consequences
- Communicates effectively with others in figuring out solutions to complex problems

Critical thinking goes beyond the acquisition of knowledge and facts that are gathered during both analytical and systems thinking. Knowing that the size of a vehicle affects both fuel consumption and safety is useful only if you critically consider how to apply that knowledge to achieve the desired outcome. Critical thinking is what helps us ensure that we more fully reflect on our analytical and systems thinking.

Next, we will see how we can apply the kinds of thinking above in our decision-making through our use of *real* arguments.

> Can you give examples of when Systems 1 and Systems 2 thinking are active in your daily life? When have you relied upon a handy heuristic that led to a faulty conclusion? What steps might you take to remain vigilant to how you are thinking about a situation and to shift your mental processes to better understand or interpret what is going on?

Real Arguments

What people commonly refer to as an *argument* can be defined as, "an exchange of diverging or opposite views, typically a heated or angry one."[133] We all have seen this kind of argument on the street, at work, on the evening news and social networks where people are going at it in angry verbal combat. Voices rise in pitch and volume, fingers thrust like daggers, and wild invectives are thrown about like feces from irate chimpanzees. We may even occasionally participate in such arguments – it seems to be normal human behavior that crosses age, race, gender, social status, and education. These are **not** the kinds of arguments that we'll examine in this section.

In this section, we'll examine *real arguments* that express "a reason or set of reasons given in support of an idea, action, or theory." This kind of argument is a less theatrical expression and more thoughtful exploration that's intended to better understand how we and others arrive at our decisions. A practical understanding of real arguments is important because it can help us make decisions that are based on well-supported reasoning.

The construction of valid and strong arguments from evidence-based premises involves various forms of thinking, including the types discussed above. Real arguments can help avoid confusion between strong opinions and facts in a diagrammatic way where we and others can *see* what we're thinking and meticulously challenge the underlying assumptions and premises that lead to our conclusions and decisions. Although the statements of the following kind may seem like real arguments, none of them are:

- **Opinions**: "Among all of the colors, green is the best!"
- **Explanations**: "We lowered the price of our product because our competitors lowered their prices"
- **Advice**: "Scrub your head with mayonnaise to grow hair."
- **Instructions**: "Turn off the main power before opening the access panel."

A real argument includes a series of *statements* that present one or more *premises* in support of one and only one *conclusion*.[134] Two conditions must be met for a real argument to be a useful argument: the premises of the argument must be true, and the premises must support the conclusion. Conversely, if the premises are false or don't support the conclusion, then the argument fails.

Deductive and Non-Deductive Arguments

Real arguments are of two kinds: deductive and non-deductive (also known as inductive). A deductive argument is a real argument for which the premises offered provide **irrefutable** support for a conclusion. A non-deductive argument is a real argument for which the premises provide **probable** support for a conclusion.

Deductive arguments are "characterized by or based on the inference of particular instances from a general law", for example,

First premise: Dachshunds are dogs,
Second premise: Ozzie is a Dachshund,
Conclusion: THEREFORE, Ozzie is a dog.

If Dachshunds are dogs (they are), and if Ozzie is a Dachshund (I know he is because he's snoozing next to me as I write this) then Ozzie **must** be a dog. There isn't any way around the conclusion of this deductive argument given the truth of the premises.

Non-deductive arguments are "characterized by the inference of general laws from particular instances", for example,

First premise: Ozzie doesn't bite me,
Second premise: Ozzie doesn't bite my wife,
Conclusion: THEREFORE, PROBABLY, Ozzie won't bite you.

If Ozzie doesn't bite me or my wife, then he may not bite you, although he might. In fact, Ozzie has nipped those who have gotten between him and his food bowl!

In both examples above, even if the real argument is properly constructed with several premises leading to one conclusion, faulty premises would lead to faulty conclusions referred to as *false* in the deductive case and *weak* in the non-deductive case.

- In the deductive argument above, if Dachshunds **aren't** dogs, but Ozzie **is** a Dachshund, then Ozzie **isn't** a dog.
- In the non-deductive argument above if Ozzie **does** bite me and my wife, then you might want to keep your distance from Ozzie.

Operating in the real world where uncertainty reigns, the modern Devil's Advocate will typically be assessing the strength of non-deductive arguments rather than the validity of deductive arguments. Business decisions must often be made in the absence of perfect information and so particular attention needs to be given to the assumptions of the argument premises – are assumptions well supported or based in wishful thinking?

Estimates of revenue growth, for example, may be based on a blend of historical performance and current market trends. The Devil's Advocate would want to not only confirm the source and veracity of such insight but also look for other interpretations of the information. Are the current market conditions similar enough to the past to support an assumption that similar revenue performance will continue forward? Are the characteristics of today's customers clearly understood, and are there reasons why customers may not respond today as they have in the past?

Diagramming Real Arguments

Diagramming real arguments as shown below can help us see how we're thinking. In the diagrams, the premises are stated to the left, and the premises lead to a conclusion to the right. Note that the only difference in these diagrams is that the premises of deductive arguments (left) lead to the conclusion with the term "Therefore" while the premises of non-deductive arguments (right) lead to the conclusion with the phrase "Therefore, probably" – a very important difference as we'll discuss below.

CHAPTER 2

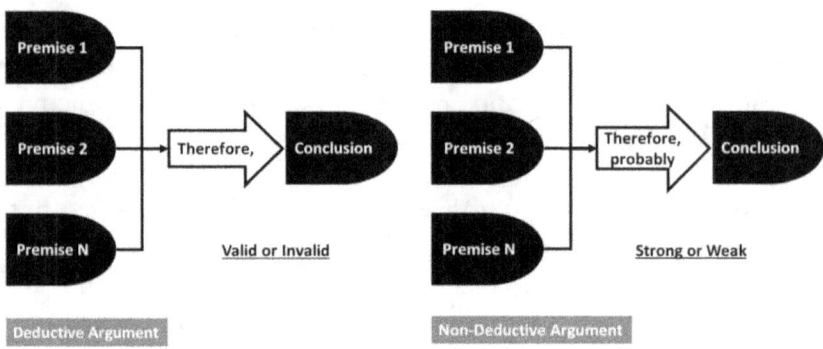

Deductive and non-deductive arguments differ by the presence of uncertainty

Deductive arguments are either *valid* or *invalid*. A deductive argument is valid "if and only if it takes a form that makes it impossible for the premises to be true and the conclusion nevertheless to be false"[135] otherwise the argument is invalid. Inductive arguments deal with uncertainty and so are deemed either *strong* or *weak*.[136] Let's apply the general diagrams above to a few examples below.

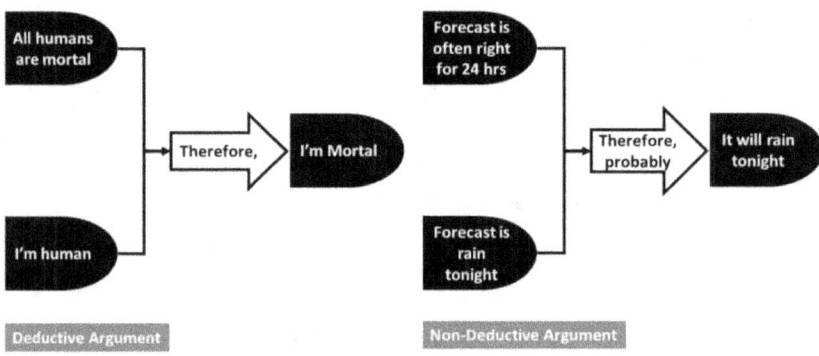

The deductive argument above (left) is based on an argument that is commonly attributed to Aristotle. The premises are that all humans are mortal and that we are human. The conclusion is that because all humans are mortal, and because we are human then we **must** be mortal. Some may suggest that Aristotle's argument isn't strictly a deductive example because we can't know with absolute certainty that all humans are mortal (although the human condition seems to support the mortality premise). If you were not strictly human (e.g. a vampire) then that condition would quash the argument because the argument is made solely for human entities.

In the non-deductive argument above (right), the premises are that a 24-hour weather forecast is generally accurate and that the current forecast indicates rain within that 24-hour window. The conclusion is that it will **probably** rain tonight, although the evening could turn out dry and clear.

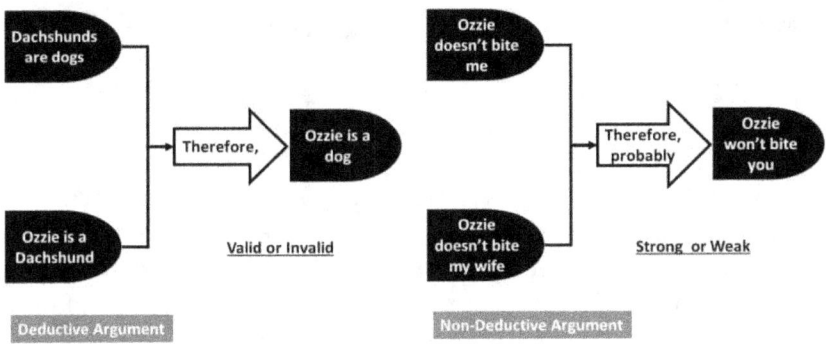

In the deductive argument above (left), I've diagrammed my earlier example about Dachshunds and Ozzie. The argument premises are that Dachshunds are a breed of dog and that Ozzie is a Dachshund, therefore Ozzie **must** be a dog.

In the non-deductive argument, the premises are that Ozzie doesn't bite me and doesn't bite my wife, leading to the conclusion that Ozzie **probably** won't bite you – but he might!

An historical example of real arguments includes those for and against a sun-centered model of the universe (below). Those supporting the earth-centered model built their premises on biblical interpretation that they claimed was indisputable while those supporting the sun-centered model built their premises on an interpretation of observed planetary motion for which various sun-centered and earth-centered models were proposed. One such observation was how some celestial bodies appeared to reverse their direction of travel, known as *retrograde motion*.[137]

CHAPTER 2

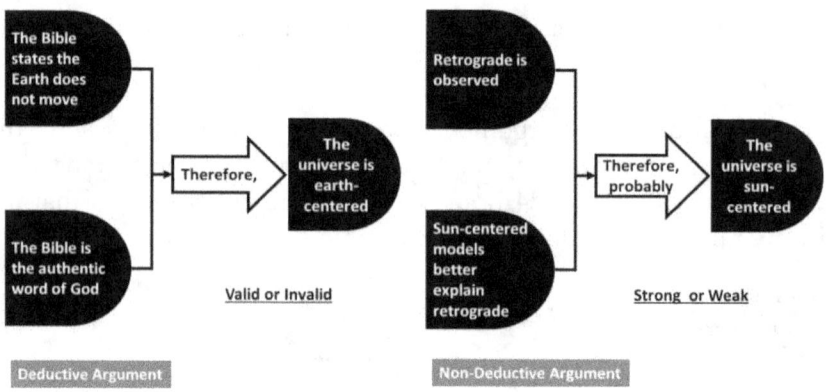

The diagram above shows simple versions of the sun-centered vs. earth-centered debate. At the left is the deductive argument for earth-centered models based on "irrefutable" biblical premises. At right is the non-deductive argument for sun-centered models based on the likelihood that the apparent reversal observed in planetary orbits is better explained by sun-centered models than by earth-centered models.

Finally, the diagram below shows a very simple non-deductive argument for a claim that I proposed in the Introduction of this book.

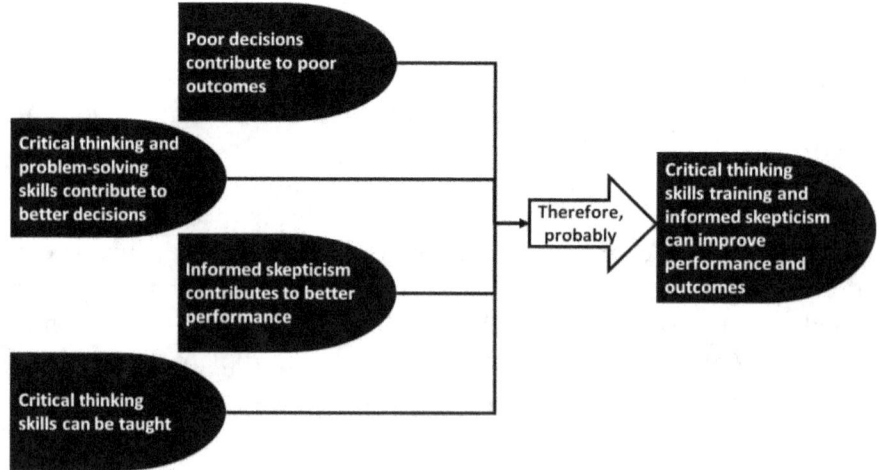

Constructing valid and strong arguments is only part of the work required when challenging a given position. Real arguments are often made in a live debate setting where parties with differing views are working to express their position in the strongest possible terms and to question the validity and strength of opposing arguments (e.g. project meetings, management reviews). The act of challenging an argument is typically referred to as *refutation* or attempting to show that an argument is false or erroneous. Several approaches are common in refutation, including challenging *relevance* or *significance* of the argument and *spinning* (also referred to as *turn* or *capture*).

A **relevance** challenge attempts to dismiss an argument (or a premise in support of an argument conclusion) because the argument or premises have nothing to do with the question being discussed. Consider the following premises used to construct arguments against and for the question, Will background checks reduce gun violence?

- **Against**: Generations of Americans have owned guns since well before the founding of the Country and without any background checks.
- **For**: The Vast Majority of Americans Support Universal Background Checks.

Both statements may be factually true but neither statement supports a conclusion about the relationship between background checks and gun violence and so neither statement is relevant to the topic. Strong arguments could be made by premises that rely upon relevant third-party evidence that demonstrates either the ineffectiveness of background checks in the reduction of violence or the effectiveness of such checks.[138,139]

A **significance** challenge on the question of background checks and gun violence would propose that one position offers more weight or importance than an opposing position. For example, one party may focus on the financial impact that background checks would have on gun sales. In response, a counter position may propose that saving even a few lives by background checks is far more important than any loss of sales revenues and so is more significant to the issue.

Spinning has become a favored pastime in our world today. In the debate domain, spinning is known as *capture* or *turn*. Spinning is like playing catch where you grab a ball that's tossed to you and then throw it back to the pitcher. In a debate, one party may willingly accept the premises of their opponent and use those same premises in a counterargument. For example, consider how a premise in support of an argument **for** background checks may be spun to argue **against** background checks.

- **Premise**: Between 1999 and 2016 there were over 550,000 gun-related deaths of which almost 60% were due to suicide.
- **Spin**: I agree that most gun deaths are due to suicide, but suicidal thoughts are impulsive and occur well after a background check and a gun purchase – so a background check won't reduce most gun-related deaths.

Modern Devil's Advocates will regularly engage in a thoughtful debate where they will challenge others' claims and have their own premises and conclusions questioned. Daily practice in the creation and critique of real arguments is intended to help develop useful thinking and debate skills. Some good sources of practice material for arguments to dissect and analyze include daily news feeds, editorials and opinion pieces, and questions available on Kialo.com and ProCon.org. Of course, debate with other Devil's Advocates would be a good practice, too, because you would occasionally be required to take a position that is contrary to your own beliefs and to create the strongest possible case that you can construct.

As we strengthen our use of real arguments, we must work to ensure that we are thinking clearly and not succumbing to common ways of thinking that are biased or fallacious. Next, we'll examine just a few of the various biases and fallacies that can lead us to faulty premises and poor conclusions.

> Download the free *7-Day Argument Challenge* at http://bit.ly/39rMOMC that encourages you to see the world through the eyes of someone whose opinion you might normally dismiss without much thought. You can also download a free *Decision Log* to help analyze your decision-making behavior at https://bit.ly/3g8A29f

> What is a common argument that you have made and how would you diagram it as discussed above? What is a recent argument that another party has presented and how would you diagram it?

Notable Biases and Fallacies

Identifying and constructing real arguments relies upon compelling premises that lead to reasonable conclusions. Our efforts to assess the premises that we and others make require that we avoid being swayed by bias and fallacy.

Bias may be defined as "an inclination of temperament or outlook, especially, a personal and sometimes unreasoned judgment".[140] Fallacy may be defined as "a false or mistaken idea"[141] which can occur due to bias. It is important to become aware of common bias and fallacy and then to remain vigilant for the presence of these forces in our decision-making.

There are scores of books, videos, and other resources that discuss the many kinds of bias and fallacy from the perspectives of cognitive science, psychology, and philosophy. While academic research from these fields can be daunting for the casual reader, other sources explain bias and fallacy in plain English. One of my favorites in this accessible category is David McRaney's book, *You Are Not So Smart*, and his website by the same name.[142,143]

There are many types of bias and fallacy – one source lists 228 common fallacies.[144] I'm including just the *notable nine* listed below because I feel that they can be particularly influential in everyday decision-making. The descriptions and commentary that I provide are not comprehensive, and while some like False Dilemma are simple and straightforward, others like Survivorship Bias offer us the opportunity to delve more deeply into related issues.

Ad Hominem	Halo Effect
False Dilemma	Framing Bias
Confirmation Bias	Appeal to Authority
Survivorship Bias	The Dunning-Kruger Effect
False Cause	

CHAPTER 2

Ad Hominem

I'm starting with the Ad Hominem fallacy, in large part, because I feel that it is in full view on social networks today and also because it can be particularly (and unfortunately) effective.

The term, *ad hominem*, is Latin for "to the person". There are various forms of ad hominem which attack a person who is making an argument rather than the quality of the premises and conclusion of the person's argument. For example, faulting a representative's policy due to her political party affiliation rather than to the specifics of the policy that she is promoting. Ad hominem is also in play when we won't take advice from someone because they don't practice what they preach (e.g. a parent who smokes while telling a child not to smoke).

Some have suggested that the ad hominem may be appropriate **if** it also applies to the argument.[145] For example, should the honesty of the little boy who has repeatedly, and falsely, cried wolf be challenged if he's claiming once again that wolves are after the sheep? I feel that this exception can be a trap door that may quickly lead to wider acceptance of the ad hominem. I urge you to entirely reject the ad hominem in all of its forms, even if revalidation of the claim in question takes some time and effort (e.g. maybe the kid really did see a wolf this time).

The following exchanges are simple examples of the kind of ad hominem that is popular in political use.

Jane: "My plan will improve the quality of life for our citizens by increasing the minimum wage which will enable people to buy more goods and services." **John**: "Jane is a Socialist who wants nothing less than the downfall of America."	**John**: "The only way for us to improve the quality of life for our citizens is by removing rules barring companies from government bids so those companies can hire more people." **Jane**: "John belongs to the one-percenters whose greed will only make the rich richer."

ARE YOU CONTROLLING WHAT YOU CAN?

There may be truth in the claims and responses offered by both Jane and John, however, neither response directly addresses the other party's argument. Rather than view these kinds of exchanges as a win/lose game, it may be more useful for both parties to explore each other's premises to find some common ground for a cooperative conclusion.

John might ask Jane how she will ensure that businesses aren't burdened by a minimum wage increase and Jane may reply that the minimum wage requirement would not apply to companies with fewer than a certain number of employees. This kind of back-and-forth exploration could eventually lead to an understanding of the real arguments that Jane and John are making rather than to engage in a verbal fight and attacks on each other's character.

As productive as this shift away from a win/lose environment might be, I doubt it will happen any time soon. Why? Because the ad hominem attack appears to be a very easy and extremely effective means to sway the opinions of others. In one study,[146] researchers investigated the effect of ad hominem attacks by exposing test subjects to certain scientific claims with and without ad hominem. Separate subject groups were then tested as follows:

- **Group 1**: was presented with the claim and an attack on the scientific veracity of the claim
- **Group 2**: was presented with the claim and an ad hominem attack on the party making the claim
- **Group 3**: was presented with the claim and an attack on both the claim and the party making the claim

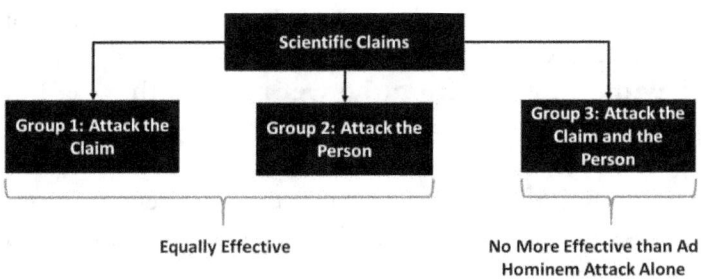

The results of the study revealed that a combination attack on the claim and the person making the claim was no more effective than an ad hominem attack alone. Further, an ad hominem attack alone was as effective as attacking the claim alone. In short, you don't need to spend any time and energy to understand a claim and then construct a strong and real counterargument to the claim. Simply attack the person making the claim – an attack that you can pull out of thin air, and you stand a good chance of swaying others to your side. Note, I'm **not** suggesting that you ever mount an ad hominem attack!

False Dilemma

False dilemma fallacy is also known as a false dichotomy. A *dilemma* may be defined as "an usually undesirable or unpleasant choice"[147] and a *dichotomy* as "a division into two especially mutually exclusive or contradictory groups or entities".[148] This fallacy can often be easily identified when options are stated in black-or-white terms like "either this or that" or authoritative declarations like "if, then".

During the COVID-19 pandemic, for example, several theories for the origin of the virus were promoted, including from so-called "wet markets" in Wuhan, China, or a Chinese bioresearch laboratory situated near Wuhan, or by other sources.[149,150] In a television interview with columnist and author Gordon Chang, however, Chang confidently offered only two possible origins of the virus (bold is mine),

> "And, by the way...there is a lot of evidence that suggests this comes from the lab. A January 24th article from The Lancet -- which is the authoritative British medical journal -- said that many of the initial coronavirus cases did not come from the wet market, which is China's theory. Well, **if they didn't come from the wet market, they had to have come from the lab.**"[151]

Note that even if the source of the virus is objectively determined to be from the Chinese wet markets or the Wuhan laboratory, Chang's comment is still a false dichotomy because it does not recognize other plausible sources of the origin.

> 💡 Reflecting on the nature of *hedgehogs* and *foxes* as mentioned at the end of Chapter 1, what are your thoughts about Mr. Chang's comments and the likelihood that his opinion will be sought in the future?

False dilemma claims are easy to find in the world of politics and I'd bet you could share examples from your work and personal life, too. Do any of the following examples seem familiar to you?

- "If you want **better public schools**, then you have to **raise taxes**. If you don't want to raise taxes, then you don't want better schools."

- "If you want to **gain market share** then we need to **lower the product price**. If you don't want to lower the product price, then you don't want market share."

The claims made above ask you to look at the world as if decisions could be decided in a coin toss that offered only heads or tails outcomes. A better mental model of the world is generally one with a wider choice of options.

- Can public schools be improved **only** by a raise in taxes? Could public schools be improved by:
    - better allocation of existing resources, or
    - better working relationships between parents and teachers, or
    - other actions unrelated to increased funding through taxes?

- Can market share be increased **only** by lowering the product price? Could you increase market share by:
    - offering additional services with the product to increase its value to more customers, or
    - changing how the product is marketed, or
    - other actions unrelated to lowering the product price?

CHAPTER 2

Confirmation Bias

Confirmation bias is the tendency to interpret certain evidence as validation for our existing beliefs. If we believe that a certain politician is a dangerous extremist (Left or Right) then we are receptive to claims that frame the politician in that way and support our belief. It's as if once a belief is established, that belief creates the shortest path to an acceptable answer, effectively bypassing active thinking.

In 2018 the Pew Research Center conducted a survey that was intended, in part, to measure "the public's ability to distinguish between five factual statements and five opinion statements."[152] Looking at the segments of respondents, the results revealed that, "Republicans and Democrats are more likely to think news statements are factual when they appeal to their side – even if they are opinions." Wouldn't it be interesting if Pew conducted another survey to learn how many Republicans and Democrats agreed with Pew that members of both parties exhibit confirmation bias?

In the article, *The Case for Behavioral Strategy*, authors Dan Lovallo and Olivier Sibony note how pattern-recognition predispositions like confirmation bias may specifically affect those in positions of authority who lean on prior experience and questionable analogies:

> "The ability to identify patterns helps set humans apart but also carries with it a risk of misinterpreting conceptual relationships...Particularly imperiled are senior executives, whose deep experience boosts the odds that they will rely on analogies, from their own experience, that may turn out to be misleading. Whenever analogies, comparisons, or salient examples are used to justify a decision, and whenever convincing champions use their powers of persuasion to tell a compelling story, pattern recognition biases may be at work." [153]

Note that confirmation bias is different from reliance on strong theories that are supported by compelling evidence while remaining open to new information and modification of existing theories.

The Cottingley Fairies offer a curious historical example of how confirmation bias can affect even those with a reputation of keen observation and intellect. The Fairies are named after Cottingley Village[154] in the UK where young cousins, Frances Griffith, and Elsie Wright produced several photographs showing fairies.

The girls took their first picture in 1917 which showed a tiny fairy posing with Frances. By one account, Elsie's father believed the image to be a trick although his wife was more believing in the supernatural. Through a series of connections, the story of the Cottingley Fairies reached Sir Arthur Conan Doyle, the creator of the master detective, Sherlock Holmes.

Doyle held a firm belief in spiritualism and wrote a slim book on the Cottingley Fairies entitled, *The Coming of the Fairies*.[155] In the preface of the book, Doyle takes a somewhat moderated stance that provides a little distance between spiritualism and "subhuman" forms of life. Perhaps he was hedging his bet; if the fairies proved to be fake, then spiritualism would not be soiled by the deceit?

> "This book contains reproductions of the famous Cottingley photographs, and gives the whole of the evidence in connection with them. The diligent reader is in almost as good a position as I am to form a judgment upon the authenticity of the pictures. This narrative is not a special plea for that authenticity, but is simply a collection of facts the inferences from which may be accepted or rejected as the reader may think fit.
>
> "I would warn the critic, however, not to be led away by the sophistry that because some professional trickster, apt at the game of deception, can produce a somewhat similar effect, therefore the originals were produced in the same way. There are few realities which cannot be imitated, and the ancient argument that because conjurers on their own prepared plates or stages can produce certain results, therefore similar results obtained by untrained people under natural conditions are also false, is surely discounted by the intelligent public.

> "I would add that this whole subject of the objective existence of a subhuman form of life has nothing to do with the larger and far more vital question of spiritualism. I should be sorry if my arguments in favour of the latter should be in any way weakened by my exposition of this very strange episode, which has really no bearing upon the continued existence of the individual."

I hope you won't be disappointed to learn that the Cottingley Fairies were a hoax to which the girls admitted before her deaths.[156]

> ⏱ Due to disputed copyright claims from outside of the United States, I'm not providing any images of the Cottingley Fairies in this book. Images are available online, however, including at the link below where you may also learn more about the curious events surrounding the images. http://bit.ly/39sn8Qn

== *The Backfire Effect* ==

Not included in my shortlist of bias and fallacy, but discussed here because of its relationship to Confirmation Bias, is the so-called Backfire Effect. The Backfire Effect has been described as, "When your deepest convictions are challenged by contradictory evidence, your beliefs get stronger."[157]

You may agree that the Backfire Effect seems to be particularly active in today's social media exchanges where readers can readily adopt some far-fetched claims, especially when political claims align with the reader's closely held beliefs? Research, however, questions the validity of the backfire effect, even for political claims. In a recent paper entitled, *The Elusive Backfire Effect*, the authors reported that,

> "results from five experiments in which we enrolled more than 10,100 subjects and tested 52 issues of potential backfire. Across all experiments, we found no corrections capable of triggering backfire, despite testing precisely the

kinds of polarized issues where backfire should be expected. Evidence of factual backfire is far more tenuous than prior research suggests. By and large, citizens heed factual information, even when such information challenges their ideological commitments."[158]

It turns out that the Backfire Effect may be relatively rare[159] but could be a potential bias to keep in mind if you encounter particularly strong opposition to an evidence-based, dissenting opinion. You can listen to an interview with Brendan Nyhan, one of the researchers behind the Backfire Effect at https://www.wnyc.org/story/walking-back-backfire-effect/

> Can you think of a simple experiment whereby you first assess a subject's belief in the Backfire Effect, then present the counterview above and see if their response suggests that the Backfire Effect is occurring?

Survivorship Bias

As the term implies, Survivorship Bias is formed when we consider only successful outcomes and then generalize from those selected instances. This bias can occur on any topic, including financial decisions that can make significant impacts on an investor's expectations,

> "Survivorship bias or survivor bias is the tendency to view the performance of existing stocks or funds in the market as a representative comprehensive sample without regarding those that have gone bust. Survivorship bias can result in the overestimation of historical performance and general attributes of a fund or market index."[160]

Common financial planning guidance relies on how the stock market value has risen over time. Some point to an historical market growth figure and propose that had you invested your money in stocks at some time in the past then you, too, would have experienced this kind of growth.[161] Numbers are available to support the stock market growth narrative but also reveal periods when the stock market value dropped dramatically.[162] So, of course, your investment growth could have been higher or lower than the historical growth, depending on your mix of actual stocks, when you bought, and when you sold.

The popular market value growth narrative isn't surprising because indices like the Dow Jones Industrial Average (DJIA) lean into a positive outlook. The DJIA includes just 30 companies that meet certain performance criteria and firms that don't meet the criteria are replaced by other firms that do qualify.[163] Fifty-four reorganizations have been made to the DJIA since its creation, including the removal of former star participants Bethlehem Steel, General Electric, Citigroup, and Sears.[164] By keeping only those firms in the DJIA that perform positively, ignoring firms that perform poorly or have gone bankrupt, certainly benefits the growth story. Remember, however, that asset management firms are required by the Securities and Exchange Commission to state that "past performance is no guarantee of future results".

It is certainly likely that the mix of assets in your portfolio won't perform well indefinitely and may dip precipitously just when you need to rely upon them for income. Occasional and notoriously unpredictable depressions and recessions have occurred in the stock market and will likely happen again. However, even experts can be blindsided by these future events,

> "In 1929, popular prognosticators like the Yale economist Irving Fisher swore that if a correction came, it would look like a harmless slump, while others predicted a jagged cliff. But nobody, absolutely nobody, could have foreseen the stock-market slaughter that happened in late October."[165]

Survivorship bias can be powerfully misleading by presenting a perspective of success that does not reflect all outcomes, including outright failures. Some may claim that such filtering is a good way to identify those characteristics that make people and companies great – and therefore you should emulate those characteristics. Such a view, however, assumes that past successes can be reliably reproduced today when conditions may be significantly different than in the past (as we considered earlier under trailing versus trailblazing processes and best practices). See also *The Creation of Modern Mythology* in the Appendices of this book.

False Cause

False Cause fallacy is also referred to as *post hoc* fallacy. Post hoc is Latin for "after this" and refers to the misconception that because one event occurred after another, the first event **must** have caused the second event. Note that the term "false" should not be misconstrued to mean that the party making the claim is intentionally lying. Rather false should be understood as "incorrect" or not strongly established.

Consider some of the claims made about what factors may have driven down the crime rate in the United States between 1993 and 2017.[166] The reasons for the reduction in crime aren't fully understood but many opinions are available. As discussed in an *Atlantic Magazine* article,[167] several proposed reasons for the reduced crime rate include the following:

- **Economic growth** in the 1990s led to less incentive for people to engage in criminal behavior.
- **The reduction of alcohol consumption** during the period led to less criminal behavior, particularly violent crime.
- **Better law enforcement** and policing with higher rates of incarceration put more criminals behind bars who could not conduct criminal behavior.
- **Affirmation of Roe v. Wade** in 1973 by the Supreme Court led to fewer unwanted pregnancies so fewer individuals were raised in environments that can contribute to criminal behavior.
- **Passing of the Clean Air Act** of 1970 which lowered toxic materials in the environment, including lead which is associated with behavior problems that may contribute to criminal behavior.

The author of the *Atlantic* article offers both support for and against the propositions stated above. While it may be true that the proposed reasons (and others not stated or known) worked in conjunction to achieve the overall reduction in crime rates, we simply can't be reasonably certain of the actual causes and effects.

CHAPTER 2

== *Correlation and Causation* ==

Neither bias nor fallacy, *correlation* and *causation* are strongly related to False Cause bias. *Correlation* is a statistical technique that indicates how strongly pairs of variables are related and change together. *Causation* is when a change in one variable causes a change in another variable (cause-and-effect). A simple example to show the difference between correlation and causation follows.

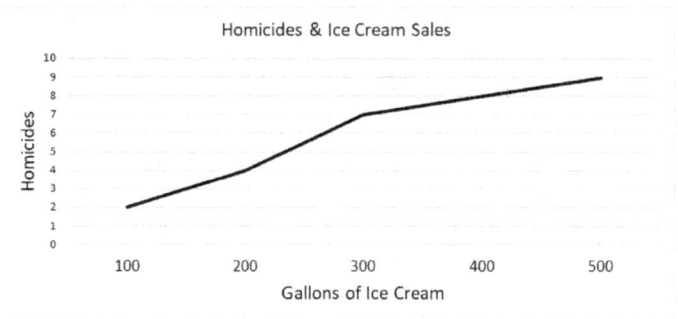

Suppose you are given the graph above which shows the number of homicides and the sales of ice cream for a given city. Your first impression may be that a cause and effect relationship exists - that an increase in ice cream sales is (somehow) causing homicides to increase! Here we see a correlation in action where the relationship between two variables reveals an upward trend. Graphs are typically created with the independent variable on the horizontal axis and the dependent variable on the vertical axis. So, you may be inclined to interpret homicides as being dependent upon ice cream sales.

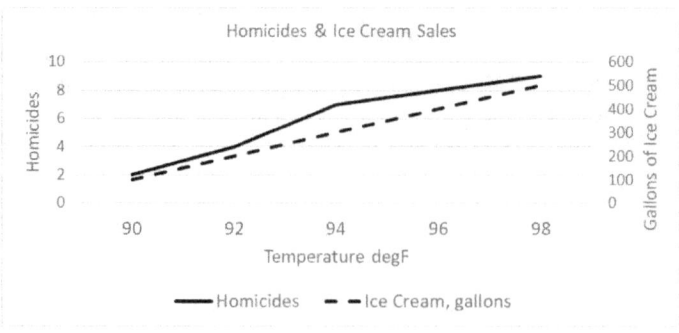

The second graph above shows the same homicide and ice cream information but plotted against a proposed independent variable, the temperature. Does it make sense that as the temperature rises so does frustration and anger – and your desire for a cold treat? The graph suggests that increases in homicides and ice cream sales are both caused by the temperature and not that ice cream sales have any direct relationship to homicides.

The Halo Effect

In broad terms, a halo defines the boundary of an area like the luminous circle of light that surrounds the moon on those evenings when ice particles are in the atmosphere. Halos may also refer to rings of light in paintings of persons who are considered worth veneration from emperors to saints.[168] This term has more recently been applied to how we perceive other people and companies.

The earliest reference to the "halo" effect is attributed to a paper written in 1920 by Edward L. Thorndike entitled, *A Constant Error in Psychological Ratings*.[169] Thorndike reported (bold is mine),

> "In study conducted in 1915 of employees of two large industrial corporations, it appeared that the estimates of the same man in a number of different traits such as intelligence, industry, technical skill, reliability, etc., etc., were very highly correlated and very evenly correlated. It consequently appeared probable that those giving the ratings were unable to analyze out these different aspects of the person's nature and achievement and rate each in independence of the others. Their ratings were apparently affected by a marked tendency to think of the person in general as rather good or rather inferior and to color the judgments of the qualities by this general feeling. This same constant error toward suffusing ratings of special features with a **halo** belonging to the individual as a whole appeared in the ratings of officers made by their superiors in the army."

CHAPTER 2

The article described how army officers were assessed by characteristics such as physical qualities (e.g. physique, neatness, voice), intelligence (e.g. ease in learning, decision-making), leadership (e.g. initiative, ability to inspire), personal qualities (e.g. loyalty, cooperation), and general value (e.g. professional knowledge, experience). The correlation among these various qualities was much higher than would have been expected or demonstrated by objective metrics. What appeared to be happening was that those who scored high in one characteristic also scored high in other characteristics, although the characteristics had no apparent commonality. Thorndike concluded that,

> "…even a very capable foreman, employer, teacher, or department head is unable to treat an individual as a compound of separate qualities and the others. The magnitude of the constant error of the **halo**, as we have called it, also seems surprisingly large, though we lack objective criteria by which to determine its exact size. As a consequence science seems to demand that, in all work on ratings for qualities the observer should report the evidence, not a rating, and the rating should be given on the evidence to each quality separately without knowledge of the evidence concerning any other quality in the same individual."

We may judge an individual's characteristics based on solely on our initial impressions

Consider, for example, the image of the businesswoman above – what are your initial thoughts? Doesn't she appear confident? Isn't she sharply dressed for success? Doesn't she exude youthful energy? Perhaps she's an executive of a successful business, or a talented medical specialist or scientist? Certainly, someone so poised and confident – someone like Theranos founder Holmes, must have other admirable qualities like technical expertise and truthfulness!

Are you able to look past the picture and conjure up any other impressions? Can you imagine that the subject is a struggling model whose life is nothing like the persona that she projects? How often might such appearances fool us, automatically positioning a *halo* of positive characteristics above the heads of people from all occupations who we don't know?

Almost one-hundred years after Thorndike's paper, Phil Rosenzweig published his seminal book, *The Halo Effect*,[170] in which he describes the halo phenomenon in the business world as,

> "The tendency to look at a company's overall performance and make attributions about its culture, leadership, values, and more. In fact, many things we commonly claim drive company performance are simple attributions based on prior performance."

Rosenzweig provides persuasive examples from the business world on this effect, including observations made by pundits on several real businesses. Examples included how pundits initially opine with great confidence that a company needs to do something *different* to achieve a certain goal like revenue growth. When the company does take innovative action but doesn't achieve the expected growth then the pundits opine with equal confidence (but in the opposite direction) that the company should have stuck its core business.

We seem to seek a narrative that appears to give a reasonable account for cause and effect that may not exist. If a company is hitting new highs in sales then we may believe that the CEO is a brilliant strategist and tactician, an empathetic leader, etc. Later we seem surprised when the company fails, or we learn about the CEO's infidelity, larcenous activities, etc. When this happens, we can quickly create a *post hoc*[171] story that explains these formerly unknown facts in retrospect, or as the old saw goes, "hindsight is 20/20" - although *hindsight* is yet another bias.[172]

CHAPTER 2

Framing Bias

Framing bias refers to the tendency for our perceptions and decisions to be influenced by how information is presented. We can look to politics to see how some work to exploit this bias to promote their agenda or ideology.

Imagine that you take two pictures of the same automobile. For the first picture, you zoom in on the front of the vehicle and focus on the sleek, highly polished lines of a luxury car. For the second picture, you zoom out to show the entire car and reveal that the vehicle has been in a serious accident, its trunk a crumpled mess. Placed side by side the two images of the same vehicle tell different stories. Another example is the email below that I received from a state representative (I've bolded certain framing text).

> **Subject**: I Need Your Feedback: Do you support Earmarks?
> "Recently, some members of Congress have expressed wanting to revive earmarks – a legislative procedure that allows for spending carve-outs for specific projects **historically fraught with waste**. Do you support or oppose lifting the ban on earmarks?"

On an initial read, you may feel as though earmarks should be avoided because you don't want your tax dollars wasted, especially when this waste has a long and well-established *history*. Consider, however, the following hypothetical version of the email that an opposing politician may send to you under the same subject.

> **Subject**: I Need Your Feedback: Do you support Earmarks?
> "Recently, some members of Congress have expressed wanting to revive earmarks – a legislative procedure that allows for spending carve-outs for specific projects that **will bring much-needed jobs to our State**. Do you support or oppose lifting the ban on earmarks?"

Hmm... jobs are good and with earmarks come jobs so maybe you ought to support earmarks? Framing bias also has the power to sway other important decisions. Consider the following example in healthcare which is based on a framing study from 1981.[173]

You are offered two experimental treatments for a serious health problem that you have. You are told that, based on clinical trials of 600 people, there is some risk in both treatments you ought to consider in choosing between two treatments:

> **Treatment A** was shown to contribute to 400 deaths of those who received the treatment
> **Treatment B** was shown to help 1/3rd of those who received the treatment

You may have noted that both treatments are equally effective. In Treatment A, 400 deaths out of 600 subjects means that 200 people were saved. Two hundred divided by six-hundred equals 1/3rd which is the same outcome as Treatment B. The study, however, found that Treatment A was chosen by 72% of respondents when it was presented with positive framing ("saves 200 lives") dropping to 22% when the same choice was presented with negative framing ("400 people will die").

Looking for framing bias can help ensure that you aren't being led astray by information that is being presented, intentionally or not, in a strongly positive or negative way.

Appeal to Authority

Appeal to Authority refers to our tendency to accept that a claim is true because an "authority" made the claim. Note that the term *authority* can apply either to someone who has the power to impose a decision or to an expert who has a high level of knowledge and experience in certain subjects. These are two very different kinds of authorities.

An example of the first kind of authority may be the CEO of a company or government official who can mandate a decision regardless of her area of expertise. An example of the second kind of authority may be a researcher who holds advanced degrees in a certain area of knowledge, who has published numerous peer-reviewed articles and who others in the field acknowledge as a thought leader. Claims made by either kind of authority

CHAPTER 2

figure may be false or weak, but as we'll examine below, it **is** reasonable to seek out the perspective of those authorities who have appropriate subject knowledge and expertise.

It is also beneficial, of course, to consider the view of several authorities when possible rather than to be led solely by a singular expert voice. Consider the business world where those who accept as *gospel* the solitary opinion of prominent individuals could be led astray.

> "$500, fully subsidized with a plan?!... That is the most expensive phone in the world, and it doesn't appeal to business customers because it doesn't have a keyboard."[174]
> *Steve Ballmer, CEO of Microsoft from 2000 to 2014, on the iPhone announcement*

> "I didn't understand the power of the model as I went along. And the price always seemed to more than reflect the power of the model at that time."[175]
> *Warren Buffett on why he didn't buy Amazon stock*

On the hot topic of climate change, various individuals with advanced science degrees have been identified as authorities on climate science.[176] Among the authorities are biologists, geologists, chemists, etc. It is certainly possible that a biologist or chemist may have deep knowledge and insight into climate change, but is it more likely that someone who has specific education and experience in climate science might be a true authority? Put another way, if you learned that you had a brain tumor, then you would presumably look for assistance from a medical doctor – but maybe not a proctologist?

An example from the healthcare arena is cigarette ads like the one below that ran from the late 1930s into the 1950s, featuring physician spokespersons.[177,178] Certainly, if a medical doctor smokes then smoking can't be harmful to you, right? Well, these ads predated the 1964 report of the Surgeon General's Advisory Committee on Smoking and Health that tied smoking to disease.[179] So while physicians at the time that the ads were created willingly participated in the messaging these physicians were expressing their subjective opinion rather than an evidence-based conclusion.

Are You Controlling What You Can?

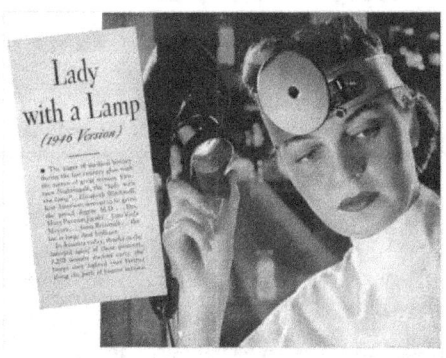

A 20th Century smoking advertisement

Similar product endorsements by non-medical celebrities are commonplace today and can create a detrimental influence on the decisions that consumers make. In one study,[180] researchers examined five-hundred and ninety endorsements by one-hundred and sixty-three celebrities in the music industry and concluded that "music celebrities who are popular among adolescents endorse energy-dense, nutrient-poor products." The researchers make a connection between the potential negative impact of celebrity endorsement on the health of those who are influenced,

> "Food and beverage marketing has been identified as a significant environmental contributor to childhood obesity. Exposure to food marketing promotes excess consumption, increased purchase requests, and higher preference for the product among children and adults."

Assessing the legitimacy of claims is particularly important when considering topics that are outside of our education and experience. In addition to product claims like those noted above, examples of dubious claims are found in so-called *conspiracy theories* that offer alternate explanations of events, featuring a scheme among a secretive group of nefarious connivers.[181] *Time* magazine provided the following conspiracy theory shortlist.

Chapter 2

Paul Is Dead	The Moon Landings Were Faked
9/11 Cover-Up	Jesus and Mary Magdalene
Area 51 and the Aliens	Holocaust Revisionism
The JFK Assassination	The CIA and AIDS
Secret Societies Control the World	The Reptilian Elite

Although we live in a time where many claims can be investigated in just a few clicks via the internet, social networks appear to be multiplying bad information at ever-escalating speed. Recently, researchers investigated over 125,000 news stories distributed more than 4.5 million times by about 3 million people on Twitter from 2006 to 2017. The researchers found that,

> "Falsehood diffused significantly farther, faster, deeper, and more broadly than the truth in all categories of information, and the effects were more pronounced for false political news than for false news about terrorism, natural disasters, science, urban legends, or financial information."[182]

The opinions and guidance from authorities who are subject matter experts are certainly useful and should be sought out. At the same time, it's important to monitor how we and others are choosing authorities.

The Dunning-Kruger Effect

Coined in 1999 by Cornell psychologists David Dunning and Justin Kruger, the Dunning-Kruger Effect is a bias where we are unable to recognize our own incompetence. Not only do we not recognize our incompetence, but we also may grossly underestimate our incompetence.

Dunning and Kruger arrived at their conclusion with findings from four studies that they conducted as reported in their article, *Unskilled and Unaware of It*[183] The four studies assessed individuals' self-assessments against standards on three categories: one in humor, two in logical reasoning, and one in English grammar. The researchers were particularly interested in how subjects who scored in the lowest quartile self-assessed.

Are You Controlling What You Can?

The graph below is a representation of the results from Dunning and Kruger's experiment. The solid line shows the results of how people believed they scored on test questions; the dashed line shows the actual test scores. The squares on the lines show the average scores in each of the four performance groups, from the lowest 25% to the top 25%.

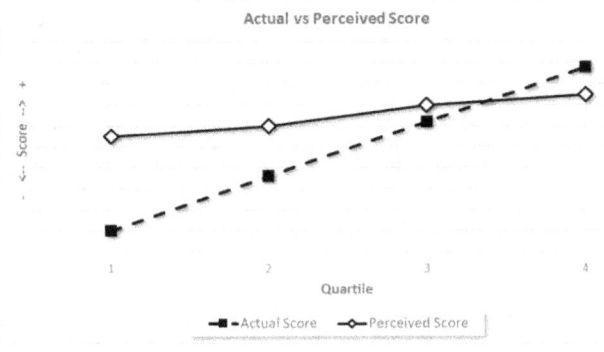

The first thing you'll notice in the graph above is that the perceived scores are higher than the actual scores in the first three groups. Those with the lowest actual scores also estimated their performance much more poorly than those with higher actual scores. A curious thing happens in the top 25% where individuals with the highest actual scores believed that they performed worse than they had. As David Dunning and an associate noted in a more recent paper:

> "When it comes to overconfident judgment, a little learning does appear to be a dangerous thing. Although beginners start with humble self-perceptions, with just a little experience their confidence races ahead of their actual performance." [184]

In case you feel as though you are better at estimating your abilities than the test subjects described, I refer you to the cautionary observation by Dr. Dunning, "The first rule of the Dunning-Kruger club is you don't know you're a member of the Dunning-Kruger club." [185] Given the potential negative consequences of such delusion – including on the part of a modern Devil's Advocate, you might wonder if there is any way to avoid this effect. Dunning offers the following advice (bold is mine),

Chapter 2

"For individuals, the trick is to **be your own devil's advocate**: to think through how your favored conclusions might be misguided; to ask yourself how you might be wrong, or how things might turn out differently from what you expect. It helps to try practicing what the psychologist Charles Lord calls "considering the opposite." To do this, I often imagine myself in a future in which I have turned out to be wrong in a decision, and then consider what the likeliest path was that led to my failure. And lastly: Seek advice. Other people may have their own misbeliefs, but a discussion can often be sufficient to rid a serious person of his or her most egregious misconceptions."[186]

 What high level of skill do you believe you possess? How will you attempt to challenge your perception of your skill today?

In this chapter, we briefly looked at different kinds of thinking and saw that analytical, systems and critical thinking are not reflexive but intentional and within our control. We examined how real arguments can help us map out our thinking to see how our premises that lead to our conclusions. We also examined how bias and fallacy can cloud our thinking as we examine others' arguments and build our own arguments.

Of course, many things are outside of our control that can impact our judgments and outcomes and we'll take a look at several of these factors in the next chapter.

Chapter 3: Are You Recognizing What's Beyond Your Control?

We opened the last chapter with an observation by the Stoic philosopher, Epictetus. Following is Epictetus' complete statement,

> "Some things are in our control and others not. Things in our control are opinion, pursuit, desire, aversion, and, in a word, whatever are our own actions. Things not in our control are body, property, reputation, command, and, in one word, whatever are not our own actions."[187]

We saw in the last chapter how we may control our impulsive tendencies by monitoring our thinking, avoiding common bias and fallacy, and making strong real arguments. You may quibble with some of the items on Epictetus' list of those things that are outside of our control, however, I'd bet that you regularly struggle to control outcomes and are frustrated when things seem to go awry as if they had a mind of their own.

In this chapter we will take a look at a few of the more common factors that can seem actively hostile to our plans and actions, in particular, we'll examine rare and disruptive events, luck, and uncertainty.

CHAPTER 3

Black Swan Events

As the statistician and financial modeler, Nassim Taleb relates, once upon a time everyone in Europe was certain that all swans were white because that's the only kind of swan they had ever seen. But then a Dutch explorer traveling to Australia witnessed something unexpected and remarkable – black swans!

Popularized by Taleb's book, *The Black Swan*,[188] Black Swan events aren't bias or fallacy but rather allude to possible bias and fallacy associated with models that improperly assume a normal distribution of probability. Also known as the *bell curve* due to its shape, an example normal distribution curve is shown below.[189]

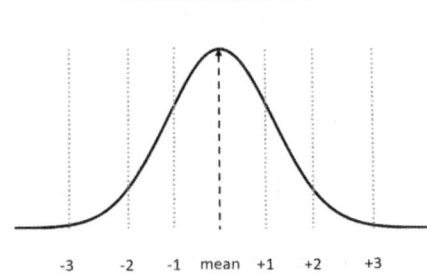

Normal Distrubution Curve

The normal distribution curve expresses how many types of data sets in our world tend to fall within a range of probabilities. For example, the curve above may represent the height of two hundred women in the freshman class of a given university. Most women included will have a height near the average (mean) height calculated from all the women's heights (referenced by the dashed black line under the peak of the curve above). The normal distribution curve drops to the left and the right of the peak as progressively fewer women will be shorter (to the left of the peak) or higher (to the right of the peak) than the mean height.

The spread of heights higher and lower than the mean height is expressed by the calculated *standard deviation* (SD).[190] In a normal distribution curve, about 68% of values will fall between one standard deviation to the left and right of the mean, about 95% of values fall between 2 SD and about 99% of values within 3 SD (these SD ranges are shown by the dashed gray lines above). In this example, there will be a minimum height and a maximum height between which all the women's heights in the measured group will be contained.

If you were to randomly choose the name of a woman out of a hat from all the women included in the height measurement example above, then the likelihood of that randomly selected woman's height being near the mean height would be greater than the likelihood that her height would fall nearer the ends of the curve. Of course, if the measurements were made of two hundred men in the same freshmen class as the women above, then the mean and standard deviation would likely be different – perhaps a higher average value with a narrower spread of heights. The characteristics of the normal distribution curve as discussed above, however, would likewise apply to those separate measurements of the men's heights.

The normal distribution curve has been so effective that it is commonly used to explain the expected outcome of a random sample for many data sets. The use of the normal distribution curve, however, is not always appropriate.

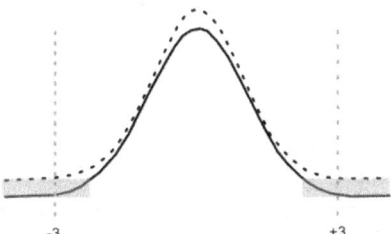

Shown in the diagram above is *fat* or *heavy* tail probability distribution (dashed black line) compared to a normal distribution (solid black line). Note how more data falls outside of 3 SD in the fat tail distribution than in the normal distribution (grayed areas). This additional data beyond 3 SD increases the chance that an unusual but possible outcome will occur.

More than a curiosity, the nature of fat tail probability distribution has real-world consequences such as those acknowledged by the investment community.[191,192] It's not that the normal distribution curve is "wrong" rather when it is improperly applied it can mask the probability of disruptive events. The Black Swan events that Taleb discusses have several characteristics, including:

Chapter 3

- They are unexpected based on experience and data
- they make a huge impact
- they are often "explained" after the fact as if the event were predictable (i.e. False Cause)

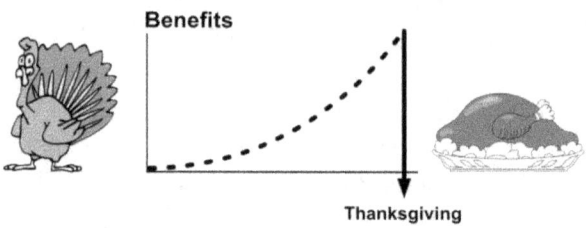

Thanksgiving is a turkey's Black Swan event

Taleb uses Thanksgiving Day as an example Black Swan event - from a turkey's perspective (diagrammed above). Every day of its life the turkey receives food and shelter from the farmer. Over time, the turkey comes to associate the farmer with food and shelter because it has no way of knowing that his demise will come with the arrival of Thanksgiving Day (the turkey's Black Swan event).

Common examples of Black Swan events include personal computers, the internet, terrorist attacks, winning the lottery, etc. Predicting Black Swan events is essentially a hopeless cause and some in the investment community have recommended abandoning complex predictive models in favor of, "Our old friends—diversification, ongoing monitoring, rebalancing and so on".[193]

A take-away is that we need to acknowledge that the unexpected, both bad and good, can happen without warning regardless of our best efforts. This affirmation may help keep our hubris to a minimum and our risk/reward goals balanced.

> You might be thinking that the COVID-19 pandemic is an example of a Black Swan event? According to Taleb, it wasn't. You can watch a video interview at Bloomberg online with Taleb entitled, *The Corona Crisis is Not a Black Swan* [194]

The Impact of Luck

In the early morning hours of January 24, 1961, a catastrophe was in the making high in the skies above North Carolina. A Boeing Stratofortress aircraft carrying two nuclear bombs was making ready to refuel mid-air when the bomber started spilling fuel from one of its wings. As the pilots abandoned their refueling task to seek safe landing below, the bomber began to tear apart.

Under the forces of an uncontrolled and violent descent, the two nuclear weapons separated from the bomber and struck impromptu targets near Goldsboro – very close to both Raleigh and Fayetteville considering that the weapons were two-hundred and fifty times more powerful than the bomb dropped on Hiroshima. During the event, three of the seven-man crew were lost but both bombs survived the impact without detonation. These weapons were designed to arm only with manual intervention, however, according to one account,

> "The military studied the bombs and learned that six of seven steps to blow up one of them had engaged, according to *The Register*. Only one trigger stopped a blast — that switch was set to 'ARM' yet somehow failed to detonate the bomb. It was only 'by the slightest margin of chance, literally the failure of two wires to cross, a nuclear explosion was averted,' a declassified 1963 memo described Robert McNamara, the secretary of defense at the time, as saying."[195]

The narrow escape of a nuclear disaster in North Carolina is a frightening example of incredibly good luck. Luck also regularly plays a role in less life-threatening situations and discounting the impact of luck can lead us to believe in strong cause-and-effect relationships that may not exist.

Earlier we looked at Survivorship Bias which can occur when we consider only positive outcomes. People who experience positive outcomes may claim that their success was due solely to their hard work and brilliant decisions. The publicity machines for such celebrities crank out well-worn narratives of the "self-made" man and woman. Once ingrained in our modern mythologies, these personas may look like roadmaps that we can follow to become rich and famous just like the celebrities.

Survivorship bias informs us that because we do not know the stories of others who have failed (or even the complete story of those who succeed), we may come to believe that success is due solely to hard work driven by personal passions. This belief may lead some to follow the narrative of celebrity success stories and thereby suffer unintentional and unwanted personal results. There is some debate about the relationship between social networks and depression, but it does appear that we may benefit by spending less time looking at all the happy and successful people on the many social networks.[196,197]

How large a role does luck play in success and failure? According to Professor Daniel Kahneman, the Nobel Prize-winning economist I mentioned earlier - who reportedly opined, "This Nobel Prize stuff, don't take it too seriously"[198] - offers two success equations,[199]

> "success = talent + luck
> great success = a little more talent + a lot of luck"

Luck, as we'll see below, is often the *elephant in the room* when discussing successful outcomes. Numerous examples of the reasonableness of Kahneman's success equations can be found in both research and from the lips of successful people.

In a paper entitled, *Talent vs Luck*,[200] investigators explored the impact of talent and luck (randomness) on success and how the allocation of funding based on merit may not yield the best outcomes. The researchers developed a Talent vs Luck (TvL) model that examined how random occurrences of lucky and unlucky events would impact successful outcomes over forty years and across a spectrum of similarly skilled individuals, who all start with the same amount of capital.

When an individual encountered a random unlucky event, their capital was cut in half; when an individual encountered a random lucky event, their capital was doubled, proportional to their talent. Their analysis suggested that while talent and hard work are certainly important factors in success "luck also matters, even if its role is almost always underestimated by successful people". The researchers also observed that the popular views of success are based on the,

> "...belief that success is due mainly, if not exclusively, to personal qualities such as talent, intelligence, skills, smartness, efforts, willfulness, hard work, or risk taking. Sometimes, we are willing to admit that a certain degree of luck could also play a role in achieving significant material success. But, as a matter of fact, it is rather common to underestimate the importance of external forces in individual successful stories...almost never the most talented people reach the highest peaks of success, being overtaken by mediocre but sensibly luckier individuals."

> The researchers suggest that their investigation, "...sheds new light on the effectiveness of assessing merit on the basis of the reached level of success and underlines the risks of distributing excessive honors or resources to people who, at the end of the day, could have been simply luckier than others."

The model created by the researchers is an example of the so-called *Matthew Effect*[201] named after a biblical parable from the gospel of Matthew. The parable describes how three servants managed gold coins put into their custody by their master while he traveled. Upon his return home, the master found that two of his servants put his wealth at risk but doubled their coins while the third servant conservatively kept the coins safe. The master expressed his happiness with the two servants who doubled their coins but was furious with the servant who didn't lose any of his coins, concluding,

> "Everyone who has something will be given more, and they will have more than enough. But everything will be taken from those who don't have anything."[202]

If you look beyond the celebrity press machines, then you will encounter successful people who acknowledge how important luck was in their

Chapter 3

accomplishment. One example is Douglas Bouton who left a six-figure job as a corporate lawyer to help build *Halo Top Creamery* and their low-calorie products. Bouton didn't have experience in the food and beverage industry or a back-up plan if the venture failed. Halo Top became a multi-million-dollar brand and was included in *Time Magazine*'s Top 25 Inventions for 2017.[203] This brief background could certainly set the foundation for yet another story of self-made success, but Bouton acknowledged,

> "I think one important thing to note that often is missed, and when entrepreneurs talk about success of their business, is luck. You can have the best idea, you can be the hardest smartest worker, and it still could fail."[204]

You may be familiar with Nate Silver whose website, *FiveThirtyEight.com*, correctly predicted the 2012 Presidential election. This outcome was taken by many as a kind of proof that people like Mr. Silver have some preternatural ability to be successful. Silver, however, acknowledged the role of luck,

> "I received a congratulatory phone call from the White House. I was hailed as 'lord and god of the algorithm' by The Daily Show's Jon Stewart. My name briefly received more Google search traffic than the vice president of the United States. I enjoyed some of the attention, but I felt like an outlier – even a fluke. Mostly I was getting credit for having pointed out the obvious – and most of the rest was luck."[205]

Likewise, Jen Rubio, co-founder of Away, the luggage company which achieved a valuation of over $1B,[206] acknowledged the significant role of luck in her life. When asked how much luck played in her success as compared to hard work, skill, and talent she replied:

> "I think it's probably fifty-fifty. For me, personally, luck and timing had so much to do with everything I've done at every single step."[207]

When she pledged half of her enormous wealth to philanthropy MacKenzie Bezos, co-founder of Amazon and former wife of Jeff Bezos conceded,[208]

> "We each come by the gifts we have to offer by an infinite series of influences and lucky breaks we can never fully understand."

Poker player and author, Annie Duke (winner of the $2 million winner-take-all, invitation-only WSOP Tournament of Champions[209]) observed,

> "We recognize the existence of luck, but we resist the idea that, despite our best efforts, things might not work out the way we want. It feels better for us to imagine the world as an orderly place, where randomness does not wreak havoc and things are perfectly predictable."[210]

Duke contrasts the games of chess and poker and the real world, making a persuasive case for the remarkable impact of luck in decision-making,[211]

> "Chess contains no hidden information and very little luck. The pieces are all there for both players to see. Pieces can't randomly appear or disappear from the board or get moved from one position to another by chance. No one rolls dice after which, if the roll goes against you, your bishop is taken off the board."

> "But life is more like poker. You could make the smartest, most careful decision in firing a company president and still have it blow up in your face. You could run a red light and get through the intersection safely – or follow all the traffic rules and signals and end up in an accident. You could teach someone the rules of poker in five minutes, put them at a table with a world champion player, deal a hand (or several), and the novice could beat the champion. That could never happen in chess."

CHAPTER 3

Duke's analogy supports her view that we can't always causally link a decision that we make today with future outcomes. You may, for example, decide today to balance your financial investments to benefit from historical returns, acknowledging that the market will occasionally take acceptable dips in performance. Your investment strategy may produce the returns that you expect – until a disruptive event like a recession occurs. Suddenly, what seemed like a reasonable choice when you made it may now appear like an awfully bad decision that you deeply regret. The fact remains, however, that at the time you made your investment decisions they were reasonably based on the available information.

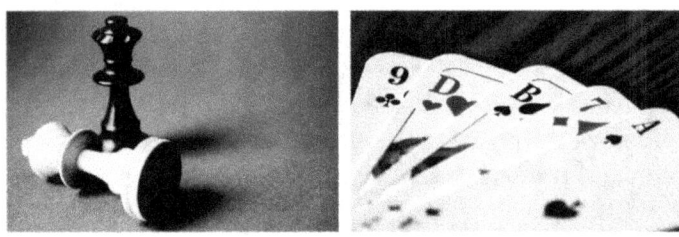

Poker is a better model for life because it is played with incomplete information and reasonable decisions can result in poor outcomes due to luck.

Of course, we should work to build and hone our skills, and to do the best job that we can in whatever endeavor we choose to pursue. However, luck (randomness) plays a significant role in the real world and so we should not view an outcome (either good bad) as a result that is due solely to our intentional actions. Consequently, no prior successes or failures should be spared a thoughtful critique and challenge, especially if such previous outcomes will be used to support premises to real arguments and future decisions.

> 💡 Can you give examples from your own life of chess-like and poker-like conditions? Can you give examples of a positive outcome that you had firmly attributed solely to your great decision-making but which may have been significantly impacted by luck/randomness? Is there a past decision that you now regret because you believed it led to a poor outcome? Would you now reconsider the regret for a poor outcome because (in retrospect) your past decision was based on the best available information at the time?

Risk and Uncertainty

The terms *risk* and *uncertainty* are often used interchangeably, however, they are different. One of the earliest explanations of risk and uncertainty is by the late economist, Frank Knight, Ph.D.,

> "The practical difference between the two categories, risk and uncertainty, is that in the former the distribution of the outcome in a group of instances is known (either through calculation a priori or from statistics of past experience), while in the case of uncertainty this is not true, the reason being in general that it is impossible to form a group of instances, because the situation dealt with is in a high degree unique."[212]

One way to think about risk is to consider the outcomes of tossing dice. The table below shows the thirty-six possible summed outcomes when tossing two six-sided dice (the diagonal lines help reveal dice combinations for eleven summed outcomes from 2 to 12).

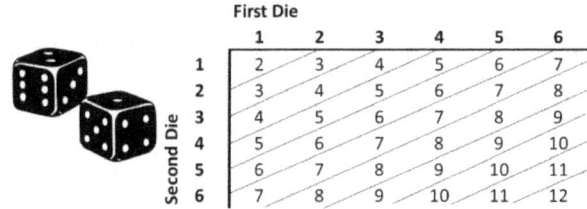

Table showing the possible totals from tosses of two, six-sided dice

These outcomes can be graphed as shown below with the probabilities for each of the eleven possible sums. For example, the number 7 can occur in six different combinations of the two dice for a probability of about 16.7% (6 combinations divided by 36 possible combinations). Knowing the probabilities of totals for these dice combinations can be used to estimate your *risk* when making bets in a dice game.[213] Let's take a quick and simple look at the dice game known as craps.

CHAPTER 3

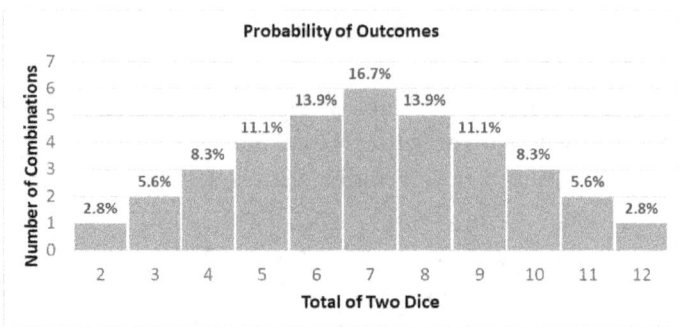

Craps is played with two, six-sided die, and the following rules,[214]

- If on your first roll the dice total is 7 or 11, then you win
- If on your first roll the dice total is 2, 3 or 12, then you lose
- Any other number total on your first roll is called the *point* (i.e. 4, 5, 6, 8, 9, or 10)
- You keep rolling the dice until you get a 7 (you lose) or your point number (you win)

What are your chances of winning on your first roll of the dice? Referring to the table above, there are 8 winning combinations for 7 or 11 out of 36 possible outcomes (or about 22%) – you can also add the probabilities for 7 and 11 from the graph and get the same answer.

Let's suppose that instead of rolling a winning 7 or 11 on your first toss, you roll a 4. Now, what are your chances that you'll roll another 4 to win before you roll a 7 and lose? This is a question of *conditional probability*, and we aren't going to delve deeper into that topic here, but the table below provides your odds of winning for different point numbers. Your chance of rolling a winning 4 before a losing 7 is about 2.8%.[215,216,217]

Your point …	Point probability…
4	2.8%
5	4.4%
6	6.3%
8	6.3%
9	4.4%
10	2.8%

Are You Recognizing What's Beyond Your Control?

If you add the probability of rolling a 7 or 11 on your first dice toss (~22%) and the combined probabilities above of rolling a winning point number if you don't win on your first roll (~27%), then you have slightly less than an even chance of winning at the game of craps.[218]

Uncertainty is different from risk in that uncertainty can't be confidently calculated as can risk. One way to think about uncertainty is to consider a dice game in which you don't know how many dice will be used for any given toss or the number of sides that each die used for any toss will have. The first toss may be with four six-sided dice, the second toss with two nine-sided dice, the third toss with one six-sided and one nine-sided die, etc. Without knowing the number and type of die that will be tossed, you have no way of constructing outcome tables and calculating probabilities as we did for two, six-sided dice outcomes above.

Outcomes can't be calculated if the type or number of dice aren't known

A take away is that it's very important to know if you are facing a situation where risk can be reasonably assessed, or an uncertain situation where your options may be limited to hedging against a complete loss should you not attain the desired outcome. It's not uncommon for people to assign a risk value that they believe is sensible but for which there is little to no objective data support. Such subjective estimates of risk are very different from determinable risk like the toss of two, six-sided dice.

In this chapter, we briefly explored factors over which we have little or no control including unexpected disruptions, luck, and uncertainty. In the next chapter, we'll consider a handful of tools that may be useful in the practice of modern Devil's Advocacy

CHAPTER 4: ARE YOU SURE THAT'S THE RIGHT TOOL?

A tool can be defined as "a means to an end" - a hammer is a means of driving a nail, MS Excel is a means to creating financial statements, etc. However, I caution you against the advice of philosopher and handyman, Red Green, that, "Any tool can be the right tool."[219] You could certainly try hammering a screw into a board but the process might be painful and the outcome less than desirable.

In this chapter, we will examine a variety of tools, starting with simple methods and ending on more advanced concepts. I've provided detour signs for those who may wish to avoid some of the more arcane discussions. Our exploration of these tools is intended to help reveal their strengths and weaknesses which will hopefully lead you to question how you have been using, or might use, such tools in your daily practice.

A strength of many of the tools that we'll be examining is that they can produce a quantitative answer based on inputs that we provide. Numbers, however, can also imply accuracy and precision that is unfounded if the validity of inputs is suspect or if the answer is blindly accepted without considering its meaning. The need to continuously question the reasonableness of tools, inputs and the interpretation of outputs is a practice requirement for the modern Devil's Advocate.

Perhaps the most important benefit of tools like those we'll be discussing is **not** the end score or result. Rather, the usefulness of such tools is that they can help raise questions, generate thoughtful analysis, create real arguments, and provide beneficial insights.

Sketches and Graphs

Both hand-drawn sketches and software-generated graphs can be very effective to explain or understand a mental model. If you've ever tried to explain a physical device to another person, then you may have put a pencil to napkin to draw the thing.

Drawings can also be useful to explain non-physical concepts like one of the processes that we discussed earlier. There are several famous sketches, including one for the Compaq Portable Computer made on the back of a restaurant placemat,[220] and another on a dinner napkin for the much-debated *Laffer Curve*.[221,222]

Graphing data with software tools can also be very helpful in explaining and understanding information rather than relying solely on certain simple indices of the overall data like the mean and range. One of the most effective examples of the power of an image is *Anscombe's Quartet*, named after the English statistician, Francis Anscombe. The Quartet refers to four sets of data that Anscombe constructed, each set having the same following characteristics:

- eleven x, y pairs
- mean for x of 9.00
- mean for y of 7.50
- variance for x of 11.00
- variance for y of 4.13
- correlation coefficient between x and y of 0.816

If I were to ask you to sketch a graph based on the information provided above, then what would it look like? Even if you saw the actual data tables you might be challenged to answer this question. I've recreated below Anscombe's Quartet graphs using his data and MS Excel.

Chapter 4

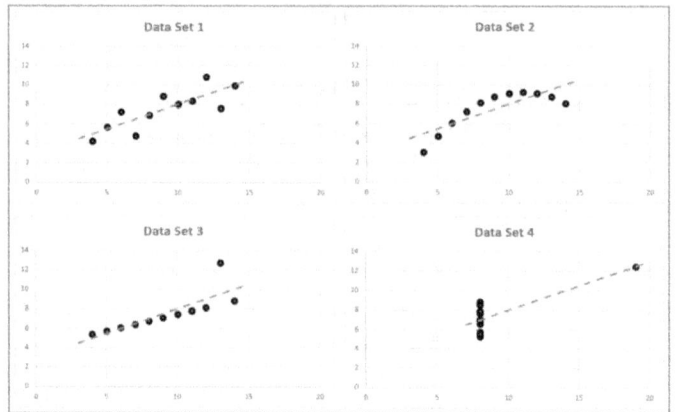

Using a straight "line of best fit" results in the same calculated indices for the four very different sets of data above

Note the very different shapes formed by the data points in the four different sets, even though the itemized characteristics are identical (e.g. mean, variance). The reason for the identical indices is because those numbers were generated by a straight "line of best fit" calculation (shown as dashed lines in the graphs above).[223]

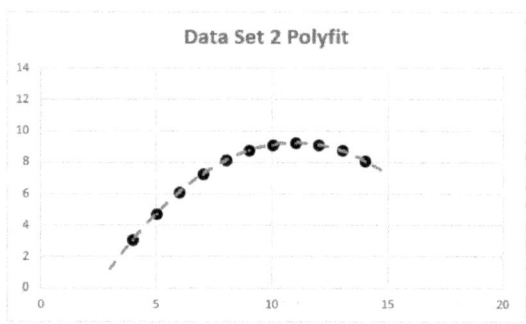

Seeing the data enables us to better understand relationships

If we had seen the shape of each data set graph, then we could have challenged the use of a straight line of best fit and the usefulness of the numbers that the fit generated. In the case of Data Set 2, for example, we may have chosen a polynomial best line fit as shown above, which would have more precisely intercepted all the data points.

An important takeaway from Anscombe's Quartet is that summary numbers alone like the mean can be very misleading. Being able to see the original data in graph form can be vital to a clear understanding of what summary numbers may not be revealing.

In the graph below we can see the cyclic rise and fall of a checking account into which a paycheck goes and from which expenses are paid. Implicit in the information are several average rates at which we deplete the account (A, B, C) over the period between paychecks. Would rescheduling certain payments to achieve a more consistent rate of depletion be of any benefit?

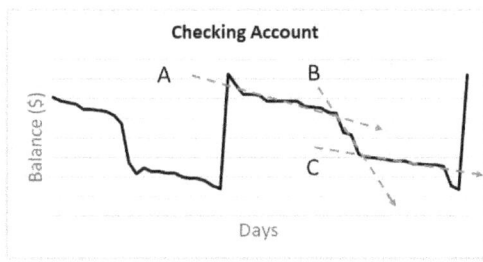

The changing rates of income and expenses in a checking account

As we will see later in this chapter, even simple sketches that show our assumptions about variables and their relationships to each other can be very important in the development and testing of our mental models.

Strengths	Weaknesses
• Quick and easy, especially when sketched by hand • Helps convey mental models • Provides basic documentation for ideas and judgments	• Not everyone sketches well • Can be misleading if quantitative information is not scaled properly or clearly presented

CHAPTER 4

Weighted Lists

One of the simplest and most useful tools is a simple list generated with a pencil and a paper pad. The act of scrawling comments, ideas, and sketches like the ones we discussed above helps us see what we're thinking. A list can help itemize the key points of a mental model, possibly in a categorical way like pros and cons or easy and difficult.

Simple lists can be formalized and quantified to help identify the relative importance of the listed items. This method of quantifying items by relative importance is referred to as *weighting* and the method is used for many purposes. The following are a few examples of various weighted lists. Note that the strengths and weaknesses of all the examples are similar due to the common method of weighting.

Simple Weighted Decision List

Let's assume that two managers, Ann, and Peter, have been tasked to recommend if time, effort, and resources ought to be employed to update a product that their company sells. They start by creating a list of factors to consider and categorizing them as either supportive of a product update or a reason not to update.

Once all the pros and cons are listed, Ann and Peter rate each. To keep things simple, they use a scale of 1 to 5. As we see in the table below, Ann rates the first stated pro at a 5 while Peter rates it at a 3, both Ann and Peter rate the first con at a 3, etc.

PROS

	Ann	Peter
Low cost decision	5	3
Quick installation	3	3
Increase Sales confidence	5	2
Totals	21	

CONS

	Ann	Peter
Limited features	3	3
More after sales support	5	2
Limited competitive effectiveness	4	1
Totals	18	

Totals are individually calculated for the pro and con scores. While the results are close, the score for the pros is a tad higher than the score for the cons – 21 to 18. This outcome could lead Ann and Peter to recommend the product update. They could also decide to seek additional participation from others to expand the pros and cons, to consider other decision-making tools, etc.

The construction of a real-world decision list, especially in a business setting, would likely include the pros and cons offered by many stakeholders. In cases where the number of options is significant, a decision list can be effective to quickly obtain a weighted score through the simple addition of scores.

Note that while a decision list offers a simple and quick method of analysis, it also has some potentially serious limitations. For one thing, the scores are likely the subjective opinion of the scorers who may be (intentionally or unwittingly) introducing their preferences and bias. Bias may be due to the participant's role in the business, for example, sales and marketing associates may lean more toward new and updated products while service and quality control may prefer to improve and better support the current products.

Bias due to groupthink is another potential weakness in the weighted list. As an employee of a firm, you may well embrace the mission and vision of the firm and have a shared opinion about what is included in the main pros and cons of any question or solution.

Further, there is likely an informal hierarchy that is not captured in formal organizational charts. One member of the team may be particularly vocal about their opinions, another may be recognized as an expert, another as the eyes and ears of executive management, etc. These kinds of human and social dynamics can all influence both the items that are included in the list and how those items are rated by those involved. Change the mix and number of participants and the scores may also change.

Strengths	Weaknesses
• Simple to understand • Quick and easy to implement • Provides basic documentation for information and decisions	• Often involves solely subjective inputs • Can become unwieldy as the number of participants and items scored increases

Weighted Sales Revenue Forecast

A weighted list approach has also been used to forecast sales revenues. Suppose that while Ann and Peter in the example above are working on their recommendation for a product update, Janet and her sales team are tasked to forecast the sales revenue for the current product in the upcoming quarter. Janet follows her company sales process as diagrammed below.

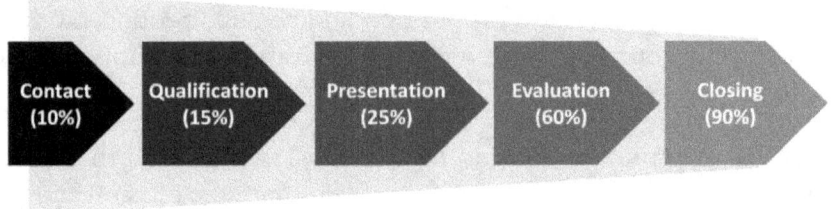

This stepwise process envisions a "funnel" of sales opportunities that starts with many opportunities at the left and narrows in number but increases in the likelihood of a customer purchase to the right. The process indicates that at the initial **Contact** step where a sales opportunity enters the funnel there is a 10% chance that the customer will eventually make a purchase. The chance of a customer purchase increases in each stage of the process, presumably because stages in the process are qualifying the customer and her needs, presenting the product features and benefits, and establishing confidence in the customer via a product evaluation (assuming the evaluation goes well).

Note that even in the **Closing** step of the sales process above the chance of the customer making a purchase is still not 100%. Experienced sales managers know that a sale isn't truly closed until the customer's funds are transferred into the company bank account **and** the product return period expires!

Using the process stages above, Janet speaks with each member of her team and constructs the table below. The table lists each opportunity, the face value of each opportunity (amount if the opportunity closes), and probability estimate (the chance of closing each sale opportunity as per the process diagram above).

Opportunity	Face Value	Probability Est	Weighted Value
A	$110,000	60%	$66,000
B	$250,000	15%	$37,500
C	$50,000	90%	$45,000
Totals	$410,000		$148,500

By multiplying each sales opportunity value at close by its chance of closing, Janet creates a weighted value for each opportunity. The total weighted value represents a kind of best guess for the upcoming quarterly sales revenues that Janet's team will close, $148,500. Note that Janet's estimate is just 36% of the total value if all of the identified sales opportunities were to close in the quarter.

This sales process concept isn't an unreasonable idea, but several features of a weighted forecast can conspire to foil the ability of the model to be of much practical use:

- What appears to be a robust sales process on the surface may be mostly aspirational and not supported by a formal and current analysis of historical performance data required to set the closure rate for each step in the sales process
- Sales representatives and their managers likely recognize that if their sales are low, then their employment may cease and so may hold out false hope of a customer purchase until the very last minute
- Although the customer may make a smaller purchase than what was originally expected, sales are won or lost – so weighting the individual

Chapter 4

potential sales does not accurately reflect either high value wins or zero value losses

If you use a weighted forecast approach for many sales opportunities, then you may find that wins do balance the losses and that the total weighted forecast is close to the actual results. If, however, you have just a few opportunities like the simple example above, especially if the opportunities include a couple of potentially high-value purchases, then the loss of just one opportunity can seriously miss the total weighted forecast. Consider the list of opportunities below.

Opportunity	Face Value	Probability Est	Weighted Value	Running Weighted Total	Wins	Actual Value	Running Actual Total
A	$183,464	90%	$165,118	$165,118	1	$183,464	$183,464
B	$228,575	90%	$205,718	$370,835	0	$0	$183,464
C	$216,156	90%	$194,540	$565,376	1	$216,156	$399,620
D	$83,745	25%	$20,936	$586,312	1	$83,745	$483,365
E	$71,357	25%	$17,839	$604,151	0	$0	$483,365
F	$54,812	90%	$49,331	$653,482	0	$0	$483,365
G	$20,179	60%	$12,107	$665,589	0	$0	$483,365
H	$23,673	15%	$3,551	$669,140	0	$0	$483,365
I	$27,285	25%	$6,821	$675,961	0	$0	$483,365
			$675,961			$483,365	

- There are nine sales **Opportunities** (A-I)
- Each opportunity has a **Face Value**, the actual sales revenue of the opportunity **if** the customer purchases ($183,464 for opportunity A, $228,575 for B, etc.)
- Each opportunity is assigned a probability estimate based on the sales process diagram above (10%, 15%, 25%, 60% or 90%)
- The **Weighted Value** of each opportunity is calculated by multiplying the Face Value by the Probability Estimate (opportunity A = $183,464 x 90% = $165,118, opportunity B = $205,718, etc.)
- The **Running Weighted Total** value is simply the sum of the opportunities beginning with the weighted value of A ($165,118), then adding the weighted value of B to A ($370,835), then the weighted value of C

to A and B ($565,376), etc. Of course, the total Running Weighted Value arrives at the same value as summing up all the individual Weighted Values ($675,961) which is the weighted forecast
- Each opportunity is either a **Win** or a loss for the forecast period (opportunities that are not won may have been lost forever or may simply be taking longer to close than anticipated)
- The **Actual Value** is what each opportunity that was won contributed to sales revenues beginning ($183,464 from opportunity A, nothing from opportunity B, $216,156 from opportunity C, etc.)
- Finally, the **Running Actual** is calculated like the Running Weighted Total and arrives at a total Actual value of $483,365

The graph below shows how the running Weighted Total value grows from $165,118 to $675,961 while the Running Actual Total value grows but falls nearly $200,000 (28%) short of the weighted forecast.

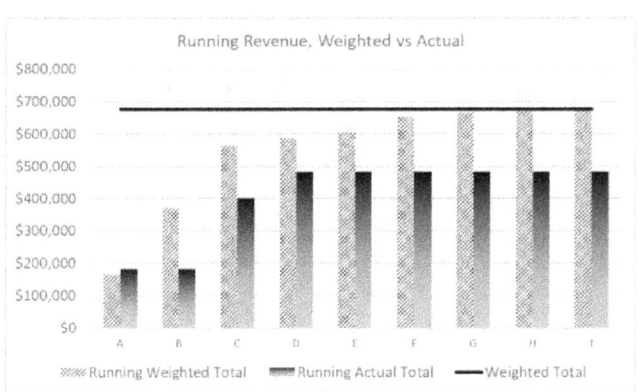

Running the model again but with a different mix of Probabilities and Wins, the situation reverses, and the Total Actual Value exceeds the forecast by about $40,000 (11%). Note, however, that this reversal occurs only if all nine of the opportunities are considered. If the forecast included just the first four or five opportunities, then the Actual total value would have fallen short of weighted forecast.

CHAPTER 4

Opportunity	Face Value	Probability Est	Weighted Value	Running Weighted Total	Wins	Actual Value	Running Actual Total
A	$198,577	15%	$29,787	$29,787	1	$198,577	$198,577
B	$247,430	90%	$222,687	$252,474	0	$0	$198,577
C	$218,259	10%	$21,826	$274,299	0	$0	$198,577
D	$70,462	25%	$17,616	$291,915	0	$0	$198,577
E	$73,349	60%	$44,009	$335,924	1	$73,349	$271,926
F	$54,976	25%	$13,744	$349,668	1	$54,976	$326,902
G	$36,286	10%	$3,629	$353,297	1	$36,286	$363,188
H	$31,014	15%	$4,652	$357,949	0	$0	$363,188
I	$47,106	25%	$11,777	$369,726	1	$47,106	$410,294
			$369,726			**$410,294**	

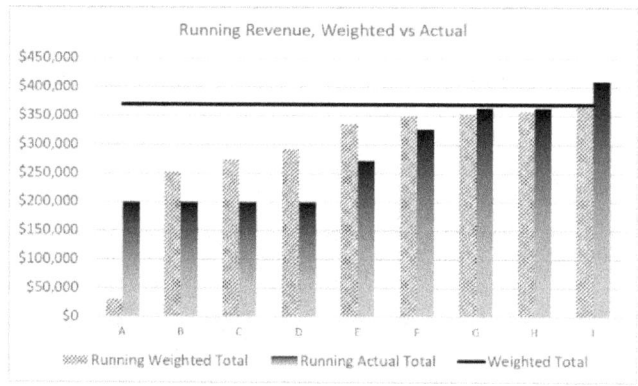

END DETOUR

The discussion and examples above underscore how the probabilities defined by the process and the win-to-loss ratio can lead to actual outcomes that are far-ranging from what was projected by the overall weighted value. Rather than weighting the individual opportunities as discussed above, perhaps a more useful analysis would be to simply categorize the total face value of the opportunities by their probabilities as shown below?

Are You Sure That's the Right Tool?

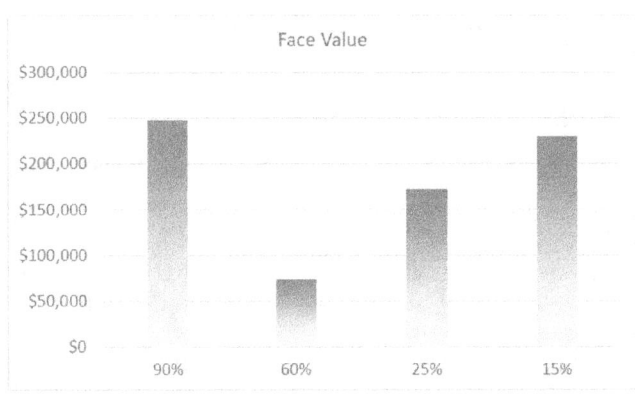

By categorizing the sales opportunities, as shown above, Janet can discuss with her team various strategies. For example, a significant portion of sales opportunities is included in the 25% and 15% probability of close. It may not be possible to increase the likelihood of closing those sales at 15%, but is it possible to increase those in the 25% category to 60% or higher? Although the face value of opportunities in the 60% category is lower than in the 25% and 15% categories, perhaps focus should be put there to try and add the 60% opportunities to the 90% opportunities?

Strengths	Weaknesses
• Easy to understand and share the assumed sales stage close rates	• Often involves solely subjective input
• Can be managed in an Excel spreadsheet	• Stages may not reflect actual sale close rates of the real-world
• Provides basic documentation for information and decisions	• The numeric output may suggest unfounded certitude
• Provides the means to categorize by sales close rates and to discuss where focus might best be applied	• Weighted calculations do not reflect the all-or-nothing win/loss nature of sales

CHAPTER 4

Failure Modes & Effects Analysis

The Failure Modes & Effects Analysis (FMEA) is another kind of weighted list that is used in product development, engineering, and quality domains. FMEA is used to "analyze potential failure risks within systems, classifying them according to severity and likelihood, based on experience with similar products or processes. The object of FMEA is to help design identified failures out of the system with the least cost in terms of time and money."[224] FMEA is a process that can be broken into five steps:

1. Identify potential failures and effects
2. Estimate severity
3. Estimate the likelihood of occurrence
4. Estimate failure detection
5. Calculate the risk priority number (RPN)

Severity and likelihood of occurrence may be rated on a scale of 1 (none) to 10 (very high). Failure detection is an estimate of the likelihood that a fault will make it through a test from the lowest chance (e.g. 1-fault would be caught by testing) to the highest chance (e.g. 10-fault would be missed by testing and make its way to the end-user).

The scores used in FMEA can be defined to help standardize estimations across teams and projects. Some definitions are quantitative (e.g. a rating of 2 means 67 incidents per opportunity). Other definitions are more general as shown in the following simple severity table example.

Rating	Definition
1	None
2	Very minor, not likely noticed
3	Moderate, minor product malfunction
4	High, significant product malfunction
5	Very high, may cause injury or death

The risk priority number (RPN) is calculated by multiplying the separate ratings for severity, the likelihood of occurrence, and failure detection.

$$RPN = Severity \times Occurrence \times Detection$$

The table below shows a simple FMEA analysis for just four items. In practice, FMEA analysis will often assign multiple opportunities for failure within key components that are being analyzed. If, for example, Item A were a gasket in an engine, then one failure mode may be cracking under pressure. The engineering team would propose various other ways in which that gasket could fail such as shrinking when very cold, dissolving in the presence of certain liquids, etc.

Note that both items B and D have relatively high RPN numbers primarily because of the high severity and occurrence estimates for those two items. Although item D has a slightly lower occurrence estimate, it has a slightly higher detection estimate and so its RPN is higher and perhaps of greater concern than is item B.

Item	Severity	Occurance	Detection	RPN
A	4	6	3	72
B	7	10	3	210
C	1	4	1	4
D	7	7	5	245

All four items in the FMEA analysis above offer opportunities to lower the RPN by lowering severity and/or occurrence scores and by improving the detection score. The example analysis above suggests that an initial focus on items B and D is likely warranted.

This kind of weighted analysis can be relatively simple to conduct and may offer reasonable consistency, provided the defined scores are properly applied by those who make the assessment. Several noted disadvantages of the FMEA approach include.[225]

- Time-consuming and tedious to trace failure through FMEA charts
- Applied too late and does not affect the decision-making of design and process
- Depends on subjective analysis and engineers' experience that are known by a small group of individuals, but fairly unknown and unmanaged at the enterprise level
- The relationship between different failure components is disregarded

CHAPTER 4

Even organizations with highly skilled personnel in possession of a wealth of information and resources can fumble risks that may lead to a major catastrophe as occurred in the 1986 *Challenger* disaster.[226] Reportedly, there was at least one dissenting voice whose warning may have helped to avoid the *Challenger* tragedy, Roger Boisjoly, an engineer who was familiar with technical issues that led to the failure.

> "In a memo dated July 31, 1985, about six months before the *Challenger* incident, Boisjoly warned Thiokol's vice president of Engineering that the O-ring issues were a disaster in the making, ominously predicting that the 'result would be a catastrophic of the highest order – loss of human life.' Boisjoly's warnings were ignored…Boisjoly was shunned and ostracized by colleagues and managers at Morton-Thiokol, who thought that his testimony during the accident investigation would cost them their jobs."[227]

In an article about the *Challenger* incident, the authors suggest that a *fuzzy* FMEA approach may have provided Boisjoly with more compelling evidence – of course, we'll never know.

> "Solid research of the challenger failure clearly captures that test analysis was regularly performed and accurately identified single point failures in the 'O' rings. However, research never revealed where potential failures were ranked and prioritized. Had fuzzy logic been applied, Roger Boisjoly would have had more decisive data that would have demanded program management."[228]

> The methods of fuzzy logic and fuzzy FMEA are outside the scope of this book, however, the interested reader may start their independent exploration of fuzziness with these endnote references[229,230]

Strengths	Weaknesses
• Easy to understand • Can be managed in an Excel spreadsheet • Provides basic documentation for information and decisions • Provides the means to quickly sort by severity, occurrence, detection or RPN	• In the absence of historical data, inputs may be subjective • The numeric output may suggest unfounded certitude

Probability of Successful Search

When someone goes missing in the woods, a search and rescue incident commander employs various search strategies.[231] A *hasty search* involves a few responders to conduct a quick exploration near the last known location of the lost person. A *grid search* requires numerous searchers to form a tight line and methodically walk back and forth over a defined area. The probability that a search might locate a missing person is calculated from two estimates:

- the probability of area (POA), which is the likelihood that the lost person is in a defined search area
- the probability of detection (POD), which is the likelihood that the lost person will be detected during a search of a defined area

Those managing the overall search effort allocate search teams and resources that are available to them based on the initial information they have gleaned. In the example search map below, search teams are dispatched to areas A, B, and C which are believed to offer the greatest likelihood of where the lost person would be located (POA). After their search, the leaders of the individual search teams estimate the likelihood that a lost person would have been detected during their team's search of their assigned area (POD).

CHAPTER 4

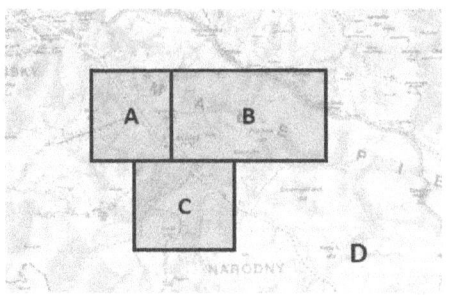

An example search map with defined search areas

The separate estimations by the search managers and team leaders reflect the different roles and kinds of information that is known to these individuals. Search managers are responsible for the overall supervision of the search, working from information like the last known location of the lost person and the resources available to search. Search team leaders are responsible for supervising the boots on the ground and making first-hand assessments like how the vegetation in the search area could obscure the detection of the lost person.

The Probability of Successful Search for each defined search area is calculated by multiplying the POA and POD for each search area. For search area A,

$$POS_A = POA_A \times POD_A$$

If the search managers estimate the likelihood of the lost person being in area A at 60% and the search team leader estimates the likelihood of detecting the lost person in area A at 80%, then the POS for area A is,

$$POS_A = POA_A \times POD_A = 0.60 \times 0.80 = 0.48 \text{ (or 48\%)}$$

Of course, the same POS_A value would be calculated had the search managers estimated a POA_A of 80% and the search team leader estimated a POD_A of 60%, although such a reversal in estimates could represent a significantly different set of search conditions.

Note that although the search managers did not dispatch search teams in area D (essentially the rest of the world), they would still make a POS estimate for area D. This rest-of-world estimate acknowledges the possibility that the lost person was never in any of the defined search areas. It's also possible that the person was lost in one of the defined areas but simply walked out on their own and is safely back home unaware of the search that's underway to locate them!

 Lost persons can and do move during land search operations and drift due to wind, currents, and waves in sea searches. How would you think about the uncertainty of location that these factors introduce to the search probability? You may wish to explore these questions further by starting on the US Coast Guard National Search And Rescue Committee site - https://bit.ly/2wTqCNM

Strengths	Weaknesses
• Easy to understand • Can be easily calculated • Provides basic documentation for information and decisions • Provides the means to quickly sort by POA, POD, and POS	• Inputs lean toward subjective assessments by team leaders • The numeric output may suggest unfounded certitude • Assumes that the subject's location is relatively fixed (i.e. not moving from one search area into another area that has already been searched and scored).

Probability of Precipitation

Weather instrumentation was developed from the 15th Century, including a thermometer by Galileo. These instruments and others enabled the coordination of observations by independent weather stations in the late 19th Century and cracked opened the door to the modern weather forecast.[232] Today, forecasters use weather data to estimate the probability of precipitation[233] which is yet another kind of weighted estimate. The probability of precipitation (POP) is the likelihood that measurable precipitation will occur in an area of forecast and is calculated from two estimates:

CHAPTER 4

- the confidence the forecaster has in his prediction that precipitation will occur **somewhere in the forecast area**
- the **percent of the forecast area** that the forecaster believes will receive measurable precipitation (0.01 inches or more)

Like the FMEA and POS calculations, the estimates above are multiplied to calculate the probability of precipitation which could suggest various points-of-view. For example, your local weather forecaster tells you that there is a 30% chance of rain tomorrow, then her forecast could mean several things.

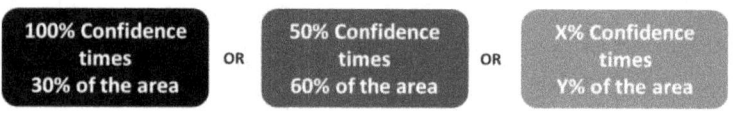

Note that the probability of precipitation is typically expressed in whole percentages. In the diagram above, for example, we would not encounter confidence of 49.3% for 61.7% of the area to arrive at a POP of 30.4%. The whole value POP estimates are accompanied by conventional expressions of uncertainty as itemized below. Somewhat akin to the *fuzzy* FMEA approach noted above, the table below reflects a certain *fuzziness* rather than a strict demarcation of expected weather.

POP (%)	Expression of Uncertainty
0, 10	*None used*
20	"Slight chance"
30, 40, 50	"Chance"
60, 70	"Likely"
80, 90, 100	*None used*

As with other weighted approaches, the probability of precipitation offers a simple method that produces an index from data and subjective estimates. The simplicity of the methodology, however, does not ensure the proper interpretation by the general public. It seems that "a five-day forecast can accurately predict the weather approximately 90 percent of the time" yet it's not uncommon to hear complaints about the reliability of a weather forecast.[234]

A take-away is that we should not confuse probabilistic estimates of precipitation with an undesirable outcome that we experience. If there is only a "slight chance" of rain but you happen to be standing within the forecast area when that chance occurs, then you will get wet. Your personal experience does not mean that the area forecast was "wrong".

Strengths	Weaknesses
• Can be easily calculated • Provides basic documentation for information and decisions • Augmented by plain English statements that may be better understood by the public	• Often misunderstood by the public • Inputs are at least partly subjective and based on the assessment of the forecaster(s) • The numeric output may suggest unfounded certitude

Kano Analysis

Kano Analysis is named after its creator, Noriaki Kano, professor emeritus of the Tokyo University of Science.[235] Kano Analysis is used to help determine what product or service features may best drive customer satisfaction.

Kano Analysis takes a somewhat similar approach to the weighted lists above, itemizing features that are then categorized by the way that customers rate the presence or absence of each feature. A difference between Kano Analysis and the simple weighted lists above is that Kano Analysis shifts the assessment onto the customer such that the results may better reflect the customer's perspective rather than the analyst's view.

Professor Kano's premise was that customers expect certain features in a product or service but may be significantly swayed by unexpected features that surprise and delight them. Kano Analysis defines five categories of features:

CHAPTER 4

1. **Attractive** features increase customer satisfaction when present but don't cause dissatisfaction when absent (e.g. free tire rotation with an oil change).

2. **One-Dimensional** (or Performance) features satisfy customers when present and create dissatisfaction when they are absent (e.g. ease of use, low price).

3. **Indifferent** (or Unimportant) features are those that typically don't matter to the customer (e.g. the color of trash bags)

4. **Must-Be** are those features that are required to meet basic customer expectations (e.g. a steering wheel in a car)

5. **Dissatisfiers** (or Undesired) features create dissatisfaction when present (e.g. slow service time). Dissatisfiers work opposite to Attractive features.

By identifying how various features fall into the attributes above, Kano Analysis may help you focus on the product and services features that will lead to the greatest customer satisfaction. The relationship feature types and customer emotional satisfaction is commonly diagrammed as shown below. Not explicitly shown is the indifferent vector which falls atop the horizontal axis between *present* and *absent*, that is, features that neither delight nor dissatisfy the customer.

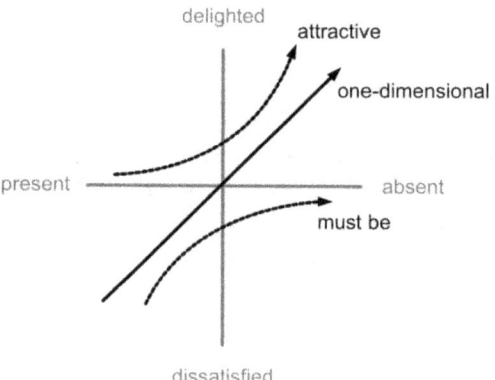

The Kano Analysis method is generally conducted as follows:

1. You assemble a list of features for analysis which would include the features of your current product or service, features that your competitors offer, and features you may be contemplating

2. You create question pairs where one question asks the customer how they feel about a feature if it is present and how they would feel if the feature was absent. Paired questions are referred to as functional when positively stated and dysfunctional when negatively stated, for example,

   Functional: How would you feel if your car had a backup camera?

   Dysfunctional: How would you feel if your car did not have a backup camera?

   Customers are limited to the following five answers for paired questions used in a Kano Analysis: I like it, I expect it, I am neutral, I can tolerate it, I dislike it

3. The customer's answers to the paired questions are then assessed by the table below to determine the attribute of each feature.

Dysfunctional Question Answer

Functional Question Answer		Like	Expect	Neutral	Tolerate	Dislike
	Like	Questionable	Attractive	Attractive	Attractive	One-Dimensional
	Expect	Dissatisfier	Questionable	Indifferent	Indifferent	Must-be
	Neutral	Dissatisfier	Indifferent	Indifferent	Indifferent	Must-be
	Tolerate	Dissatisfier	Indifferent	Indifferent	Questionable	Must-be
	Dislike	Dissatisfier	Dissatisfier	Dissatisfier	Dissatisfier	Questionable

Note that answers to the paired questions can appear contradictory as indicated by the table cells above labeled *questionable*. There are a variety of reasons for these contradictory answers, such as an unintentional answer by the customer, or some misunderstanding due to the way the question was stated. A few such results are not uncommon, however, if you are

CHAPTER 4

seeing more than a few then it may indicate that you need to take a closer look at your paired questions.

Armed with the results of the analysis, you would then ensure that you maintain must-be features, avoid dissatisfiers and indifferent features, and increase both one-dimensional and attractive features.

Remember that the Kano Analysis method is yet another model and so is a simple representation of customer dynamics. Further, the attributes identified by Kano Analysis are a "snapshot" of customer perspectives at the time that the analysis was conducted. Customer expectations change over time, and features that were once deemed attractive or one-dimensional may now be basic requirements.

Kano Analysis can be a useful tool in decision-making to help assess and confirm what is important to customers. It may be informative to compare the results from older Kano Analyses with results from a current analysis in search of potentially important trends.

Strengths	Weaknesses
• Straightforward to administer (once the questions are established)	• Assumes that the model accurately reflects customer preferences
• May be managed in an Excel spreadsheet	• A snapshot in time that can change after the results are calculated
• Provides documentation of questions and answers	• Not specifically designed to ask questions regarding innovation about which the customer is unfamiliar
• Comparison of recent results to past results (of the same questions) provides a means to detect trends	

Financial Returns

A common question in business is, will an investment I make today be worth the risk over the long run? Included among the various assessments of investment returns is the calculation of **Net Present Value** (NPV) and **Decision Trees**. These methods express different mental models, each with its own strengths and weaknesses. When using either method, however, we'll want to consider risk and uncertainty as we make our assumptions to help ensure that our models adequately reflect real-world conditions. Let's start with a look at an example Net Present Value calculation followed by a Decision Tree example.

Net Present Value

Net Present Value (NPV) gets its name from its intention to estimate the *time-value* of an investment today, considering the value of the future returns on the investment. Simply put, the time-value of money means that the money you have today is worth more than the money you will receive in the future. There are two reasons commonly given for the time-value of money: *inflation* and *opportunity cost*.

Inflation occurs when increases in the price of goods and services lead to a fall in the purchasing power of money. The inflation rate in the United States between 2009 and 2018, for example, was between 0.7% and 3%, and the inflation rate for the 12 months ending in April 2019 was 2%.[236] If the cost an item increases by 3% over a year, then a dollar today would purchase only 97% of that item a year later.

Opportunity cost occurs when your money isn't creating additional value that it might generate. If you keep your money in your mattress rather than in an interest-bearing account, then you are losing out on the interest that you could be generating. Likewise, if your money is tied up in an investment that isn't doing well, then it isn't available for investments that may offer a higher return.

NPV provides a means to compare different investments to see which ones might offer the greatest return on your money, considering the impact of inflation. Following is a simple example of a Net Present Value calculation for a project that requires an initial investment of $500,000 and generates annual returns of $131,312 in each of four years following the initial investment.

Year	0	1	2	3	4	Totals	Returns
Cash Flows	-$500,000	$131,312	$131,312	$131,312	$131,312	$25,248	5%

A total return of $25,248 (5%) may or may not be acceptable to you, depending on other investment options, risk tolerance, etc. What appears to be fixed returns for the four years, however, does not reflect the impact of inflation. If we assume that the inflation rate during this project will be 2%, then the present value of those future returns can be calculated with the following formula.

$$\text{Present Value}_n = \text{Future Value}_n / (1 + \text{Discount Rate})^n$$

In the equation above, "n" is the year for which the Present Value is being calculated and the Discount Rate is our assumed inflation rate of 2%. Applying this calculation to the table above results in the present values shown in the table below. The Net Present Value of $25,248 is calculated by adding up the present values for each of the years which "nets out" the original investment from the discounted returns.

Year	0	1	2	3	4	Totals	Returns
Cash Flows	-$500,000	$131,312	$131,312	$131,312	$131,312	$25,248	5%
Present Values	-$500,000	$128,737	$126,213	$123,738	$121,312	$0	0%

As you can see, what appeared to be a constant return of $131,312 decreases over the years due to the impact of inflation. Consequently, what originally looked like a 5% return on your investment turns out to be a 0% return because of a 2% annual inflation.

A more valuable use of the NPV calculation may be to rank competing projects based on the financial return of each project. The table below contains the cash flows and present values of those cash flows for three projects A, B, and C. Note that each project requires a different investment amount and produces different returns on the investment made. Which project may generate the greatest financial return based on NPV?

- Project A requires a $500,000 investment as in the example, generating a fixed annual return of $144,443 for an overall return of 10%
- Project B requires a lower investment of $432,500 and generates rising returns in each following year but achieves a lower return of 8%
- Project C requires a higher initial investment of $575,000 and generates decreasing returns in each following year but achieves a higher return of 12%

Project	Year	0	1	2	3	4	Totals	Returns
A	Cash Flows	-$500,000	$144,443	$144,443	$144,443	$144,443	$77,772	16%
	Present Values	-$500,000	$141,611	$138,834	$136,112	$133,443	$50,000	10%
B	Cash Flows	-$432,500	$119,111	$121,493	$123,923	$126,401	$58,427	14%
	Present Values	-$432,500	$116,775	$116,775	$116,775	$116,775	$34,600	8%
C	Cash Flows	-$575,000	$182,125	$173,019	$164,368	$156,150	$100,661	18%
	Present Values	-$575,000	$178,554	$166,300	$154,888	$144,258	$69,000	12%

The NPV model, of course, has its limitations. The NPV calculation is based on your estimates for initial investment, the project duration, returns for the project, and the discount rate. Fixed conditions may be reliable when the NPV analysis is applied to certain situations like comparing different annuities.[237] When applied to projects where the conditions are uncertain, like the development of a new product or service, estimation errors, and variability in any of these inputs can create misleading results.

It isn't uncommon for a project NPV analysis to be used to obtain a *green light* from management to start the project. Likewise, this method of calculating NPV can also be used to help support a claim that a project should not proceed. If, for example, the return required by management is not achieved by the calculated NPV then that result could contribute to a decision to kill the project.

It's been my experience that once a project is given approval the analyses used to obtain the approval are filed away and never reviewed during or after the project. Regular review of the original NPV analysis, however, may help ensure transparency and encourage frank discussion about actions that may be required to ensure the desired return is achieved. If a review reveals a shortfall relative to the initial analysis, and if someone proposes corrective action, then you'll want to ensure that the claimed outcomes of such action are accompanied by strong supporting evidence and arguments.

Strengths	Weaknesses
• Straightforward to build in Excel (Excel also provides a built-in NPV function)	• Generally, relies on subjective estimates of future income (unless terms are fixed by agreement)
• Enables a simple financial comparison of several investment or project options	• In its basic form, assumes a fixed discount rate which may not reflect the real world
• Addresses the issue of the time-value of money	• The numeric output may imply unfounded certitude
	• Assumes all other issues are equal (e.g. that all investments or projects are equally strategic for the business goals)

Decision Trees

Decision trees offer a way of looking at choices when the likelihood of different outcomes can be reasonably estimated. Decision Trees are often used for financial modeling as we'll see below but can be used to analyze non-financial questions. For a nice overview of decision trees from 1964, see *Decision Trees for Decision Making* by John F. Magee.[238]

Decision trees are so named because they are diagrammed like a tree that branches out from the basic question being considered, through different options to the likely outcomes for each option. The simple decision tree example below considers three different investment options: Investment A, Investment B, and Do Nothing. The Do-Nothing branch should not be overlooked when building a decision tree because taking no action is always an option that has its own consequences.

 Download a free copy of the decision tree below in MS Excel format at https://bit.ly/2ZxhWbo

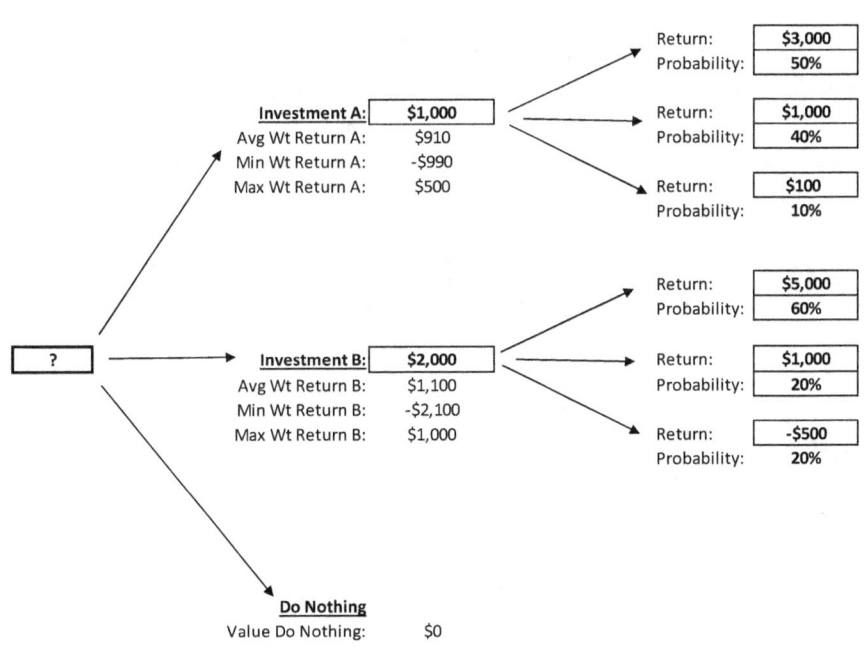

CHAPTER 4

In this example, Investment A and Investment B will require a commitment of money by you to achieve one of the outcomes shown. Note that we're considering only three outcomes for Investment A and Investment B but there could be any number of outcomes identified.

Each investment option outcome includes the likelihood (probability) of a specific monetary return, and the total of all probabilities for the estimated returns of each option must equal one hundred percent. Referring to the diagram you will see that Investment A has three options with probable outcomes of 50%, 40% and 10% respectively and the total probability of these three outcomes is 100%. There could be many other possible outcomes, but we're only considering the three shown. Likewise, the total probability of the three outcomes for Investment B is 100%.

In the example, the Do-Nothing option does not require any commitment of money and is assumed to result in neither a gain nor loss. In the real world, there are likely positive and negative outcomes if no action is taken. Your first impression may be that a decision list already accomplishes the same end as a decision tree. Both decision lists and decision trees use a "weighting" approach to analysis, but a decision tree enables you to calculate an overall value of different decisions that are based on the likelihood of different outcomes within each option that is identified. The calculated outcomes of each option may then be compared to assess which decision results in the best outcome. Let's walk through the example decision tree above.

In the first case, you are presented with two investment opportunities. Investment A will require a commitment of $1,000 and Investment B will require a commitment of $2,000. Based on the money commitment alone, you can't make a reasoned decision to go with either investment – or to pass on both investment opportunities. After some research, however, you determine that each investment has three likely returns as shown in the model below.

Investment A	Investment B
50% likelihood of a $3,000 return	60% likelihood of a $5,000 return
40% likelihood of a $1,000 return	20% likelihood of a $1,000 return
10% likelihood of a $100 return	20% likelihood of a $500 (loss)

For this simple model, we assume that the Do-Nothing option results in a neutral return – neither a gain nor a loss – but remember that in the real world doing nothing can have both positive and negative outcomes.

Your initial impression may be to avoid Investment B and the possibility that you could lose $500, but let's take a look at the returns that the model calculates for each option based on your estimates of the likelihood for various returns to see if the results change your mind. The weighted average return is calculated by adding up all the piecewise (individual) returns for each investment and then subtracting the original investment amount. For Investment A the average weighted return is $910:

$$\$3000 \times 50\% + \$1000 \times 40\% + \$100 \times 10\% - \$1000 =$$
$$\$1500 + \$400 + \$10 - \$1000 = \mathbf{\$910}$$

By inspection, you can quickly determine the lowest piecewise weighted return for Investment A is $10 and the highest is $1500. Subtracting out your $1000 investment, you are left with two weighted extremes to either side of the weighted average return: $500 in the best case or a loss of $990 in the worst case. Considering Investment B in the same way as above, the average weighted estimated return is $1100:

$$\$5000 \times 60\% + \$1000 \times 20\% - \$500 \times 20\% - \$2000 =$$
$$\$3000 + \$200 - \$100 - \$2000 = \mathbf{\$1100}$$

By inspection, the lowest piecewise weighted return for Investment B is a $100 loss (-$500 x 20%), and the highest is a $3000 gain ($5,000 x 60%). Subtracting out your $2000 investment, you are left with two estimated weighted extremes to either side of the weighted average return: a **gain** of $1,000 or a **loss** of $2,100.

CHAPTER 4

What do these outcomes "mean" and what is the "right" decision? It depends on your tolerance for risk and if you are considering a one-time investment or a group of similar investments. If you are making a one-time investment, then you need to acknowledge that only one of the expected outcomes could occur. So even if the likelihood of a negative outcome is low, that unwanted outcome certainly could happen and result in a large loss. Likewise, an unlikely positive outcome could happen and result in a large gain for you.

Look again at the piecewise returns of Investment A without *weighting* to provide a real-world perspective – that is, any **one** of the three returns would occur independently of the others. These unweighted returns would be:

- $2,000 if you get the $3,000 unweighted return minus the $1,000 investment
- $0 if you get the $1,000 unweighted return minus the $1,000 investment
- A loss of $900 if you get the $100 unweighted return minus the $1,000 investment

[END DETOUR]

Rather than a one-time investment, the decision tree model might represent a group of similar investments that you will make repeatedly over time – as in an investment portfolio. In this case, the actual returns ought to approach the weighted average return if you've gotten your assumptions right, the conditions don't change, and if you make enough investments over time. The model considers that you will win some and lose some, but your overall portfolio performance will likely average out over time.

The calculations resulting from a decision tree can be confounding to interpret. A strength, however, is that the construction of such trees can help you think through various outcomes to decisions and the probability of those outcomes. As with any modeling tool, obtaining solid support for your assumptions can make the critical difference between an evidence-based decision and one founded on pure speculation and wishful thinking.

Strengths	Weaknesses
• Offers a graphical representation of decision-making that may help others' understanding • Offers several perspectives of outcomes (best, worst, average) • May be most useful when applied to numerous same-as instances (e.g. a portfolio of investments with the same historical probabilities of outcomes)	• Generally, relies on subjective estimates of outcome probabilities • The calculated weighted outputs do not reflect the impact of a one-time outcome (i.e. an outcome that is the worst rather than the average) • Can become difficult to manage as the number of decision branches increase • Assumes all other issues are equal (e.g. that all investments are equally strategic to the business goals)

 How does the NPV example above differ from the decision tree example we just examined? When might you be inclined to use a decision tree over NPV or vice versa? How might you misinterpret the results of either a decision tree or NPV analysis?

CHAPTER 4

Causal Loop Diagrams

A simple but useful tool is the causal loop diagram (CLD) which is another kind of sketch. I've placed the discussion about Causal Loop Diagrams here rather than under Sketches and Graphs because it will serve as a good introduction to our discussion about Stock and Flow Simulations later in this chapter.

As the name indicates, this tool is a way to visually state what you know (or believe) are the causes-and-effects among variables and to seek out loops that can reinforce or balance the cause-and-effect outcomes. Let's jump right into the simple causal loop diagram below that proposes relationships between **Total Customers**, **Customer Referrals**, and **Buyers** of a product or service.

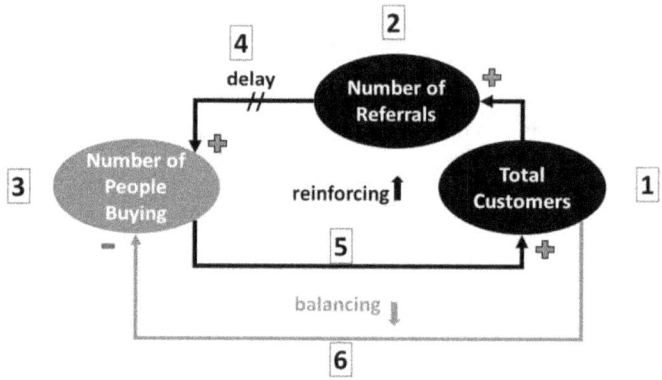

The following points explain what the diagram above proposes:

1. Start with the oval at the right that represents the number of **Total Customers** – people who own your product

2. As the **Total Customers** increases, so do the **Number of Referrals** represented by the oval at the top of the CLD – presumably, customers are satisfied and tell their family and friends about the product and thereby generate referrals. The plus sign near the arrowhead pointing at the **Number of Referrals** proposes that as **Total Customers** increases so do **Number of Referrals**

3. As the **Number of Referrals** increases so do the number of **Number of People Buying** represented by the oval at the left of the CLD

4. The "//" symbol along the path from **Number of Referrals** to **Number of People Buying** indicates that referrals don't immediately make a purchase and that a delay exists between the time that a referral decides to buy the product

5. Buyers become your customers and increase the number of your **Total Customers** as indicated by the arrow that runs from **Number of People Buying** back to **Total Customers**. The cause-and-effect between **Total Customers, Number of Referrals** and **Number of People Buying** creates a reinforcing loop that drives growth

6. As the number of **Total Customers** grows, the **Number of People Buying** the product starts to slow down (because there are fewer buyers available) as shown by the arrow that connects the **Total Customers** to **Number of People Buying** which creates another loop that balances increases in **Total Customers**. This balancing loop keeps the reinforcing loop from running away toward an infinite number of **Total Customers**

Causal loop diagrams can help spur discussion and insight into our mental models by revealing to others (and to ourselves) what we believe are cause-and-effect relationships. This kind of transparency can enable a more robust analysis and critique of the model to expose the strengths and weaknesses.

We will shortly discuss simulation methods that can generate quantitative data based on causes and effects diagrammed in your causal loop diagrams. Along the transition from a static causal loop diagram to a dynamic simulation lies an important bridging step that incorporates sketching to explain your mental model. The sketch below, for example, suggests how the simple causal loop diagram above might affect the growth of **Total Customers** over several years of sales.

CHAPTER 4

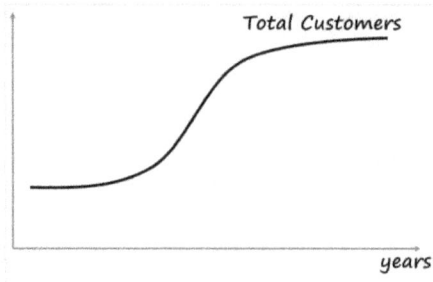

The kind of S-shaped curve sketched assumes that you will have relatively few **Total Customers** initially which increases as **Number of Referrals** grows the **Number of People Buying**, and the number of **Total Customers**. If the number of possible customers was infinite, then you might expect that the curve would continue upward along an exponential growth path. Because the market of customers is limited, however, then (all other things being equal) the curve levels off to some reasonable number of **Total Customers** that the company might achieve.

Your sketch may look significantly different if your model anticipates future events over time such as price increases, the introduction of a replacement product, etc. Of course, it is also possible that outside factors would cause the actual number of **Total Customers** to veer off from your sketch – such as a disruptive competitive product entering the market or change in customer needs and wants. As we discussed under the section on Black Swan Events, these kinds of incidents are practically impossible to reliably predict and factor into your model.

> Note that including a lot of "best guesses" won't make the model better and may likely introduce more noise and uncertainty into models. I recommend creating simple models that include the main variables and relationships that describe the system and clearly state the key evidence-based assumptions that reflect the real-world.

A handful of causal loop diagrams have been adopted as useful *archetypes* (templates) for recurring themes in our world as listed below. Rather than reproducing those archetypes diagrams below, I refer you to two websites that offer detailed examples. *The Systems Thinker* website[239] provides a series of free pocket guides, including diagrams of the common archetypes (https://bit.ly/3eooOgL). The *Thinking Tools Studio*[240] website offers free online courses, including on archetypes (https://bit.ly/3epIdxQ).

- **Drifting Goals**. An example of this archetype is when a project falls behind schedule and to catch up, the goals are reduced. To hit the launch date for a new product, for example, features that were originally deemed important are dropped. Drifting goals can help ensure that the desired launch date is achieved but the product may suffer and fail because it no longer offers features that the customer values.

- **Escalations**. Escalations occur in retaliatory situations where one party takes an action that provokes a reaction by another party and this second party's action causes the original party to take a more severe step. Suppose, for example, that a competitor lowers the price of their product to entice your customers to switch from your product to their product. You counter your competitor's price reduction with your price reduction, your competitor reduces their price again and so do you as you both engage in a headlong race to the lowest price. As these exchanges continue, you and your competitor are lowering your profit and thereby reducing your ability to sustain your business operations. One or both of you may go out of business while a third competitor positions themselves as the high-value, high-price option, and benefits handsomely.

- **Fixes that Fail**. If you've ever acted to "fix" a problem that either didn't work or that made the problem worse, then you are familiar with this archetype. An example might be if the CEO of your company demands that resources are shifted from what was originally deemed a critical project to address the concerns of a major customer who the CEO fears will depart and create a major loss of revenue. By doing so, however, the broad issues of your larger customer base are not addressed, and revenues drop even further than they would have done if the major customer had departed.

- **Growth and Underinvestment**. This archetype describes a situation where to achieve further growth, further investment is required but such investment is not made. Consider the situation where your product is selling well in the market and to expand sales further you need to invest in development but don't make that investment because management is complacent with the status quo. Due to lack of investment, the performance of the product line stagnates or drops which is then used to justify avoiding further investment. A downward spiral created by lack of investment and poor product line performance continues until the product line is of no further value.

- **Limits to Success**. Somewhat related to the growth and underinvestment archetype above, this archetype examines how a goal can remain out of reach due to certain constraints. One example is going on a diet to lose weight which works initially but then plateaus as your body adjusts. Unlike growth and underinvestment, a temporary halt in a dieter's weight loss may have more to do with human physiology and changes in metabolic rate caused by the diet rather than the dieter's faithful adherence to the diet.

- **Shifting the Burden**. This archetype addresses how the application of external solutions can weaken the ability to address problems forwardgoing. Consider, for example, the child of doting parents who give him whatever he wants, using their connections rather than demanding their child take responsibility. In this case, the *burden* of becoming a functional adult in society is shifted from the child to the parents and so the child never develops important skills for adulthood.

- **Success to the Successful**. This archetype explores how greater resources can lead to greater success which in turn creates more resources and success. Children from wealthy backgrounds, for example, have greater access to the best schools and connections than those from poorer families. As one successful businessman conceded, "What became of my life was as much a factor of the inequities that exist in our society today as it was my skills, my talents, and my work ethic."[241]

- **The Tragedy of the Commons**. The *tragedy* referred to in this archetype is how individual pursuits that utilize common resources can diminish everyone's ability to achieve and maintain desired outcomes. An original analogy was a pasture where cattle graze (also known as a *common*). As more people put more cattle into the pasture the ability of the pasture to sustain the cattle decreases until it is overgrazed and unusable to all users of the pasture.

While the archetypes listed above can be helpful to think about and *ballpark* an issue that you are analyzing, strictly following an archetype as if it were a trailing process may obscure key causes and effects that apply to your **specific** issue. Note, too, that causal loop diagrams are more like a snapshot than a movie and so these diagrams show *qualitative* rather *quantitative* relationships. Variable A may increase Variable B in a causal loop diagram but because casual loop diagrams do not stipulate time or quantities it is not possible to clearly express rates of change or scale of such causes and effects.

 Can you give examples from your own personal or business life of the archetypes listed above? What insight might you gain from the archetype that would help you form and critique corrective actions? What limitations might accompany archetypes and how would you ensure that any archetype accurately reflects an actual situation that you are facing?

Strengths	Weaknesses
• Straightforward to create • Encourages diverse team involvement • Diagrams help convey cause and effect relationships	• Lacks quantitative information and timing • Can become unwieldy as the number of variables grows

CHAPTER 4

Stock and Flow Simulations

As stated above, causal loop diagrams are like snapshots of your mental models. Stock and Flow Simulations are like movies of your causal loop diagrams. Simulations dynamically run your cause-and-effect assumptions during a period (e.g. revenues in the third month, revenues per quarter).[242] In this section, we'll discuss how to simulate the causal loop diagram above and generate a time-based output for the number of Total Customers.

To create dynamic simulation models, you will require a software tool. Microsoft® Excel is a popular tool that can be used to generate useful simulations from financial projections to various scientific topics.[243,244] A less-known class of software tools offers a visual approach to simulation that more closely aligns with causal loop diagrams. Several of the more popular software simulation tools include the following.

- **Analytica**, a product of Lumina Decision Systems that runs under MS Windows and is available in a free and fee-based version - https://lumina.com/products/free101/
- **InsightMaker**, an open-source online tool that also offers team sharing - https://insightmaker.com/
- **Sheetless (formerly Sysdea)**, an online tool that has both free and subscription options - https://sheetless.io
- **Simantics System Dynamics**, an open-source, Windows-based tool available - http://sysdyn.simantics.org/
- **Vensim**, a product sold by Ventana Systems that runs on Windows or Macintosh computers. A free limited features version is available by download for learners - https://vensim.com/free-download/

> Online tools may operate differently under different browsers. If an online tool doesn't seem to work properly then try using a different browser (e.g. Firefox, Chrome, Edge, Opera, etc).

The kinds of visual modeling tools noted above work in a way that can be described by the bathtub analogy below. In this analogy, water flows from some source through a faucet valve and into a tub. Water in the tub flows out through an adjustable drain and on to some other location.

For the bathtub analogy, we do not need to know the exact source of the water flowing into the tub (e.g. public water or well) and we do not need to know the exact place where the water from the tub goes (e.g. public sewer or septic tank). Likewise, other models of the real world often do not need to include the countless minutiae that will not likely make a significant difference in the cause and effect relationships or the outcomes that the model generates.

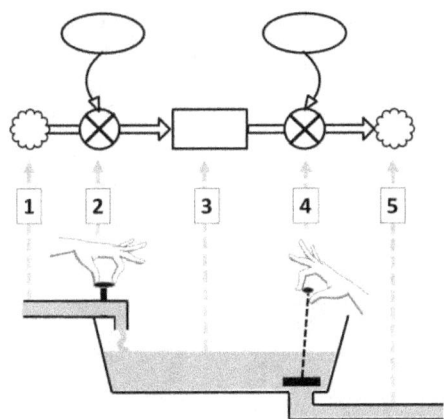

A bathtub analogy to stock and flow model simulations

Simulation software represents the elements of the tub analogy by symbols which differ from program to program but typically look like the ones shown above:

1. The cloud symbol at the left represents the source of the water

2. A circle with an X represents a valve like the one on the tub faucet, and the oval symbol represents a variable like a hand on the faucet

3. A rectangle represents the tub that holds the water, the level of which is determined by the water flowing into the tub and out of the tub

4. The X and oval represent the control of the water out of the tub

5. The cloud symbol at the right represents the destination of the water draining from the tub

CHAPTER 4

To give you a flavor of how these software tools enable you to move from causal loop diagrams to simulations, I've used InsightMaker to generate the following simulation example.[245] This simulation is based on the customer growth model that we discussed and sketched in the Causal Loop Diagram section.

For this example, I've added some additional inputs, including a **Conversion Rate** and the **Total Market Size**. You can access this simulation online at the InsightMaker website - http://bit.ly/338vKcv Let's look at this simulation model, working from left to right and top to bottom.

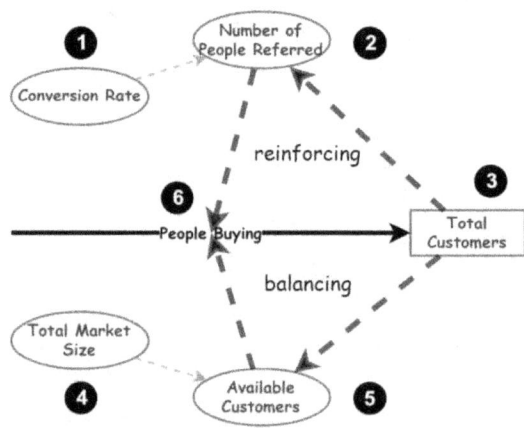

- The **Conversion Rate** (1) is the rate at which people who have been referred to our product buy the product (the value can be set between 5% and 15%)
- The **Number of People Referred** (2) is calculated from the **Conversion Rate** (1) and the **Total Customers** (3)

Number of People Referred =
Total Customers x Conversion Rate

- **Total Market Size** (4) is the number of people who could be customers for products like what you are offering, including competitive products (can be set from 25,000 to 50,000)

Are You Sure That's the Right Tool?

- **Available Customers** (5) are calculated from **Total Market Size** (4) and **Total Customers** (3)

  Available Customers = Total Market Size - Total Customers

- In the center of the diagram is an arrow named **People Buying** (6) that is pointing to **Total Customers**. **People Buying** is calculated from the **Number of People Referred** and **Available Customers**

  People Buying = People Referred + Total Customers
  (note when Available Customers = zero then no more customers are added to Total Customers)

The value of Total Customers is initially set to 1,000 (assuming we've had a soft launch to seed the market). When this simulation is run in InsightMaker the 36-month graph below is produced. The line nearest the horizontal axis is the **Number of People Referred** on a month-to-month basis. The higher, rapidly rising line is the number of **Total Customers**.

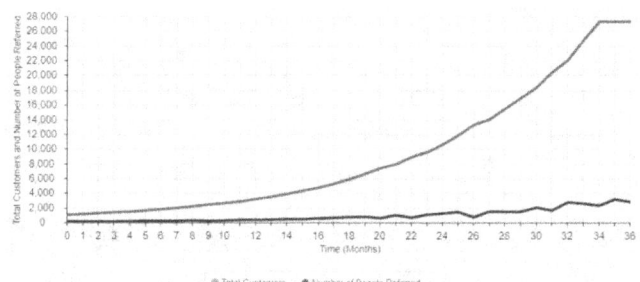

You can see the *reinforcing* loop in action, compounding the growth of **Total Customers** – more total customers lead to a higher **Number of People Referred** which leads to more **Total Customers**.

Note, too, that the simulation graph from InsightMaker above looks like the growth that we sketched under the Causal Loop Diagram section. Unlike the smooth S-shape in the growth sketch, however, there is a sharp termination of growth at 34-months. This abrupt change is because at that point all the people who would buy our product have done so and the number of **Available Customers** is set to zero in the simple model. In the real world, we would expect a slowing period as we reached market saturation which would create a more S-shaped curve.

Note that while simulation can offer the means to predict outcomes, such predictions are limited by the stability of the model and the reliability of variables and relationships. We can, for example, simulate the motion of planets and predict with accuracy the positions of the planets at a future date.[246,247] By contrast, attempts to predict the future in the business domain can be frustratingly fruitless due to uncertainty.

In cases of high uncertainty, models can be used to seek insight into actions we might take and how those actions might affect outcomes. Methods like Exploratory Modeling and Analysis (EMA),[248] robust decision-making (RDM), and scenario discovery (SD) have been used to address uncertainty in some rather complex systems like global container transport[249] and activities related to international security operations.[250]

While these advanced methods are outside the scope of this book, the example of a simulation that we will consider ahead suggests a simple approach to explore useful cause and effect scenarios rather than to predict outcomes.

 What are several possible strengths and weaknesses in our model regarding the growth of Total Customers? What other cause and effect relationships is this simple model not considering?

Strengths	Weaknesses
• Provides the means to explore actions to improve outcome (if the system is well understood) • Provides the means to consider a variety of scenarios for more robust decision making (when facing a highly uncertain system)	• Requires software to build and run • Requires time and effort to learn and become proficient • Can become more difficult to manage as the number of variables increases • The numeric results and graphs may suggest unfounded certitude

Monte Carlo Simulation

Let's now explore a tool that you may find both challenging and useful, Monte Carlo simulation. I've positioned this topic here because you can leverage the information we've covered up to this point, incorporating thinking skills and considering bias and fallacy as we construct a couple of example simulation models.

I'll take a step-by-step approach, working from simple concepts to a full example of Monte Carlo simulation in the business world. If you are already familiar with Monte Carlo simulation, then I hope that the following discussion will be a useful refresher. If you are new to the topic then you may want to read this section and then return when you can work with the online models (links provided in the examples below).

Named after the city in Monaco that is famous for gambling, Monte Carlo simulation is a method used to estimate a range of likely outcomes based on ranges of likely inputs. By popular accounts, Monte Carlo methodology originated during the development of the atomic bomb by scientists at the Los Alamos laboratories during the 1940s. A problem that these scientists faced was determining the complex behavior of atomic collisions which was difficult to calculate by direct methods. The scientists realized that they could make reasonable estimates if they took a probabilistic approach.

The Monte Carlo method has gone on to be successfully used for problems in other domains, including engineering, finance, and business. Even if you never use a stock-and-flow modeling tool or Monte Carlo simulation, just knowing that such tools exist and can be employed may be of significant benefit to the modern Devil's Advocate. Rather than coldly explaining the Monte Carlo method and the associated mathematics that the method employs, let's work toward an understanding by starting with simple concepts and then a more advanced business example.

CHAPTER 4

Strengths	Weaknesses
• Offers a way to scope a range of likely outcomes that better reflects a probabilities-based real world • Provides both tabular and graphical output	• Output accuracy and meaning is only as good as the quality of the inputs and mapped relationships • The numeric results and graphs may suggest unfounded certitude

A Simple Monte Carlo Example

If I asked you for the sum of 2 plus 3, then I am confident that you would quickly respond with the answer of 5. The inputs of 2 and 3 are fixed and the calculation of adding those two numbers together is straightforward. But what if I asked you for the sum of two variable numbers with the following characteristics:

- The first number (**A**) could be any value between 1.75 and 2.25
- The second number (**B**) could be any value between 2.50 and 3.25, but the most likely value is 3 — and the likelihood of that value decreases linearly from 3 to both 2.50 and 3.25

This may seem a confusing and pointless puzzle to you but in a way, it touches on common problems of estimating risk and managing uncertainty that business and financial planners face every day. These planners, for example, don't know with perfect certitude how well products will sell over the next quarter or which way an investment will trend over the year ahead. Planners may, however, make reasonable estimates by applying Monte Carlo methodology, using historical data and current indicators.

Let's continue by first sketching out the probability profiles for **A** and **B**; that is, the likelihood that a specific value will be randomly chosen across the given range of possible numbers while adhering to the characteristics noted above.

Are You Sure That's the Right Tool?

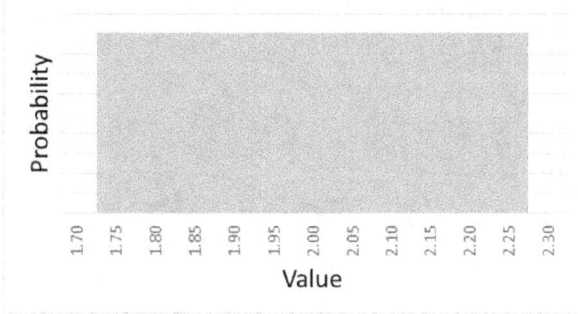

The value of **A** can be any number between 1.75 and 2.25 with no number being any more likely than its neighbors. This probability landscape (diagrammed above) defines a "box" that encompasses an area between the defined range of 1.75 to 2.25 (along the X-axis) with each number in that range having an equal chance of being randomly selected (along the Y-axis).

One way to think about a probability distribution is to imagine that the box is a small area rug on the floor, and you throw confetti into the air above the rug. As the confetti falls it will be randomly, and more or less evenly, distributed across the rug (we will ignore any confetti that falls outside of the rug because that confetti doesn't meet the range and probability boundaries as defined by the shape of the rug).

The probability landscape for **B** (diagrammed below), is in the form of a triangle that encloses an area between the defined number range of 2.50 to 3.25 with a peak at 3. Unlike the even distribution of **A** diagrammed above, the value of 3 is the most likely outcome with decreasing chance for other values being selected that are closer to 2.5 and 3.25. Referring again to the rug and confetti analogy, you can imagine that the falling confetti will also distribute evenly across the triangular rug but that the greatest amount of confetti will be under the peak of the triangle (ignoring again any confetti that falls outside the area of the rug).

Probability distributions can assume many shapes, and one of the most used is the normal distribution curve as was briefly discussed earlier. We, however, will be using the triangular probability distribution function in this example because it provides simplified variability using the example conditions described above. The triangular probability graph below may

CHAPTER 4

remind you of the triangular probability distribution graph in our earlier discussion about Risk and Uncertainty but it is not the same.

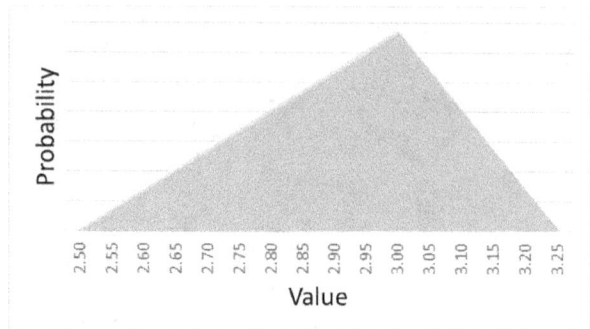

Remember that the probable outcomes by two, six-sided dice rolls are limited to thirty-six discrete possibilities – you can't roll any summed number below 2 or above 12 or a fractional number like 5.25. Further, because the dice have no "memory" of prior tosses, these probabilities remain fixed for every toss.

By contrast, we were able to set the conditions of the triangular probability function above specifically for this example. Like the dice rolls, the probability distribution cannot extend beyond the minimum and maximum results, however, it does include fractional values in between. Unlike the dice rolls in problems faced by modern Devil's Advocates, past outcomes may influence the probabilities of future outcomes. Thanks to real-world uncertainty, we often have no way of knowing if we have enough information to make a reasonable estimate of probable outcomes.

Returning to our summation question, we could use the probability landscapes for **A** and **B** and construct a Monte Carlo model in Excel. Instead, we're going to use InsightMaker.com which includes both the random number generators we need and a Monte Carlo function (referred to as a Sensitivity Testing by InsightMaker). The model for the summation example in InsightMaker is very simple as shown below.

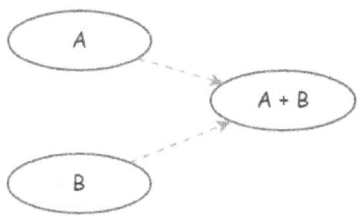

See http://bit.ly/2VVZ0Sf for this Stock and Flow model example

- Using InsightMaker, values for **A** will be generated by the uniform random function **Rand(Minimum, Maximum)** where the minimum and maximum values in our example are 1.75 and 2.25, respectively. This function will randomly select a value between 1.75 and 2.25, assigning an equal chance of selection to all values between 1.75 and 2.25.

- InsightMaker will generate values for **B** with the triangular random function **RandTriangular(Minimum, Maximum, Peak)** where for our example the minimum, maximum and peak values are 2.5, 3.25, and 3. This function will randomly select a value between 2.5 and 3.25, assigning the greatest chance of selection to values near 3.

- InsightMaker will then sum the outputs of the randomly selected values for **A** and **B**.

If we run a basic simulation for one-hundred examples in InsightMaker then we will see a graph that looks like the one below. You may notice how the values for **A** (bottom of the graph) that are calculated from a uniform distribution fall pretty evenly over the defined range. The values for **B** (middle) that are randomly calculated by the triangular distribution function tend to fall nearer the peak value of 3, with an occasionally value near the range extremes of 2.50 3.25. The sum of **A** and **B** (top) exhibits the characteristics of the random number generators used to select **A** and **B**.

CHAPTER 4

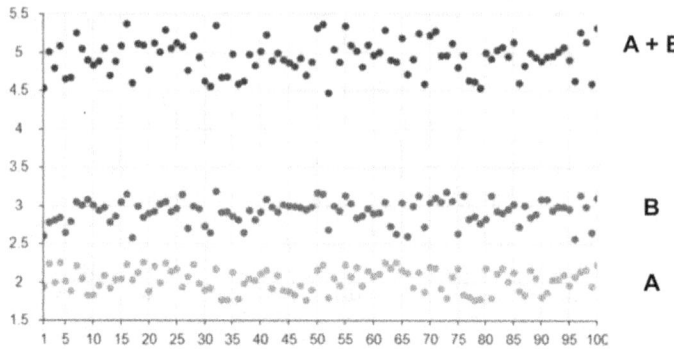

At this point, we have confirmed that the variables **A** and **B** and their sum are expressed as we would expect, based on the characteristics of these numbers as stated above. Had we seen straight lines or variables outside of the defined ranges, then we would know that we've made a mistake somewhere along the way. We will now run the Sensitivity Testing function to see how these probabilistic input values lead to estimates of likely outcomes.

The graph below is the output of the Sensitivity Testing function from InsightMaker. I generated the same number of runs as for the graph above and set InsightMaker to calculate five-hundred instances for each run. This means that for each of the one-hundred steps InsightMaker made five-hundred separate calculations for **A + B**, using different randomly selected values for **A** and **B** from their assigned random function generators.

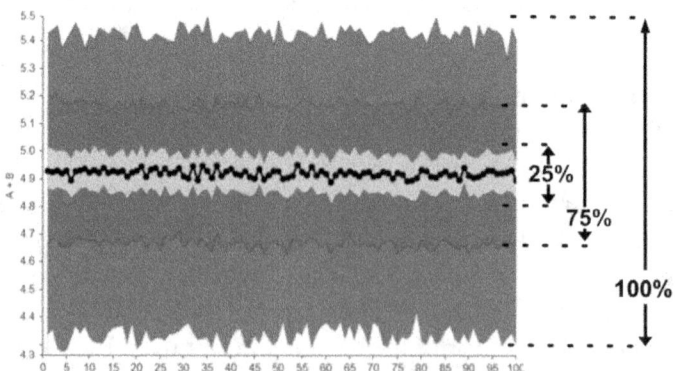

Each of the black dots that create the black line in the middle of the graph above indicates the median value of the five-hundred calculations for **A + B** for each of the one-hundred steps. The band nearest the line of black dots indicate where 25% of all the calculated values for the sum of **A+B** fell, the next widest band is where 75% of **A+B** sums fell, and the outermost band is where 100% of all the calculated values for the sum of **A + B** fell.

InsightMaker enables you to export the actual tables behind the graph in CSV format so you can view the data in a program like Excel (below are the exported numeric tables for the graph above). What we can see is that the median values for **A + B** fell within a range of 4.89 to 4.95, three-quarters of all the calculated values for **A + B** fell within a range of 4.63 to 5.21 and all of the calculated values for **A + B** fell between 4.26 and 5.49.

	100% Lower	100% Upper	75% Lower	75% Upper	25% Lower	25% Upper	Median
Min	4.26	5.33	4.63	5.13	4.81	4.95	4.89
Max	4.41	5.49	4.71	5.21	4.88	5.02	4.95

At this point, you might be thinking, "So what?" Well, provided that we have properly constructed the model in InsightMaker, we could use the outputs to answer the original summation question with, "I expect the sum of **A** and **B** to be about 5, and I'm very confident that the sum will be between 4.26 and 5.49" (because **all** the calculated results fell within this range). If you were pressed for a narrower estimate, then you might answer, "I'm fairly confident that the sum will be between 4.63 to 5.21" (because 75% of all calculated sums fell within this range).

[END DETOUR]

You may understandably ask if generating the Monte Carlo analysis was worth the effort just to answer a question like the one posed? After all, you could have likely guessed close to the results above.

For simple examples like the one above, I agree that Monte Carlo simulation isn't the best tool, but a more advanced business case that follows may help demonstrate the benefits of Monte Carlo simulation.

CHAPTER 4

A Monte Carlo Business Case Example

Now that you have a sense of how Monte Carlo simulation works, let's take a look at a more advanced example. Note, the discussion that follows may appear complicated and confusing, however, I'm confident that you can follow along with the step-by-step explanation below. If you get frustrated, then just set the example aside and return later with a fresh perspective.

> The Stock and Flow Simulation Model I'll be referring to below is available at https://bit.ly/3ixeO62 It may be helpful to have the model running as you read through the discussion that follows.

Let's say you are a Program Manager who has been tasked to work with associates and create a projection of gross profit for a given product. The calculations related to gross profit are straightforward and can be stated as follows:

- Gross Profit = Revenue – Total Cost of Goods Sold (COGS)
- Revenue = Units Sold x Sale Price
- Total Cost of Goods Sold = Units Sold x Unit Cost of Goods Sold

A typical solution to a gross profit projection is to use an Excel spreadsheet to make the calculations above. Let's assume that you have historical data for the average price that customers paid for the product and the average COGS to make the product. Armed with this data, you could enter your estimates for Units sold into the Excel spreadsheet and easily calculate the Revenues and Gross Profit as shown below.

Month	Jan	Feb	Mar
Units	9,256	8,219	9,761
Unit ASP	$5.04	$5.04	$5.04
Revenues	$46,650	$41,424	$49,195
Unit COGS	$18,660	$16,570	$19,678
Gross Profit	$27,990	$24,854	$29,517

It's not unusual for financial targets like revenues and gross profits to be set by a mandate from the C-suite (e.g. achieve $49MM revenues in three years). Such mandates may be heavily influenced by outside forces like shareholders' expectations and board members' opinions. These mandates and outside forces aren't necessarily based on the historical data you are using or market feedback that you are regularly receiving from your customers and the sales teams.

Starting with the mandated outcomes for revenues and gross profit, it's not unheard of for managers to create a spreadsheet like the one above that *backs into* the mandated targets. This approach has everyone involved working towards a mandated "one right answer". The numbers generated by such a spreadsheet can have a persuasive effect on people, especially when a lot of numbers are presented with apparent high precision.

Looking at the table above, one might take at face value that future sales of the product will be reliably achieved down to the individual unit and that the forecast ASP and COGS will be similarly managed to the penny. Of course, "everyone knows" that the actual future outcomes won't be identical to the projection, but organizations may still move forward with the expectation (hope) that actual outcomes will be close to or exceed the projected figures.

In contrast to simple Excel spreadsheet projections, a Monte Carlo simulation can provide a more realistic expression of uncertainty in the real world (provided the inputs and their relationships are reasonably supported). Running a model that projects the future based on relationships and probability estimates may help resist the *gerrymandering* of calculations to arrive at a desired or mandated result. To demonstrate these points, let's move further in our example starting with the causal loop diagram below that shows the basic relationships.

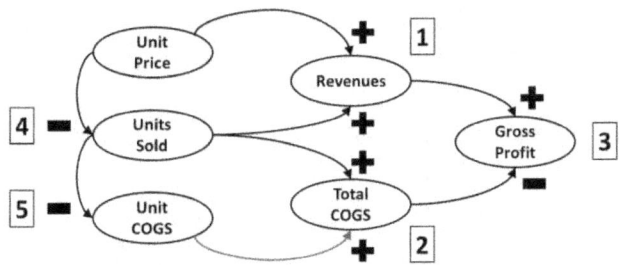

1. **Revenues** are calculated from the **Unit Price** and the number of **Units Sold**, increasing as either **Unit Price** or **Units Sold** increases

2. **Total COGS** are calculated from the number of **Units Sold** and the **Unit COGS**, increasing as either **Units Sold** or **Unit COGS** increases

3. **Gross Profit** is calculated from **Revenues** and **Total COGS**, increasing as **Revenues** increase and decreasing as **Total COGS** increase

The first three references to the diagram above are the basic relationships for Revenues, COGS, and Gross Profit. The next two references are for assumptions that we will introduce in the model to reflect real-world causes and effects for our Monte Carlo simulation, which are:

4. We plan to intentionally lower our **Unit Price** over time from its initial price, believing that as the product becomes affordable to more customers, more customers will purchase the product and the number of **Units Sold** will *increase* as **Unit Price** *decreases*

5. We also believe that as the number of **Units Sold** increases so will our production operational efficiencies improve and the **Unit COGS** *decreases* as **Units Sold** *increases*

If our assumptions above hold then we could make an *educated guess* at how these changes might look over time as sketched below. The downward trending curve represents decreases in **Unit Price, Unit COGS,** and **Total COGS** and the upward trending curve represents increases in **Units Sold, Revenue,** and **Gross Profit**.

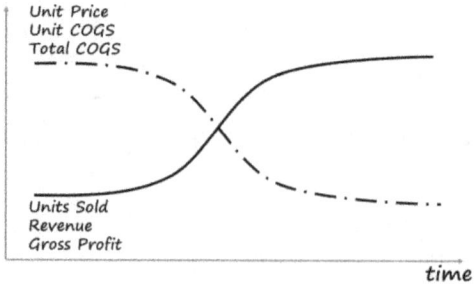

Are You Sure That's the Right Tool?

Our sketch above is certainly "wrong". For one thing, neither the rate of change nor scale for any variable considered is known at this point, and not all variables would rise and fall at the same rate or scale. It is also very unlikely that changes will be nearly as smooth as the curves suggest or that the trends would continue indefinitely in the real world. After all, there is not an infinite number of customers who will buy our product or service regardless of the price, COGS will never be zero, etc.

The shapes of the sketched curves, however, are useful. The curves represent the expected outcome of our assumptions and provide us with a visual *guardrail*. If as we develop our model further, we see that the calculated outcomes are not in line with our sketched expectations, then we ought to be alert and very interested to learn the reason for the discrepancy. Are our original cause and effect assumptions incorrect? Did we fail to include a variable that is required to properly represent the real world? Did something outside the boundaries of our model change such as a competitive product or service, regulation, market trend, etc.?

In addition to the causal loop diagram and our initial assumptions as stated above, we're going to also assume that we have historical data and other useful information (e.g. the expected number of Units Sold based on different Retail Price points). We are now ready to build a stock-and-flow model in InsightMaker and simulate outcomes.

Let's begin by looking at each component of the InsightMaker model below starting with the oval at the top left labeled, **Year**.

- In InsightMaker, ovals represent variables that can serve either as inputs or calculated outputs. In the case of the **Year** variable, it is being used simply to drive calculations incrementally over a term of five years. We could have set InsightMaker to drive calculations over months or weeks, but I chose to model a five-year horizon for this example.

CHAPTER 4

Stock and flow model diagram

- Directly below the Year variable is a hexagon symbol labeled **Retail Price Likely**. Hexagon symbols in InsightMaker indicate "converters" – essentially a table of values that are used as are the lookup functions in Excel. The **Retail Price Likely** lookup table states the retail price that the company intends to set for each of the five years in the model. Specifically, as the **Year** variable increments from 1 through 5, the value of the **Retail Price Likely** variable decreases annually according to the underlying lookup table which is shown below. Note that the **Retail Price Likely** value moves linearly and reflects our decision to initially offer the product for $15 in the first year and then to drop the price by $1 every year to $11 in the fifth year.

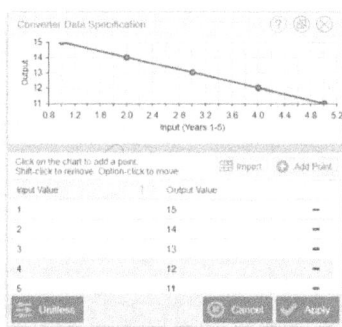

Retail Price Likely lookup table

- Directly below the **Retail Price Likely** hexagon are two ovals labeled **Retail Price Max** and **Retail Price Min**. These variables are percentages represented as fractions that will be used to multiply the **Retail Price Likely** value to calculate the range of possible retail price values in a year. If we set the **Retail Price Max** value to 1.10 and the **Retail Price Min** value to 0.95 then the range of possible values for the **Retail Likely Price** of $15 in the first year will be from $16.50 ($15 x 1.10) to $14.25 ($15 x 0.95).

- Note that the **Retail Price Likely, Retail Price Max** and **Retain Price Min** variables are all connected to the **Retail Price** variable. Our model will calculate the **Retail Price** variable for each year with the **RandTriangular(Minimum, Maximum, Peak)** function that was discussed above.

- Look now at how the **Retail Price** variable output is input into a white hexagon symbol labeled **Units Sold**. The lookup table behind the **Units Sold** hexagon is shown below and reflects our assumption that as the **Retail Price** decreases, more customers will be able to afford our product and so the number of **Units Sold** will increase.

CHAPTER 4

*The **Retail Price** lookup table*

- The table above shows how when the **Retail Price** is $15 the expected number of **Units Sold** is 972,000 units and when the **Retail Price** is reduced to $11 the expected number of **Units Sold** rises to 11.5 million units. Note that the **Units Sold** lookup table includes retail prices of $10 and $16 which are outside the range established in the **Retail Price Likely** lookup table. These retail prices of $10 and $16 are included to acknowledge the variability that we will introduce using the **Retail Price Max** and **Retail Price Min** settings.

> In a real-world setting, the estimates provided above for the relationship between price and unit sales might come from the Marketing Manager based on her analysis of historical information and market insight gained through discussion with customers and sales teams, competitor news, market trends, etc.

- Look next at the hexagon symbol labeled **Unit COGS Likely** and the ovals beneath that symbol labeled **Unit COGS Max** and **Unit COGS Min**. We've taken a similar approach to calculate the **Unit COGS** variable as we did for the **Retail Price** variable, setting the **Unit COGS Likely** value and enabling the means to introduce a range for **Unit COGS Likely** by setting the **Unit COGS Max** and the **Unit COGS Min** variables. An important difference, however, is that where the **Retail Price Likely** value is determined by **Year**, the **Unit COGS Likely** value is determined by the number of **Units Sold** as shown in the table below.

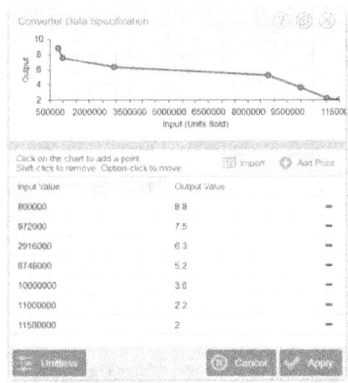

Unit COGS Likely lookup table

- Note our assumption that the **Unit COGS Likely** will decrease as the number of **Units Sold** increases because our manufacturing operations become more efficient. Our stated assumptions are that **Unit COGS Likely** will decrease from $8.80 at 800,000 **Units Sold** to $6.30 at 2.91MM units, then a shallow decrease to $5.20 at 8.74MM **Units Sold**, and then a significant decrease to $2.00 as sales approach 11.5MM **Units Sold**. The table values set upper and lower boundaries so the cost of manufacturing the product can never be zero.

> In a real-world setting, the estimates provided above might come from the Buying Manager based on his analysis of historical information and further insight gained through discussions with Manufacturing, vendors, market trends, etc.

Our model now has variability introduced for **Retail Price** and **Unit COGS** and can use the outputs from **Retail Price, Unit COGS,** and **Units Sold** to calculate the **Revenues, Total COGS,** and **Gross Profit**.

We next confirm that the model works as we would expect from our assumptions to help identify any mistakes that we may have made in building the InsightMaker model. To do so, we will first use the sliders in the model to reduce variability near zero as shown below. By reducing the variability, the model will work much like a traditional Excel spreadsheet that uses fixed values.

CHAPTER 4

Retail Price Min %

○ 0.99

Retail Price Max %

1.01

Unit COGS Min %

○ 0.99

Unit COGS Max %

1.01

Next, we will run the model, looking specifically at the output from **Retail Price**, **Units Sold,** and **Unit COGS**. InsightMaker displays the graph shown below which does reflect our assumptions; for example, as we lower our **Retail Price** linearly every year the **Units Sold** increase in the expected S-shape and the **Unit COGS** decreases as anticipated.

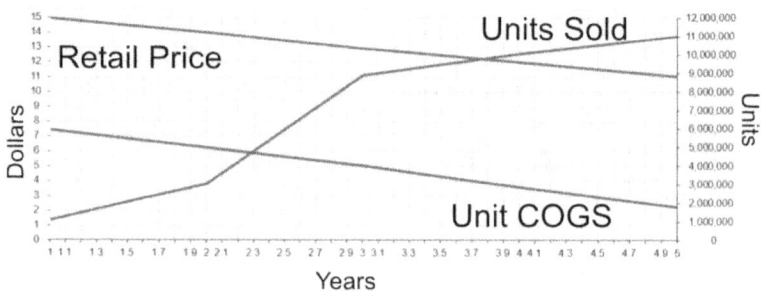

Next, we will look at the impact of our assumptions on the **Revenues, Total COGS,** and **Gross Profit**. InsightMaker displays the graph below that shows how our **Revenues** grow toward a plateau following the S-shape in our assumptions, while our **Gross Profit** increases in an S-shape as the **Unit COGS** decrease. At this point, the model appears to be generating the kind of results that our assumptions would support.

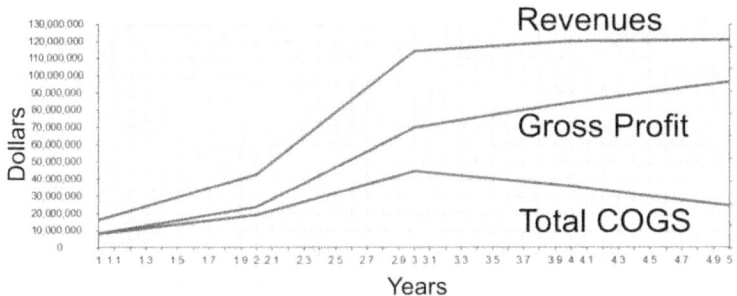

The two graphs above are unremarkable and could have been easily generated in a simple Excel spreadsheet. Now, however, let's look at what the InsightMaker Sensitivity Testing function may reveal.

Let's assume that the Product Manager believes that within any of the five years forecast the product may recognize an upside pricing potential of 5% over the **Retail Price Likely** estimate but that there may also be heavy discounting that could reduce the **Retail Price Likely** by 15%. Meanwhile, the Buyer believes that within any of the five years forecast it may be possible to drive the **Unit COGS** lower by 5% but **Unit COGS** could also increase by 12%. How might these independent variability assessments combine to impact our simulated forecast of **Gross Profit**?

Before we run the Sensitivity Testing function, we first use the sliders in the InsightMaker model to set the variability estimates provided above from the Product Manager and Buyer as shown below.

Retail Price Min %   0.85
Retail Price Max %   1.05
Unit COGS Min %   0.95
Unit COGS Max %   1.12

We will also set the parameters for the Sensitivity Testing function as shown below to focus on the Gross Profit results and to set the way that the Sensitivity Testing function will calculate and report results.

CHAPTER 4

Monitored Primitives:	Gross Profit ×
Number of Runs:	50
Confidence Regions (%):	25, 50, 100

Based on our simulation model and setting the sliders and parameters as shown above, when we run the Sensitivity Testing function, Insight-Maker will:

1. Find the **Retail Price Likely** for the first **Year**

2. Use the **RandTriangular(Minimum, Maximum, Peak)** function with the **Retail Price Likely** as the peak, 85% of the **Retail Price Likely** for the minimum and 105% of the **Retail Price Likely** for the maximum

3. Use the calculated **Retail Price** to find the number of **Units Sold** in the **Units Sold** lookup table

4. Use the number of **Units Sold** to find the **Unit COGS Likely** in the **Unit COGS Likely** lookup table

5. Calculate **Unit COGS** using the **RandTriangular(Minimum, Maximum, Peak)** function will with the **Unit COGS Likely** as the peak, 95% of the **Unit COGS Likely** for the minimum and 112% of the **Unit COGS Likely** for the maximum

6. Calculate the values for **Revenues**, **Total COGS** and **Gross Profit** for the **Year**

For each **Year** (1-5) InsightMaker will repeat steps 1 through 6 above fifty times and store the resulting calculations. It will then use these stored results to determine the median value for **Gross Profit** and the confidence regions (25%, 50%, and 100% of all calculations made for the **Year**).

The graph created from the Sensitivity Testing function, in this case, is shown below. At first glance, this graph may look very odd, indeed. What accounts for its cornucopia shape with a very wide range of possible outcomes for **Gross Profit** in the first **Year** that narrows over the five-year forecast?

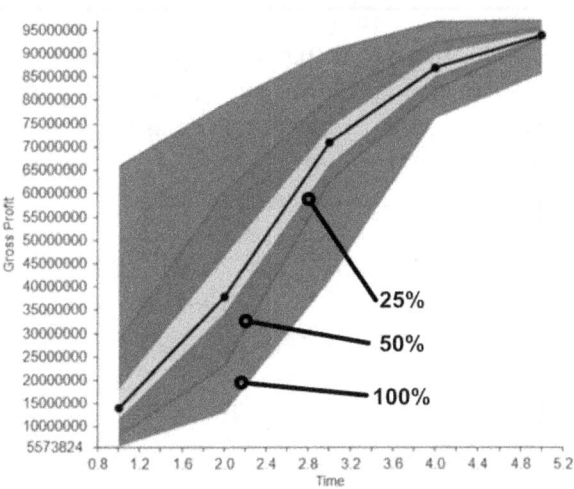

First, note the S-shape of the median value line which reflects the projected growth of **Units Sold** based on our assumption that our intentional lowering of **Retail Price Likely** will increase the number of units sold. Next, note that the light area surrounding the solid median line represents the 25% confidence band (where 25% of all calculated **Gross Profit** values fall). The next darker area represents the 50% confidence band and the outermost area the 100% confidence band.

Remember that over the five-year forecast both the **Retail Price Likely** value and the **Unit COGS Likely** value are decreasing, so the range of likely values is also decreasing. For example, the **Retail Price Likely** value of $15 in the first **Year** reduces to $11 in the fifth **Year**, shifting the minimum value for **Retail Price** from $12.75 to $9.35. Consequently, the variability calculated as a percentage of these diminishing values is also getting smaller.

CHAPTER 4

What the model permits us to do is to think more deeply about our assumptions and consider steps we may be able to take to narrow the anticipated variability and better control outcomes.

Let's suppose that faced with the results of the Sensitivity Testing function the Product Manager and Buyer pursue avenues to tighten their initial estimates of variability. The Market Manager may propose that the product will never be sold at a price lower than a few points below the **Retail Price Likely** value. The Buyer may be able to negotiate a purchase agreement that secures a lower price for a five-year purchase commitment. Their new estimates of variability are set with the model sliders and the Sensitivity Testing function updates the graph (shown below).

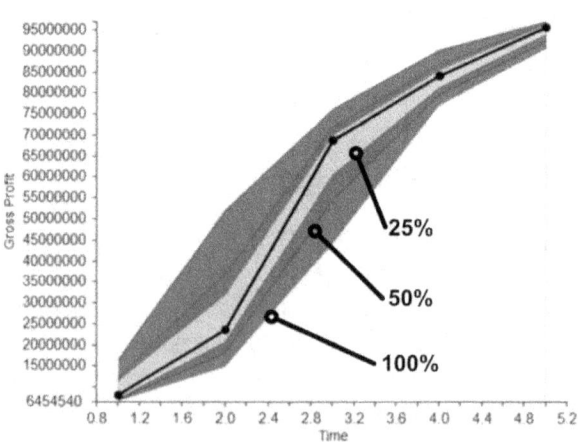

The tighter pricing and cost of goods conditions lead to a narrower estimated range of **Gross Profit** over the term of the forecast. Different decisions could also be reflected in the model such as changes in the **Retail Price Likely** and **Unit COGS Likely** lookup tables **if** good evidence is available to support such changes.

Note that the decisions made by the Product Manager and Buyer to narrow variability also have consequences. Fixing a basement sale price for the product could lead to fewer **Units Sold**, especially if a competitor drops their price and draws customers toward those lower prices. Committing to a longer purchase agreement could mean excess inventory if the number of **Units Sold** falls short of expectations due to the Product Manager's decision to set a basement sale price. Of course, the model could be altered further to advance it past the simple relationships it now reflects which would open the door to other scenarios and possible outcomes.

The current model considers only simple **Retail Price** as the driver of **Units Sold**. Businesses may sell through distributors who can purchase the product at a lower wholesale price which introduces additional variability. In this case, you might construct a model that includes the new variable, **Wholesale Price** which would drive a separate lookup table for the number of units sold through distributors. The total number of units sold through direct and distributor sales would then drive the **Unit COGS** estimate.

> A common question about Monte Carlo analysis is, How many samples are enough? Too few samples may not adequately represent the variability of the model, while very many samples could take a long time to calculate. Somewhere between 500 and 1,000 samples are commonly used, however, other factors may need to be considered depending upon the specific case. These considerations are well outside the scope of this discussion but a brief primer is available on the Vose Software website at http://bit.ly/2PeyU8P

[END DETOUR]

CHAPTER 4

Remember that in cases of high uncertainty, models can be used to seek insight into actions we might take and how those actions might affect outcomes, rather than to calculate highly accurate predictions. The example above provides a very basic approach to exploration rather than prediction. Using tools like InsightMaker, rather complex systems can be modeled – but there are several important cautions to keep in mind.

First, a relatively simple model that reflects a system well enough to produce useful insights is preferred over a complicated model that can quickly become confusing, unmanageable, and useless. Adding more variables and guessing at their values will add layers of *noise* that have little or no worth to the analysis. As we discussed above, *uncertainty* exists when we don't know the "distribution of the outcome in a group of instances". In the face of uncertainty, we shouldn't fool ourselves into believing that we can create certainty through casual conjecture.

Second, remember that the goal is not to *game the system* to deliver a mandated outcome (e.g. a **Gross Profit** target). The goal of the simulation is to better understand the relationships among variables and how those relationships and variables may drive results. The insight from the simulation may identify options that we can pursue in our attempt to achieve a mandated target. Through regular monitoring of our activities, we can confirm that our model reasonably reflects the real world.

Third, we shouldn't be lulled into a sense of certitude that our models and simulations can unintentionally convey by the numbers and charts they generate. Rather, our models and simulations should help remind us of uncertainty in the real world. This uncertainty may create anxiety and fear, but it can also be embraced as a useful catalyst that helps actively reexamine our mental models and to incorporate new information as it becomes available.

Fourth, if a model or simulation isn't getting us close to a mandated outcome after evidence-based actions are taken, then the responsible thing to do is advise those who have set the mandate that success appears unlikely within the current boundaries (e.g. budget, resources, timeline). This is easier said than done, of course, because speaking truth to power can lead to unpleasant outcomes, including jeopardizing one's job. At the same time, failed projects can also lead to financial instability in a company, bankruptcy, and the loss of many jobs.

Modeling for uncertainty works best in an environment where everyone from the CEO to team members understands the purpose and benefits of such work and support the effort. On the path to company-wide support for Devil's Advocacy, you may want to look for ways to quietly incorporate modeling and simulation into your activities without belaboring your efforts, and to informally share the insights that modeling can offer (e.g. water cooler chats with your peers, one-on-one status updates with your manager).

> 💡 Can you give examples of a projection that you created which was similar to the example above? If you did not factor in the uncertainty of key variables like price and COGS then do you see merit in considering a Monte Carlo analysis in the future?

As we conclude this section on several analytical tools, I recommend that you read *The Too Fleet-Footed Mercury* in the appendices for an example of how a set of very good tools in the hands of some very bright people were the "wrong" tools for the problem they were trying to solve.

CHAPTER 4

Group Decision-Making

We conclude this chapter of the book with a discussion about group decision-making. Modern Devil's Advocates will rarely opine on the decisions made by one person but rather will examine how a group of individuals has made judgments and reached conclusions. Of particular interest will be signs of rote decision-making tendencies of individuals and teams that may indicate groupthink bolstered by dogmatic processes and methods. When modern Devil's Advocates interact directly with the individuals whose work they are analyzing, they may (understandably) be treated as an unwanted nuisance and troublemaker.

Any method of decision-making has its strengths and weaknesses and various decision-making methodologies may be employed depending on factors like the group composition and the environment in which the group operates. When interacting with multicultural teams, unexpressed but existing miscommunication issues within the stakeholder entity may be common and confound the Devil's Advocate efforts.[251] Although it may be a natural desire of group members to get along and reach harmonious decisions, groups may benefit by enabling (if not encouraging) thoughtful dissent. As the late Supreme Court Justice Antonin Scalia acknowledged,

> "I probably believe that the worst opinions in my court have been unanimous. Because there's nobody on the other side pointing out all the flaws."[252]

It's important to understand that the modern Devil's Advocate is **not** the decision-maker but rather acts as a *prosecutor* who builds and presents a dissenting opinion. Consequently, even a strong case made by a modern Devil's Advocate can be ignored (see *Verde vs. Thérèse* in the appendices). Let's look next at three types of decision-making approaches used in group settings (mandated, consensus, and consent) their strengths and weaknesses.

Mandated Decisions

Mandated decisions are those that are made by one person (or a small number of people) on behalf of others. We'll be considering mandated decisions in groups (e.g. imposed a CEO), however, the pros and cons of mandated decisions also apply when you are making decisions for yourself.

If you are the CEO at the top of a hierarchy, then you may welcome autonomous authority, feeling that "nothing would happen" if you didn't explicitly tell others what to do. Even if you aren't a *micro-manager* you may believe that leadership demands regular direct control over operations. Although you can make decisions more quickly if you make the call by yourself, there are potentially damaging downsides to such direct, authoritarian control.

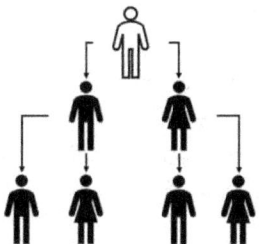

Mandated decision-making imposes the judgment of the one (or the few) on the many

As the CEO of a company, you may have little to no understanding about how to design, build, or sell your company's products and services, even if you had such understanding and skill earlier in your career. Limiting decisions to just yourself and a couple of close advisors does not benefit from a diversity of opinion, information, and expertise. A common analogy for the benefit of diversity is seeking the highest mountain peak – where the peak represents an optimal decision.

In the mountain peak analogy, you look around and see a mountain peak in your vicinity (A) that you deem is highest (i.e. the best decision). Had you asked others who reside beyond your locality, then you may have learned about an even higher mountain peak (B) (i.e. a better decision). Intending to drive activities faster or in a different direction, however, you may forego seeking wider input and mandate actions based on your limited

CHAPTER 4

perspective. Your mandated decision is not optimal, and it will impact design, manufacturing, and sales activities — all of which can directly affect the customer.

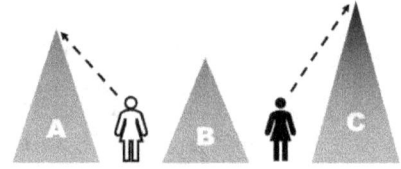

Solo decision-making can lead to sub-optimal choices

Mandated decisions can also create an acrimonious environment as employees throughout the firm try to figure out how best to implement a decision in which they were not involved, don't understand, and don't support. Depending on your temperament as the CEO, employees may publicly support you while quietly agreeing among themselves that you are misguided, and your goal is unachievable. Further, it may take months of implementation effort until the full shortcomings of your mandated decision surface, during which time other related decisions have been made, each contributing to the overall outcome.

An extreme case of how badly mandated decision-making can go is Theranos, the company noted in the Introduction of this book. The CEO, Elizabeth Holmes, reportedly had a direct hand in all decisions, leading right up to the point where the firm collapsed.

At the same time, mandated decisions may be required, depending on the environment, personnel, time-constraints, and other factors. Consider, for example, situations where the implications of an overarching *mission* are so broad that those at the extremities must comply even though they may not fully understand their assigned tasks. Warfighting is one such example where *mission command* is critical. As noted in the Introduction to the Army Field Manual, *Commander and Staff Organization and Operations*,[253]

> "*Mission command* is the exercise of authority and direction by the commander using mission orders to enable disciplined initiative within the commander's intent to empower agile and adaptive leaders in the conduct of unified

land operations. Mission command is both a philosophy and a warfighting function... As a warfighting function, mission command assists commanders in blending the art of command with the science of control, while emphasizing the human aspects of mission command."

Note, however, that the purpose of "authority and direction" is not for the commander to make all of the decisions in every case. Rather, the commander's authority and direction are intended to empower others in the attainment of the mission. One approach discussed in the manual is the concept of *running estimates* which is defined as,

"the continuous assessment of the current situation used to determine if the current operation is proceeding according to the commander's intent and if planned future operations are supportable...The commander and each staff element maintain a running estimate."

Throughout the manual, the importance of transparency and teamwork is constantly reinforced,

"The higher headquarters solicits input and continuously shares information concerning future operations through planning meetings, warning orders, and other means. It shares information with subordinate and adjacent units, supporting and supported units, and unified action partners. Commanders encourage active collaboration among all organizations affected by pending operations to build a shared understanding of the situation, participate in course of action development and decision making, and resolve conflicts before publishing the plan or order."

Notwithstanding any of the formal planning and decision-making guidance contained in the manual, it is acknowledged that "In extremely compressed situations, commanders rely on more intuitive decision-making techniques."

CHAPTER 4

When time is of the essence, the commander may be compelled to bypass more thorough planning and examined decision-making. In these cases, the manual points to a streamlined process that includes,

- **Increasing the Commander's Involvement** to make more rapid decisions - even though with less input from staff

- **Limiting the Number of Courses of Action (COA)** with the commander selecting one of many possible paths – although the manual warns that "this technique should be used only when time is severely limited."

- **Increasing Collaborative Planning** in real-time between the commander and those tasked to carry out orders, noting that "taking advantage of subordinates' input and knowledge of the situation in their areas of operations often results in developing better COAs quickly."

Although as CEO you may never face the same kinds of life-and-death decisions that commanders of military operations do, you may well find yourself confronted by thorny problems that need to be quickly addressed by a mandated decision. Such instances may include product failures that cause injury or death, sudden disruptions in supply chains that halt the production of products and revenue generation, or unforeseen competitive challenges that diminish the importance of products and services in the development pipeline. As the Army field manual advises, however, mandated decisions should be reserved and used only when timeliness is a significant issue.

> What might it mean if mandated decisions are being made regularly? Could an executive be a micro-manager? Could the staff lack the skills required to get the job done? Might the project be so out of control that a robust and honest reassessment needs to be made? What other unseen political and influential issues might be occurring? How might you offer a constructive opinion in a way that is palatable to those who can mandate a decision?

Unanimous Consensus Decisions

Consensus decisions seek unanimity or harmony. The general idea is that a proposed decision is opened to discussion and when everyone agrees then the decision is accepted. We've all had common experiences in consensus decision-making like choosing a restaurant.

Consensus decision-making seeks unanimity, but a mandated decision can be imposed if the group cannot reach a harmonious decision

If you (the outlined figure above) are tasked to choose a restaurant that will appeal to your good friends, then attaining unanimous consensus may be quick and easy. Knowing everyone well, you would not propose restaurants that are likely to fail (e.g. no Moroccan which Frank dislikes or Italian which Mary dislikes).

Note that within a certain circle of friends, you may always go to one of a handful of restaurants because experience indicates that those restaurants are where everyone seems happiest (even if the menu options have grown stale). This rote behavior is a *red flag* in Devil's Advocacy because it indicates *groupthink* and an imposed limitation of alternate options. Even if groupthink is not occurring, the consensus process can be long and contentious.

Consider, for example, that you are the manager of a team that is tasked to decide which of two proposed product innovations should be pursued. The innovations differ in their reward/risk profile, where the first innovation is relatively simple to accomplish with a small but acceptable return while the second innovation would be a significant challenge but could offer a much higher reward. In these kinds of cases, the team composition and environment can make consensus very difficult.

Those who would be responsible for the development of the innovation may want to create something new but feel overwhelmed due to the high level of support they currently provide for existing products. This group may be very reluctant to take on any new development work and grudgingly opt for the simpler innovation option. Meanwhile, those responsible for sales are desperate for new products to sell and so enthusiastically want the more difficult innovation option. Other team members like marketing and operations may be more neutral in their views and could support either option.

Round after round of discussions may lead developers and sales associates to harden their positions. Marketing and operations associates may be swayed to one side or the other, in part, because of personal relationships and preferences (e.g. marketing's empathy for sales' perspective and operations affinity for the developers' perspective).

As the team manager, you likely have the responsibility of mediator to help achieve a unanimous consensus, working to keep the team focused and reduce emotional conflicts. You likely also have the authority to force a mandated decision if the team efforts to arrive at a unanimous consensus fail – in which case you face the same benefits and shortcomings of a mandated decision as discussed above.

Consent Decisions

An alternative to both mandated and unanimous consensus decision-making is the *consent* method.[254] Consent requires that parties "give assent or approval". The consent decision-making approach is **not** seeking unanimous agreement among all parties in the group. The general idea in consent decision-making is that everyone participates in creating a decision that everyone can support, even if everyone doesn't agree that the group's decision is the "best" decision.

On the surface, consent may seem like an insignificant difference compared to a unanimous consensus, but I've found that consent can be a refreshingly effective approach. Consent decision-making also seems well suited for modern Devil's Advocacy because it permits strong dissenting views to be expressed while maintaining forward motion on decisions.

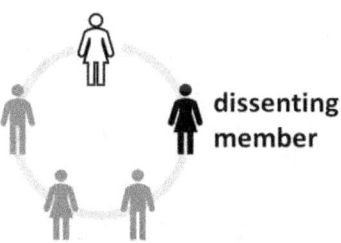

Consent decision-making enables dissent while maintaining forward motion and timely decisions

There are three main roles in the consent decision-making method: sponsor, facilitator, and group.

- **Sponsor.** The sponsor is the person who is proposing a decision to the group. The sponsor prepares the proposal after fully researching the question and related issues, speaking with associates off-line, and with consideration of the larger goals and constraints of the entity and its stakeholders. The sponsor can hold any title within any department of the organization.

- **Facilitator.** The facilitator is the person who is responsible for the consent method being followed. The facilitator takes notes but doesn't "take sides". In addition to ensuring that everyone is heard during the review of a proposed decision, the facilitator is also tasked to ensure that all *paramount objections* are addressed. A paramount objection is not a strong opinion or an attempt to "pull rank" over others in the group. Rather a paramount objection is some reason the proposed decision would either work against the aims of the group or would somehow prevent the party objecting from supporting the decision.

- **Group.** The group includes everyone participating in the decision. In a typical project team, these group members would include representatives from engineering, marketing, sales, operations, legal, finance, etc.

CHAPTER 4

== The Consent Decision-Making Method ==

Let's suppose that a decision needs to be made on the feature set of a new product. Marketing and Sales have their views based on competitive products and where they believe the market is heading. Engineering and Operations have their views based on current capabilities and target cost of goods. Legal, Finance, and others also have their perspectives, based on their roles and responsibilities.

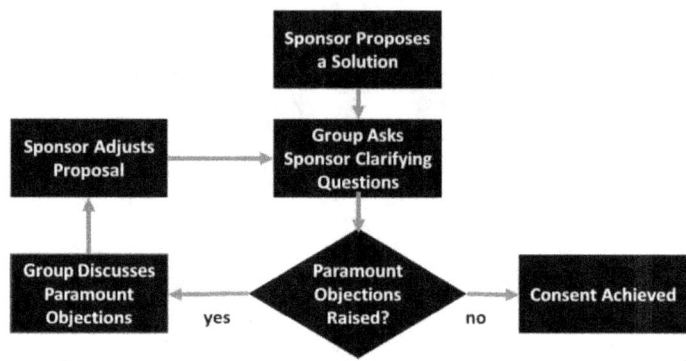

Consent decisions are made through a process as diagrammed above

A Marketing Manager is tasked as the Sponsor to propose the final feature set and the group is tasked to reach a consent decision. The Marketing Manager presents the proposed feature set and provides the rationale behind a decision to go with the proposed features. The Facilitator, who could be selected from any department, ensures that everyone, in turn, gets the opportunity to ask the Sponsor questions about the proposal.

An initial round of questions is solicited from each participant. This round is solely intended to ensure that the proposal is fully understood by everyone - no paramount objections are offered, and no decision is sought.

After everyone's clarifying questions are addressed by the Sponsor, the Facilitator asks individuals of the Group in turn if they have any *paramount objections* to the proposal by the Sponsor – note that asking for **objections** rather than agreement is fundamental for consent decisions. Remember that paramount objections are **not the opinions** of an individual but the reasons why the proposal could reasonably interfere with the individual's ability to support the proposal.

For example, a Group member who represents the legal department might object because one of the proposed features may infringe on a competitor's patent. Likewise, other members of the Group may have paramount objections within their specific domain. A Group member who represents the Sales Department may have a strong opinion about a legal issue, however, she likely lacks the legal knowledge of her associate from the legal department. In such a case of differing viewpoints, the sales representative could consent while still voicing her opinion.

Paramount objections are addressed by a revision to the proposed decision. In the example above, the potential patent-infringing feature may be dropped from the proposed decision provided it does not raise another paramount objection. Marketing, for example, may raise a paramount objection to drop the feature because doing so would weaken the final product and cause reduced revenues and profits that no longer meet the requirements of the company. The paramount objection could also be addressed outside of the meeting; for example, legal may agree to a closer examination and if they find a way to avoid infringement then would consent to the decision.

Through a series of rounds, the paramount objections are addressed and a consent decision is made. Note again that a consent decision is **not** one of universal agreement – some in the Group may have decided differently if the decision was theirs alone. Consent decisions permit everyone to be heard and help to ensure that no one will stand in the way of the decision which meets the aims of the company while permitting everyone to serve their role and responsibilities. Consent decision-making may also help maintain an awareness of uncertainty in decisions and a willingness by the group to reexamine decisions as new information and insights are obtained.

While the example above led to a successful consent decision, we recognize that in the real world our human nature will likely cloud our thinking and actions, especially when highly emotional conditions exist. If a team member simply refuses to participate in the consent decision-making method, or if an executive with the authority overrides a consent decision, then participants may find themselves unwilling and unhappy actors in either the unanimous consensus or mandated methods discussed above.

CHAPTER 4

> ⏱ Consent decision-making is a key element in *Sociocracy* (aka *Dynamic Governance*)[255] which in the United States is unfortunately confused with *Socialism*. For more information, see https://www.sociocracy.info/ https://sociocracy30.org/ and Ricardo Semler's book, *Maverick*.[256]

> 💡 The consent decision-making approach discussed above included a process diagram – what are your thoughts based on our previous discussion of trailing vs trailblazing?

Decision Method	Strengths	Weaknesses
Mandated	• Decisions can be made quickly • Can be implemented when necessary	• Often lacks a diverse perspective • May create hidden animosity
Unanimous Consensus	• Helps maintain harmony • Can be quick depending on relationships in the group	• Can enable groupthink • Can be time-consuming as the number of participants increases
Consent	• Permits dissent and diverse views • Enables progress without unanimous consensus	• Requires that participants follow the process and intentionally seek consent

In this chapter, we explored a variety of tools, including some of their strengths and weaknesses. We also considered the importance of *interpreting* the answers that such tools provide to assess their practical usefulness. Finally, we considered three approaches to decision-making in groups, acknowledging that while each approach could lead to well-reasoned decisions, the consent method offers the ability to encourage useful dissent while not impeding progress.

In the next and final chapter, we'll consider how to apply the topics covered in the previous chapters to the practice of modern Devil's Advocacy.

Chapter 5: Welcome to Wonderland

As I noted at the beginning of this book, I intended to introduce you to the world of modern Devil's Advocacy and to offer you a "red pill" with the hope that you would stay in Wonderland and see how deep the rabbit-hole goes. The key points that we explored included:

- Soft skills like critical thinking and problem-solving are becoming more important in our increasingly complex world that creates a flood of information which often lacks context or meaning

- We understand our world through mental models that are simplified representations and "wrong" - but "some are useful" when they provide us with valuable insights

- Our written and diagrammed processes are expressions of our mental models and can be helpful by providing structure to achieve our goals. Even so-called best practices, however, may be more articles of faith rather than rigorously proven processes and so should never be excluded from examination and critique

- We rely on a variety of thinking types that can help us control those things that are within our control, including monitoring our impulsive responses to make rational decisions

- Real arguments can be powerful tools to help ensure that our premises support reasoned conclusions and can be diagrammed so we can see what we are thinking

CHAPTER 5

- Bias and fallacy can distort our understanding of the world by unconsciously swaying the information we receive toward our established beliefs. Further our lack of knowledge can lead us to become overly confident in our competence

- Luck plays a significant role in Life and good decisions today can still lead to unwanted outcomes tomorrow, consequently, we should seek ways to explicitly express risk and uncertainty in our models and analyses

- Various tools may be applied to analyze problems and opportunities in support of decision-making, however, it's important to consider the limits of our tools and to take into consideration the practical meaning of the results that our tools produce

- Consent decision-making can enable diversity and dissent in group decision-making while achieving decisions in a timely fashion

Remember that there is no prescribed procedure for Devil's Advocacy. The modern Devil's Advocate must maintain an open, flexible, and skeptical perspective rather than follow a strict formal process like the ones that she will be challenging. In the absence of a prescribed process, I offer below some guidance that is based on my experience as a *de facto* modern Devil's Advocate.

Suggested Guidance

- Identify the Position to be Challenged and its Origin
- Collect & Organize Facts, Assumptions, Beliefs & Bias
- Validate Facts and Construct Real Arguments
- Create a Strong Position Case
- Create Your Opposing Case
- Present Your Opposing Case
- Authoritatively Communicating with an Authority
- Move on

Identify the Position to be Challenged and its Origin

Of course, you will need to know what position you'll be challenging, and where your participation can be beneficial. In general, the position will be something that "everyone knows", for example, that a new product idea will be a *slam-dunk* success or that a stumbling service offering is doomed to fail. These kinds of majority views are the typical targets for Devil's Advocacy, however, what may appear to be a majority view on the surface can be misleading.

Identifying the origin of the position and the level of support for the position can help you determine if you are dealing with a majority view or not, and the kind of contribution you may be able to make. Consider the following table.

Type → ↓Support	Mandated	Unanimous Consensus	Consent
Minority	C	B	B
Mixed	E	D	D
Majority	A	A	A

It's important to determine the type of decisions that have been made and the support for the decisions

The table above categorizes the three types of decision-making that we looked at in the last chapter (mandated, unanimous consensus, consent) and the underlying support for the decision (minority, mixed, majority). What may we infer about the intersecting cell types (A-E)?

A. Regardless of the decision-making method, if the majority supports a position then that is the position that Devil's Advocacy would typically challenge.

B. By definition, a unanimous consensus is the majority view. Similarly, consent decisions would indicate majority support because even those who feel that the decision isn't necessarily the "best" have acknowledged that they have no paramount objections to the decision. If you encounter minority support for either unanimous consensus or consent

CHAPTER 5

decisions, then you would need to understand why an apparent discrepancy exists before proceeding. Was the decision forced by group dynamics, or mandated, or did something change after the decision was made?

C. A mandated decision that is not supported by the majority can be difficult to confirm, in part, because individuals will likely be reluctant to openly question the decision made by a figure of authority. At the same time, this situation provides you with the opportunity to obtain a lot of material for your opposing case from dissenting individuals who may be happy to provide you with that information - as long as you don't disclose them as your source.

D. Mixed support for either unanimous consensus or consent decisions may indicate that you simply haven't identified a strong position to challenge or, as with (B) above, that something changed after a decision was made. In any event, you would want to understand the reason for the mixed support. You may also be able to frame the position in such a way that there is a shift in support from mixed to a majority.

E. As with (D) above, mixed support for a mandated decision could mean that you simply haven't identified a strong position to challenge. You may also have found a common *fracture line* in the political structure of the enterprise where some support the current leadership and others do not. Here, again, you would want to understand the reason for the mixed support or to frame the position in such a way that may cause a shift in support from mixed to a majority.

As you explore the position you will learn that perspectives often depend on who you ask, especially as you cross departments, levels of authority, and experience. For example, marketing and engineering views will likely differ as will the views of managers versus executives, and the "old guard" versus the recently hired. By speaking with those who are invested in the position you will be better able to see the "big picture" and to seek both common themes and extreme views among the stakeholders.

As you speak with more stakeholders it will be important to update and state what you believe the majority position to be. You'll want to get confirmation from the stakeholders, including from the parties with whom you spoke initially. Note that you'll likely encounter at least a few individual stakeholders who will willingly share their disagreement with the majority view, and you'll want to explore their reasons and judgments, incorporating their dissent within your Devil's Advocacy case as may be useful.

Collect & Organize Facts, Assumptions, Beliefs & Bias

Your challenge to a position will require evidential artifacts such as process diagrams, reports, and other physical materials. However, you will also be looking beyond objectively verifiable facts for the assumptions, beliefs, and biases that individual stakeholders may reveal through their verbal responses to questions and their body language. If, for example, you ask the same question to five individuals and one reacts angrily then you'll want to explore further not only the angry reply but also why others didn't seem similarly affected by the question.

A straightforward way to manage your collection of information is by a simple list that categorizes the types of information that you are collecting, e.g., the first column for facts, the second column for assumptions, the third column for beliefs and bias. These lists can be created in Excel for each source of information (i.e. persons interviewed) and later sorted to seek further insight (e.g. common themes in each department, level of authority, etc).

Validate Facts and Construct Real Arguments

Validation of facts includes checking the accuracy of figures, reports, references, and such. If someone verbally states last year's revenues, for example, then you ought to be able to confirm those figures through official financial statements. If you are given a field report summary, then you ought to be able to get the full report to confirm the summary with the party who created the report and the customer about whom the report was written.

The construction of real arguments can help assess the premises and conclusions that others believe. If someone tells you that an increase in a product price **will** lead to lower sales (a deductive argument) then you can discuss how they are certain of that cause and effect relationship. If your question causes the person to acknowledge that an increase **may** lead to

CHAPTER 5

lower sales (a non-deductive argument), then you can discuss how they are assessing the likelihood of the cause and effect relationship.

Note that while simple diagramming of real arguments may be instructive for you and those you interview, you should not expect that anyone will easily accept or acknowledge that they may have made poor assumptions, hold any unfounded beliefs, or have let bias influence their premises and conclusions. To avoid a confrontation, you can try asking individuals to consider what other plausible premises may be available, how premises could be confirmed as strong or weak, what the impact would be on the conclusion if the weaker premises were removed, etc. This kind of informal Q&A may create a cooperative tone where the stakeholder is effectively "thinking aloud" and using you as a helpful *sounding board*.

Create a Strong Position Case

To make a strong case against a position, you need to ensure that you are considering the strongest case **for** the position. Using the materials that you have collected; you should first make the strongest case for the position that you will be challenging. Try to strengthen weaknesses in the way that the position was originally stated to you (without offering alternate views).

This approach is similar to the *Red Team* and the *Red Hat* methods that attempt to get inside the minds of opponents to help ensure that you aren't casually dismissing the foundations of the original position. Starting with the strongest position case may also help you better anticipate where and how those who support the position will push back on your opposing case. You can use some of the tools in Chapter 4 and others outside of this book to help create a strong position case.

Create Your Opposing Case

Examine the strongest case for the position and again look for weaknesses in factual matters and claims that you can exploit. The exploitation that we're considering is not of the minor and inconsequential kind – it's easy to nit-pick but doing so is also lazy and petty.[257]

It's possible, for example, that an unexpected, breakthrough competitive technology would create a market disruption, but is it more likely that a competitor would acquire a product that could also disrupt plans? You're looking for scenarios that are not only possible but plausible.

You can consider a Black Swan event but only as a reason to maintain a hedge against an all-in bet that could bankrupt the company if such a rare event were to occur. The goal is not to predict the future but to generate alternate scenarios based on evidence and analyses that differ from the original assumptions and premises of the position that you are challenging. Again, you can use some of the tools in Chapter 4 and others outside of this book to help create and support your opposing case.

Present Your Opposing Case

As does any good lawyer or educator you'll want to present your case in a concise, easily understood, and memorable narrative. You can use PowerPoint for your presentation which will enable you to address an assembled audience and also to share your case with individuals who may be absent from group presentations. Take time to create impactful slides that are uncluttered by dense text or complicated graphs. Your slides will provide visual cues to the spoken narrative that you will deliver.

Your goal is to challenge the position at all levels from the basic facts to the strongly held beliefs of those who support the position that you are challenging. You'll need to be able to back up your pretty-looking top-level presentation with the underlying information that you collected and analyses that you performed. You should make sure that those materials are handy, perhaps as a few extra slides at the end of your PowerPoint deck, and organized in readily accessible folders.

PowerPoints Notes can capture and convey your evidence and narration

CHAPTER 5

If you do use PowerPoint, then I recommend that you use the Notes section to capture the simple narrative that you'll tell when showing the slide. While you'll need to know your case cold and won't refer to the notes during your presentation, Notes can be printed out with slides to share with individuals who can't attend a group presentation. Slides with concise narrative notes can help explain what each slide means to reviewers when you aren't making a live presentation to them (and can jog your memory if you need to return to the presentation at a later date). See a recommended reference regarding data presentation under Workbooks in the Suggested Reading and Resources section of this book.

Authoritatively Communicating with an Authority

One of the challenges that Devil's Advocates face is communicating with figures of authority like a pope, CEO, or senior manager who can simply dismiss an alternate perspective and mandate decisions. You may encounter authority figures who are self-absorbed and don't want to hear other opinions, but I believe that many more understand the benefits of diversity and critical thinking in good decision-making. Sometimes, however, the pressures of the job can put authority figures into a reactively defensive mindset.

Executives who may normally be open to frank feedback can become far less receptive when under pressure that they apply to themselves or which is applied from others who they serve (e.g. board members, shareholders). Further, executives understand that their decisions can lead to very poor outcomes like bankruptcy, the loss of jobs, and suffering by individuals and communities. These pressures can create a tendency for an executive to be wary of any activity that may seem to jeopardize their vision, goals, position, and authority.

Taking a gentle approach in your practice of Devil's Advocacy can help mitigate volatile, emotional responses in those who you hope to help. As Kelly Weeks, negotiation and communications consultant observed, when dealing with figures of authority, "You want to show respect to the person while maintaining your own self-respect."[258]

I've summarized Weeks' further advice into the simple table below that you may find helpful when interacting with authority figures.

Do...	Don't...
• Explain that you have a different opinion and ask to voice your view • Restate the executive's point of view or decision so it's clear that you understand it • Speak slowly — talking in an even tone calms you and the other person down	• Assume that disagreeing is going to damage your relationship or career — the consequences are often less dramatic than we think • State your opinions as facts; simply express your point of view and be open to dialogue • Use judgment words, such as "hasty," "foolish," or "wrong," that might upset or incite others

Move On

Once you've made your strongest opposing case and presented it, others will decide what action (if any) will be taken - not you. Because you've put in the time and effort to build your strong counter case it's only natural that you would want to receive accolades for a job well done. Understandably, you may experience bewilderment, regret, or other negative emotions when others disparage or dismiss your case.

To ready yourself for others' comments, reflect on Epictetus' observation, "Some things are in our control and others not." You can certainly control how you practice Devil's Advocacy, but you have little to no control over how others respond. You can, however, keep your emotions in check and move on with the knowledge that you performed to the best of your abilities.

> If you haven't yet read *Verde vs. Thérèse* in the appendices, then I urge you to do so before putting this book aside. I also recommend reading the story again from time to time to remind yourself about the unpredictable results of Devil's Advocacy.

CHAPTER 5

Closing Thoughts

I hope you have found this book to be enjoyable and thought-provoking and that the content presented will be useful in your work and personal life. If you decide to embrace the role of a modern Devil's Advocate then I caution you to be careful, particularly when it comes to personal relationships. I've too often made the mistake of offering a well-intentioned dissenting opinion to friends and family only to inadvertently offend and cause unnecessary heartache.

To avoid such unintended offense, it may be useful to always first ask the other party, "Are you *sharing* or *seeking*?" Particularly in stressful personal situations we often need to share our feelings or hardships with someone who will patiently listen to us and tell us that they understand even if they disagree with us. Other times, we may be actively seeking a frank opinion and an honest critique. By asking the "sharing or seeking" question, you may be better able to determine if your role in a situation should be that of Devil's Advocate or compassionate *angel*.

The sharing or seeking question can also be useful in the business world where Devil's Advocacy may be viewed as an unnecessary and unwanted attack on a company's vision and mission, its projects, and the executive leadership. If you are approached by management regarding an issue, then asking the seeking-sharing question can help you determine if Devil's Advocacy has a role before taking the time and effort to pursue a challenge. What, exactly, are management's issues and expectations and how might Devil's Advocacy address those issues and expectations? Just remember that if you "fake it" to not ruffle any feathers, then you could end up reinforcing unfounded assumptions, weak arguments, and poor decisions.

> Note that it isn't always necessary to openly ask another party the "sharing or seeking" question. You may benefit by asking yourself this question when assessing the needs of others. By employing this kind of internal check in daily practice, you may be better able to moderate your response, particularly in an emotionally charged environment, and thereby avoid an unnecessary and contentious exchange.

Finally, I encourage you to share your thoughts with me. I'm interested of course, in errors or omissions that you find in this book, and I welcome any suggestions you make for additions or improvements to the material. I also expect to receive a fair share of dissenting opinions from readers about what I've written – I wouldn't expect anything less from modern Devil's Advocates! You can reach me by either link below.

- LinkedIn - https://www.linkedin.com/in/robertkoshinskie/
- Email – https://ringbolt.net/contact/

> What are your main take-aways from this book? Are you considering taking on the role of a modern Devil's Advocate? Who else might you engage in discussion about this book and Devil's Advocacy, and what other next steps will you take?

SUGGESTED READING & RESOURCES

We covered a lot of territory in this book and many topics would easily fill a book of their own. Following is a list of some other books and resources, organized alphabetically, that I recommend to those who may wish to continue their journey as a modern Devil's Advocate.

== Books ==
for the general reader

Conspiracy Theories and the People Who Believe Them. Joseph E. Uscinski (editor). Oxford University Press.

Exuberant Skepticism. Paul Kurtz (Author), John R. Shook (Editor). Prometheus.

How to Measure Anything: Finding the Value of "Intangibles" in Business. Douglas W. Hubbard. Wiley.

In Defense of Troublemakers: The Power of Dissent in Life and Business. Charlan Nemeth. Basic Books.

Nonsense on Stilts. Massimo Pigliucci. University of Chicago Press.

Superforecasting: The Art and Science of Prediction. Philip E. Tetlock, Dan Gardner. Random House.

The Halo Effect: ... and the Eight Other Business Delusions That Deceive Managers. Phil Rosenzweig. Simon and Schuster.

The Hunt for Vulcan: ...And How Albert Einstein Destroyed a Planet, Discovered Relativity, and Deciphered the Universe. Thomas Levenson. Random House.

The Model Thinker: What You Need to Know to Make Data Work for You. Scott E. Page. Basic Books.

The Signal and the Noise: Why So Many Predictions Fail- but Some Don't. Nate Silver. Penguin Press.

Thinking in Bets: Making Smarter Decisions When You Don't Have All the Facts. Annie Duke. Penguin Group.

Thinking in Systems: A Primer. Donella H. Meadows. Chelsea Green Publishing.

Warnings: Finding Cassandras to Stop Catastrophes. Richard A. Clarke and R.P. Eddy. HarperCollins Publishers.

== *Workbooks* ==
for those who want to dig into the more technical and computational aspects of modeling and analysis

Business Dynamics: Systems Thinking and Modeling for a Complex World. John Sterman. McGraw-Hill.

Case in Point: Complete Case Interview Preparation. Marc P. Cosentino. Burgee Press.

Introduction to Computational Science: Modeling and Simulation for the Sciences. Angela B. Shiflet, George W. Shiflet. Princeton University Press.

Microsoft Excel Data Analysis and Business Modeling. Wayne Winston. Microsoft Press.

Storytelling with Data: A Data Visualization Guide for Business Professionals. Cole Nussbaumer Knaflic. Wiley Publishing.

Structured Analytic Techniques for Intelligence Analysis. Richards J. Heuer and Randolph H. Pherson. Sage Publishing.

Suggested Reading & Resources

== *Websites* ==

Decision Making in a Complex and Uncertain World, free course from The University of Groningen, the Netherlands via FutureLearn - https://bit.ly/3eRTp5K

InsightMaker, free systems, and agent modeling platform - https://insightmaker.com/

Kialo, debate platform, https://kialo.com

Kumo, mapping software - https://kumu.io/

Logical and Critical Thinking, free course from The University of Auckland - https://bit.ly/2MAxCDb

Model Thinking, University of Michigan course via Coursera - https://bit.ly/2Y5VYKq

ProCon, debate platform, https://procon.org

Sheetless (formerly Sysdea), an online simulation tool that has both free and subscription options - https://sheetless.io

Systems Thinking World, dynamic map of systems thinking related topics - https://bit.ly/34BJYDu

Sociocracy 3.0, a body of Creative Commons licensed learning resources, synthesizing ideas from Sociocracy, Agile and Lean - https://sociocracy30.org/

The Systems Thinker, a repository of articles and information available free of charge - https://thesystemsthinker.com/

APPENDIX A: GENERIC DECISION-MAKING PROCESS

Following is an expanded description of the simple decision-making process diagram from Chapter 1.

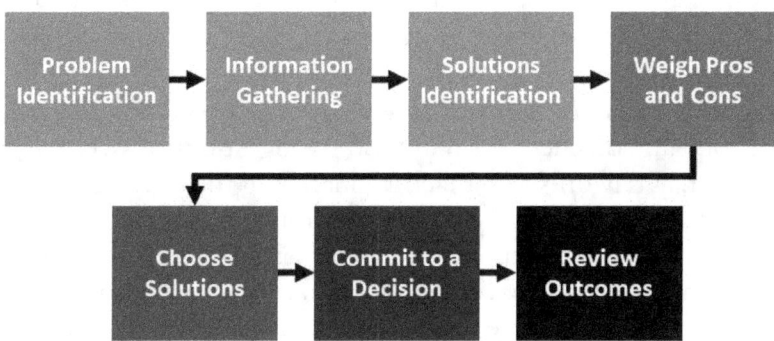

- **Problem (Opportunity) Identification.** The identification of a problem or opportunity for which decisions are required is an activity that you may agree would be a reasonable first step in decision-making. Clear problem identification should be particularly useful to help ensure that teams of people are all on the same page. There may be disagreement on how the problem or opportunity was chosen, but if anyone is unclear on the selection then should there be any surprise if participants go off in many directions and confusion reigns? See group decision-making methods in Chapter 4.

- **Information Gathering.** Once the problem or opportunity is identified then a reasonable next step would be to gather up information that will help make an informed decision. Wrongly assuming that the selected problem or opportunity is understood well enough to start solving it can lead to a lot of lost time, energy, and resources. The kind of information needed will depend, of course, on the selected problem or opportunity. Technical issues will likely require supporting specifications, technical data, test results, etc. Sales and marketing issues will likely require market surveys, competitive materials, customer interviews, etc.

- **Solutions Identification**. After the information you have gathered is thoroughly reviewed, analyzed, and discussed then several possible solutions would likely surface. If only one solution appears, then it may be a red flag that *groupthink* is active and limiting your options. Solutions options may be increased by inviting input from more stakeholders who can also help you see the information you have gathered differently.

- **Weighing Pros and Cons**. Once you have several possible solutions, then you can consider which are the strongest options. The *strength* of options may rely on several factors, including the expertise and experience of team members and vendors, company financial resources, risk tolerance, etc. It's also possible to combine features of solutions options for a solution that is stronger than any individual solution considered. In the Tools chapter, we'll look at a few methods that may help determine which options to pursue.

- **Choosing Multiple Solutions**. Limiting a decision to just one solution option may be necessary due to practical matters like staffing, finances, etc. In some cases, however, it may be possible and beneficial to pursue a couple of solutions until such time that one solution is fully implemented. Having a backup solution on the back burner can be viewed as an insurance policy if the execution of your first choice is foiled.

- **Committing to a Decision**. Commitments will be required to implement the chosen solution(s), not only commitments for company funding of resources but also a commitment of those who will execute the solution (typically the core project team members). See in Chapter 4 how team members may consent to decisions even if individual members feel that the chosen solution is not the best.

- **Review Outcomes**. The final stage in the decision-making process diagram above is to review outcomes. This review isn't something that can be conducted immediately upon the implementation of the solutions. Time would need to pass to assess if the implemented solution achieved the desired outcome (e.g. increased revenues and profits, improved customer engagement, and satisfaction). Formal post-launch evaluations may be subsumed within customer relationship management (CRM) systems that can produce data to help identify issues via trends in the number of customer complaints and metrics like the net promoter score (NPS).[259]

A generic process like the one above needs to set clear goals that both contribute to the overall purpose of the process and which have a reasonable chance of being achieved. A common approach is the use of the SMART framework, an acronym for **S**pecific, **M**easurable, **A**chievable, **R**elevant (or **R**ealistic), and **T**ime-bound.

Specific	Measurable	Achievable	Relevant	Time-bound
What is to be done and how will you know it is completed	How you know an objective meets the desired outcome	The objective can be achieved in the time frame and with available resources	The objective contributes to overall goals	When the objective will/must be completed

As a simple example of the SMART framework, suppose you've been tasked to propose a new product to expand your existing line of products – perhaps a product that can be acquired from another entity.

- Your specific attribute example, "Propose product acquisition candidates."

- Your measurement statement, "Completion of candidate products search in our current market space."

APPENDICES

- Your achievable statement, "Identification of two possible acquisition candidates."

- Your relevant/realistic statement, "Identified candidate products apply to our current market and product portfolio, have low market penetration that we can expand, and are owned by firms that may be receptive to our overtures."

- Your time-bound statement, "Identification will be completed over the next ninety days."

All the statements above may be combined into a unified declaration like the following,

> "Within the next ninety days, we will propose two possible product acquisition candidates. We will achieve this goal through a search of our market to identify candidates that apply to our current market and product portfolio, have low market penetration that we can expand, and are within firms that may be receptive to our overtures."

The SMART framework may help you and your team clarify what you hope to accomplish in a reasoned and reasonable way that everyone can understand and acknowledge their consent (see Group Decision Making in Chapter 4).

APPENDIX B: VERDE VS. THÉRÈSE

In 1914, while serving in the role of Promotor of the Faith for the Roman Catholic Church, Monsignor Alexander Verde completed his examination of the case for the canonization of Sister Thérèse of the Carmel of Lisieux.[260] Sister Thérèse had died some thirteen years earlier and Verde was assigned the task of creating a dissenting position to the majority view that Sister Thérèse should be granted sainthood. In his adversarial role as Promotor of the Faith, men like Verde were commonly known as the *Devil's Advocate*.

Monsignor Verde and Sister Thérèse[261,262]

The basic facts about Thérèse were unremarkable and not disputed. She was born as Marie Françoise Thérèse Martin in Alençon, France, January of 1873, to Louis Martin and Marie Azélie Guérin. Thérèse and four older sisters all became nuns; Thérèse enter the Carmelite convent at Lisieux, France when she was fifteen years old. To complete his assignment, Verde needed to look closely and critically at the life of Thérèse and the evidence offered in support of her beatification.

Verde reviewed the case materials that were available to him, including Sister Thérèse's popular autobiography and nearly fifty witnesses' interviews. Focusing on the key requirements for the elevation of a person to sainthood, Verde itemized various troubling issues that he had identified, including the following:

- A significant amount of supporting testimony on behalf of Sister Thérèse seemed to rely on excerpts from Sister Thérèse's autobiography[263] rather than from first-hand accounts
- The great support for Sister Thérèse had emerged after the publication of her autobiography and her death rather than from observations that others offered during her lifetime
- Fellow nuns who may not have held Sister Thérèse in high regard when she was alive could not testify because they were deceased
- Sister Thérèse had made comments that suggested she may have embraced Quietism (a kind of mysticism not condoned by the Catholic Church)
- Sister Thérèse's confessor, who may have provided some insight into her character and opinion about her views on Quietism, was also deceased
- Sister Thérèse's autobiography was actively promoted through *indulgences* offered by some parishes to those who read the book (an indulgence is a "remission before God of the temporal punishment due to sins whose guilt has already been forgiven" which can be applied to living person so their time in purgatory after death may be reduced)[264]
- Before her death, Sister Thérèse reportedly told other nuns caring for her that they should save items related to her which would be sought out as relics after her death (like the writing of an autobiography, such a suggestion is not a typical expression of saintly humility)

Verde concluded that Sister Thérèse lacked a reputation of holiness in her lifetime and that her saintly character resulted primarily from the promotion by others of Sister Thérèse's autobiography after her death. Verde's case against Sister Thérèse seemed solid on its face and you might reasonably expect that Sister Thérèse didn't achieve sainthood – but reason alone did not win out over popularity and politics in this case.

It seems that Pope Pius X disagreed with Verde's findings and advanced Sister Thérèse's cause. Later, Pope Benedict XV provided additional support and in 1925 Pope Pius XI canonized Sister Thérèse who took her place among other saints. By one account, Verde's involvement in the process continued to the end of Thérèse's canonization, and he was one of the signatories of the official documents favoring Sister Thérèse!

Thérèse's burial place has become a pilgrimage site and includes an impressive basilica that was erected in her name. The idea for her basilica was reportedly[265] "met with much opposition from the local clergy" who "thought that devotion to Thérèse, which enjoyed great popularity among the French soldiers during the First World War, had had its day." Pope Pius XI felt differently and pressed for her new basilica that would be "very big, very beautiful, and as soon as possible!" In 1997, Thérèse was named a doctor of the church by Pope John Paul II, further solidifying the durability of her written autobiography.[266]

Verde's story is a good example of the vital role that a Devil's Advocate can play in creating a reasoned, dissenting perspective. Faced with a significant and popular majority view in support of Sister Thérèse, Verde was able to look past the rosy façade and to state several compelling reasons to reject the case for Sister Thérèse's canonization. This kind of objectivity in the face of a widely held and popular belief, especially a belief that was supported by several popes, is a necessary characteristic of a Devil's Advocate.

It's certainly possible that Popes Pius X, Benedict XV, and Pius XI firmly believed in Sister Thérèse's cause. It's also possible that they factored into their decisions how a ruling against the beloved Sister Thérèse could create a lot of messy conflict between the Catholic Church authorities and Sister Thérèse's many supporters.

Verde's story reminds us how even a well-crafted argument made against the majority view can be easily dismissed by the majority and those with the authority (and incentive) to reject the argument.

APPENDIX C: THE TOO FLEET-FOOTED MERCURY

At the dawn of the 20th Century, the planet Mercury was misbehaving, and no one could explain why. This ill-mannered performance by the planet near our sun was not new and was known at least since the 17th Century. The kind of odd planetary motion exhibited by Mercury was seen before in Uranus and planetary laws effectively solved that earlier problem.[267]

Our seventh planet, Uranus, was officially discovered in March 1781 by the British astronomer, William Herschel. Over the following decades, astronomers noticed that the planet was moving in a perplexing manner. Astronomical tables for Uranus that were based on planetary laws of motion were published by the French astronomer, Alexis Bouvard, in 1821. Bouvard's tables should have accurately predicted Uranus' orbit but that was not the case. Among the various hypotheses proposed for the discrepancies was the presence of an unknown planet as sketched below.

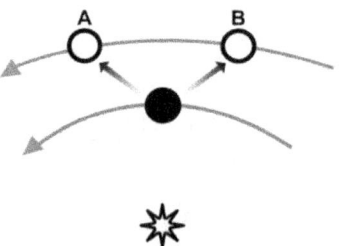

The star at the bottom of the diagram represents our sun, the black circle Uranus, and the white circle an unknown, hypothetical planet that may pull on Uranus as the planets pass near each other

If another planet, were rotating in its orbit beyond Uranus, then as this hypothetical planet passed near Uranus its gravity could pull Uranus faster forward when in position (A) and slow down the travel of Uranus when in position (B). Starting with the observed motion of Uranus, it should be possible to calculate the mass and location of the unknown planet, which may then be confirmed by telescopic observation.

French astronomer and mathematician, Urbain Jean Joseph Le Verrier made calculations that pointed to the general area of the sky where a new planet might be observed. John Couch Adams and Johann Gottfried Galle (both mathematicians and astronomers), likewise took up the challenge of solving the whereabouts of such a planet. On the evening of 23 September 1846, using the prediction by Le Verrier, Galle and his student Heinrich Louis d'Arrest confirmed the existence of Neptune![268]

Le Verrier was also aware of confounding motion in Mercury's orbit, particularly, the rate of Mercury's *precession*.[269] Mercury, named after the fleet-footed Roman god, demonstrated a precession that was a bit too quick according to the established laws of planetary motion. As he had done for Neptune, Le Verrier calculated the mass and position of a planet that would account for Mercury's motion. French physician and amateur astronomer, Edmond Modeste Lescarbault, reported to Le Verrier "a small, regular dot, just inside the edge" of the sun which he estimated to be "about one quarter the apparent diameter of Mercury."[270] Le Verrier concluded that Lescarbault's observation was factual and accurate and shortly thereafter a new planet was proposed and named Vulcan.

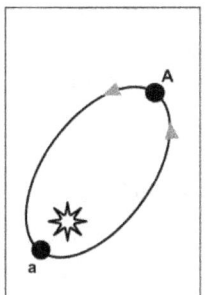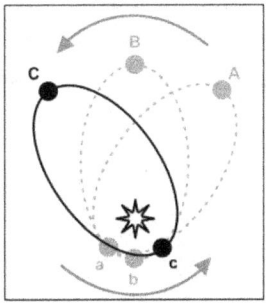

Left: *a planets elliptical path with a maximum distance from the sun (A) and a minimum distance (a).* **Right**: *precession whereby the elliptical path also rotates so the point nearest the sun shifts forward over time from (a) to (b) to (c).*

Others attempted to confirm the existence of Vulcan through additional observation. Even Thomas Edison was among the many who assembled in Wyoming in the summer of 1878 to observe a solar eclipse during which additional observations of Vulcan would be attempted. The negative results of those efforts, however, led to a broad agreement that the planet Vulcan did **not** exist.

A solution for Mercury's movement was finally found in the early 20th Century when Einstein proposed that heavenly bodies warped the space and time in their vicinity.[271] In Einstein's model, gravity is the result of deformations in space-time which was causing the orbit of Mercury to *dip* into the cup of warped space-time near the sun and thereby create its hurried precession.

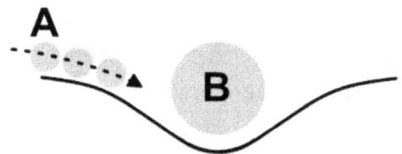

Simplified representation showing the large mass of the sun (B) warping space-time and creating a depression into which Mercury (A) dips on its near approach

It wasn't that the prior laws of planetary motion were wrong, rather those normally reliable laws alone could not fully explain the special case of Mercury. Einstein's work provided a new tool with greater usefulness than what had come before. A lesson learned from the story of the search for Vulcan is that even the best tools may not be the "right" tools for a given task.

> ⏱ For a comprehensive accounting of the search for a new planet near Mercury, I recommend Thomas Levenson's book, *The Hunt for Vulcan*.[272]

APPENDIX D: THE CREATION OF MODERN MYTHOLOGY

The history of microcomputers offers another good example of Survivorship Bias. A Google search will return many popular narratives about the success of Steve Jobs and Apple Computer, for example, but do you know the stories of Jobs' contemporaries and their competitive products, including the few listed below?

- Adam Osborne, Osborne Computer Corporation, the Osbourne computer
- Jack Tramiel and Chuck Peddle, Commodore International, the Commodore PET computer
- Mike and Charity Cheik, Ohio Scientific Inc., the Challenger 2 computer
- Charles Tandy, Tandy Corporation, the TRS-80 computer

In the early days when Apple was formed these other founders, firms, and products were also competing in the emerging market for personal computers. It was not at all clear at the time if microcomputers were just a *fad* and if any of those involved in this emerging market would survive. Today's popular narratives about why Apple lasted while the others did not, likely also suffer from False Cause fallacy as discussed in Chapter 2. These simplified narratives about Apple obscure a larger, systems thinking understanding of the factors that were in play in those early days of personal computers.

Although Jobs is often associated with the high-profile successes of Apple over the years, you may know less about Jobs' questionable decisions. An article in the HBR article notes, *Five of Steve Jobs's Biggest Mistakes*,[273]

1. Recruiting John Sculley as CEO of Apple (who later moved to fire Jobs)

2. Believing that Pixar would be a great hardware company (not understanding the highly successful animation business that evolved)

3. Not knowing the right market for NeXT computer (the article claims, "It's clear that even Jobs was confused.")

4. Launching numerous product failures (Lisa, Macintosh TV, Apple III, Powermac g4 cube)

5. Trying to sell Pixar numerous times (reportedly for as little as $50 million when it finally sold to Disney for $7.4 billion)

Notably, the five questionable decisions proposed in the article did not include Jobs' opposition to what would become a core product for Apple, the iPhone![274]

Survivorship bias may be enhanced through promotion by the publicity machines that create modern mythologies with glowing and inspirational narratives about founders, companies, and products. Entertainment vehicles, too, can further distort history as may be the case regarding the movie, *Steve Jobs*.[275]

As noted in Chapter 2, Survivorship Bias can be powerfully misleading by presenting a perspective of success that does not reflect all outcomes, including failures. Some may claim that looking solely at successes is a good way to identify those characteristics that make people and companies great, and therefore you should emulate those characteristics. Such a view, however, assumes that we know all of the causes and effects. Further, some may propose that past successes can be reliably reproduced today even when conditions are likely significantly different (as we examine under trailing versus trailblazing processes and best practices in Chapter 1). The takeaway is to consider the untold stories when presented with examples of heroic and sterling success.

Appendix E: Little Green Army Wo(men)

The proposed benefits from challenging process is a recurring idea in this book. This challenge, however, is **not** meant to suggest that no process is useful. Sometimes, a robust process is very useful as has been shown in the plastic injection molding process.

Plastic injection molded products surround us from those little green army men (and now women)[276] to medical devices. Making parts quickly while keeping the number of unusable parts low avoids the associated wasted time, effort, and cost due to bad parts. In the case of medical devices, the quality of the parts may also have a direct impact on the safety and therapeutic benefit of the product.[277]

Six Sigma methods are used to increase the rate of production while keeping errors low, and statistical analysis is employed to confirm that defects are, in fact, low. How low? When Six Sigma methods like Design of Experiments (DOE) are employed in manufacturing you can expect less than four defects out of every one-million opportunities for a defect to occur.[278] A branch of applied statistics, DOE helps establish the relationships between inputs in a process and high-quality results.[279] DOE is common in the development of injected plastic molded parts.

On the surface, injection molding may appear simple. There is a hollowed-out metal *mold* that is shaped like the part you want to make. There is a *press* that injects fluid plastic into the mold. The press must maintain the plastic at a certain temperature, force the heated plastic into the mold with a certain pressure and at a certain rate, keep the pressure applied for a certain amount of time, release the molded part and then start the process all over again. The simplified diagram below represents an injection molding station.

APPENDICES

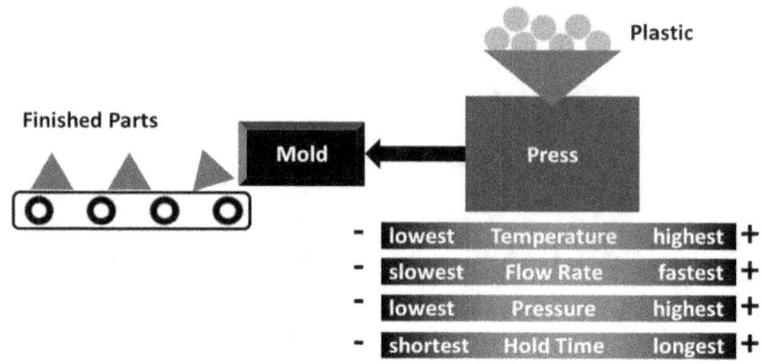

DOE enables high volume, high-quality products in production like injection molding by finding an optimal mix of input settings

Engineers have become proficient at designing molds for plastic products using advanced software modeling tools. These software systems inform the engineers as to the ideal parameters needed to produce millions of parts within Six Sigma quality standards. The virtual design, however, is not the real world and so fine-tuning is typically required to ensure that the product quality suggested by software modeling is achieved. DOE translates the ideal virtual world into the physical factory.

On the factory floor, engineers set the press parameters to the theoretical ideal settings for plastic temperature, rate of injection, pressure, etc. The engineers then change each of these settings individually while maintaining all the other settings and monitor the parts that result. The engineers learn the lower and upper acceptable settings for each manufacturing parameter, for example, the slowest and fastest rate of injection over which acceptable parts are created.

This kind of production process that can be objectively shown to yield reliable results should not be confused with the kinds of processes proposed for more *fuzzy* situations like innovation creation, project management, etc.

In the example given above, the production off of a mold can be optimized on a press in the United States to demonstrate Six Sigma performance. That mold can then be shipped to any country outside of the

United States that provides a molding facility with an identical press. Once set up at the ex-US location, assuming the same materials and press are used, the setup ought to achieve Six Sigma performance. If performance at the two sites isn't to the same high level, then something is amiss. Either the original DOE in the States was not as reported, or the DOE in the ex-US site has a problem.

In more fuzzy situations like innovation creation and product management such strictly controlled experiments cannot be practically performed. Some, have explored the effectiveness of processes in complex projects.[280] Others who have examined the effectiveness of project management in clinical trials observed (bold is mine),

> "It is also suggested that project management could reduce a proportion of fund waste. However, there is still no **randomized controlled trial to compare trial projects progressed with and without the use of project management.** We recommend such a comparison to provide a high level of evidence in this regard."[281]

Consequently, practitioners may be presented with "proof" of process performance in the form of compelling but anecdotal narratives or a handful of uncontrolled case studies. The fact that a proposed process for a fuzzy situation claims to yield reliable results does not necessarily mean that strong evidence exists to support such a claim.

⏱ If you are aware of research that provides rigorous, controlled examination of the effectiveness of processes like project management, then please do share them with me. My contact info is available under the *About the Author* page in this book.

ABOUT THE AUTHOR

Robert Koshinskie is the principal of Ringbolt Consulting where he helps clients with business analysis and strategy, product marketing, and program management.

Experienced in complex inter-company alliance relationship management, with a degree in Biophysics and an MBA, he moves comfortably among technical, clinical, and business circles, lending his real-life experience to help reduce risks and optimize outcomes. He has co-founded startups and has held a variety of positions in both small firms and large enterprises, including Philips Healthcare, Laerdal Medical, and Datascope (now Mindray).

He shares his experience through various activities, including the mentoring of participants in the NSF I-Corps Program (UNCG) and as an instructor through NC State University's Division of Continuing and Professional Education where he teaches a Decision-Making seminar that he created. You can contact Bob via the following links.

- LinkedIn - https://www.linkedin.com/in/robertkoshinskie/
- Email – https://ringbolt.net/contact/

ENDNOTES

[1] PRINCE2 (PRojects IN Controlled Environments) is a process-based method for project management [online 7Jul20> https://www.prince2.com/usa/what-is-prince2

[2] [online 7Jul20> Ringbolt Consulting, https://ringbolt.net ; NSF I-Corps Program, https://www.nsf.gov/news/special_reports/i-corps/ ; "Improve Your Decision-Making Skills", http://bit.ly/2TCzkG0

[3] "The first mention of anyone fulfilling the role of an *advocatus diaboli* was during the preliminary work in preparing for the beatification of St. Lawrence Justinian (1381-1456). The office appears to have been assigned by Leo X, although the beatification did not occur until 1524 under Pope Clement VII. The role became official under Sixtus V in 1587 and in 1708 the advocatus diaboli (technically called the Promotor Fidei) became the most important office in the Roman Congregation of Rites." History of the Devil's Advocate. Unam Sanctam Catholicam. [online 24Apr20> http://www.unamsanctamcatholicam.com/home/about-us.html

[4] "A similar legal development paralleled the assumption of canonizations by the Holy See: the emergence of the Courts of the Inquisition, first episcopal and then papal. If canonization was law applied to saint-making, the inquisitorial courts were law applied to dealing with heresy." History of the Devil's Advocate. Unam Sanctam Catholicam. [online 24Apr20> http://www.unamsanctamcatholicam.com/home/about-us.html

[5] Ronald C. Finucane. *Contested Canonizations: The Last Medieval Saints, 1482-1523*. Catholic University America Press. 2011. P.5

[6] Promotor Fidei. William Henry Windsor Fanning, SJ. Catholic Encyclopedia (1913). [online 24Apr20> https://en.wikisource.org/wiki/Catholic_Encyclopedia_(1913)/Promotor_Fidei

[7] Kathleen Manning. "How many saints are there?" *US Catholic* [online 21Mar20> https://www.uscatholic.org/articles/201310/how-many-saints-are-there-28027

[8] Richards Heuer and Randolph Pherson. *Structured Analytic Techniques for Intelligence Analysis*. CQ Press. p260

[9] Note that unlike Devil's Advocacy both Red Hat and Red Team analysis rely upon more than one analyst, require more resources, and follow prescribed procedures

[10] Robert D. Blagg. "The Bystander Effect". Encyclopædia Britannica. [online 6Jun20> https://www.britannica.com/topic/bystander-effect

[11] Subra Tangirala. "How the Bystander Effect Keeps You Silent While Problems Fester". University of Maryland. [online 6jun20> https://www.rhsmith.umd.edu/smithresearch/research/science-open-secrets-work

[12] Megan Cerullo. "Influencer marketing fraud will cost brands $1.3 billion in 2019". CBSNews [online 7Jul20> https://www.cbsnews.com/news/influencer-marketing-fraud-costs-companies-1-3-billion/

[13] Wood, M., Corbett, J., & Flinders, M. (2016). Just like us: Everyday celebrity politicians and the pursuit of popularity in an age of anti-politics. The British Journal of Politics and International Relations, 18(3), 581–598. https://doi.org/10.1177/1369148116632182

[14] Sara Ashley O'Brien. "Elizabeth Holmes surrounded Theranos with powerful people". *CNN Business*, March 15, 2018 [online 2Feb20> https://money.cnn.com/2018/03/15/technology/elizabeth-holmes-theranos/index.html

[15] Lydia Ramsey. "The rise and fall of Theranos". *Business Insider*, Apr 11, 2019 [online 2Feb20> https://www.businessinsider.com/the-history-of-silicon-valley-unicorn-theranos-and-ceo-elizabeth-holmes-2018-5

[16] Paul Szoldra. "Defense Secretary Mattis Has Some Questions to Answer About A Company Just Charged With 'Massive Fraud'". *Task and Purpose*, March 14, 2018 [online 2Feb20> https://taskandpurpose.com/mattis-theranos-questions

[17] Deepa Seetharaman, Emily Glazer. "Mark Zuckerberg Asserts Control of Facebook, Pushing Aside Dissenters". *Wall Street Journal*. April 28, 2020 [online 18May20> https://www.wsj.com/articles/mark-zuckerberg-asserts-control-of-facebook-pushing-aside-dissenters-11588106984

[18] Mike Isaac, Sheera Frenkel, Cecilia Kang. "Now More Than Ever, Facebook Is a 'Mark Zuckerberg Production'". *New York Times*. May 16,2020 [online 18May20> https://www.nytimes.com/2020/05/16/technology/zuckerberg-facebook-coronavirus.html

[19] "Coronavirus disease 2019 (COVID-19) is defined as illness caused by a novel coronavirus now called severe acute respiratory syndrome coronavirus 2 (SARS-CoV-2; formerly called 2019-nCoV), which was first identified amid an outbreak of respiratory illness cases in Wuhan City, Hubei Province, China." David J Cennimo, MD. "What is COVID-19?". *Medscape*. [online 22May20> https://www.medscape.com/answers/2500114-197401/what-is-covid-19

[20] Matt Field, John Krzyzaniak. "Why do politicians keep breathing life into the false conspiracy theory that the coronavirus is a bioweapon?". *Bulletin of the Atomic Scientists* [online 14Mar20> https://thebulletin.org/2020/03/why-do-politicians-keep-breathing-life-into-the-false-conspiracy-theory-that-the-coronavirus-is-a-bioweapon/

[21] Ryan Broderick. "QAnon Supporters and Anti-Vaxxers Are Spreading A Hoax That Bill Gates Created the Coronavirus". *Buzzfeed News* [online 14Mar20> https://www.buzzfeednews.com/article/ryanhatesthis/qanon-supporters-and-anti-vaxxers-are-spreading-a-hoax-that

[22] "5WPR Survey Reveals 38% of Beer-Drinking Americans Wouldn't Buy Corona Now". *PR Newswire* [online 14Mar20> https://www.prnewswire.com/news-releases/5wpr-survey-reveals-38-of-beer-drinking-americans-wouldnt-buy-corona-now-301012225.html

[23] Kate Gibson. "Corona beer maker shrugs off misinformation on coronavirus". *CBS News* [online 14Mar20> https://www.cbsnews.com/news/corona-beer-virus-misinformation-on-coronavirus/

[24] Matthew S. Schwartz. "Missouri Sues Televangelist Jim Bakker For Selling Fake Coronavirus Cure". *NPR* [online 15Mar20> https://www.npr.org/2020/03/11/814550474/missouri-sues-televangelist-jim-bakker-for-selling-fake-coronavirus-cure

[25] Timothy Johnson. "Alex Jones is telling his viewers that the toothpaste he sells kills coronavirus". *Media Matters for America* [online 14Mar20> https://www.mediamatters.org/coronavirus-covid-19/alex-jones-telling-his-viewers-toothpaste-he-sells-kills-coronavirus

[26] John M. Carey, Victoria Chi, D. J. Flynn, Brendan Nyhan, Thomas Zeitzoff. "The effects of corrective information about disease epidemics and outbreaks: Evidence from Zika and yellow fever in Brazil". *Science Advances 29 Jan 2020: Vol. 6*, no. 5, [online 15Mar20> https://advances.sciencemag.org/content/6/5/eaaw7449/tab-pdf

[27] *A Report on the Spread of Fake News*. Zignal Labs. Harris Poll. 2017. [online 30May20> https://zignallabs.com/blog/fake-news-epidemic/

[28] Jianing Li, Michael W. Wagner. "When are readers likely to believe a fact-check?" The Brookings Institution. [online 31May20> https://www.brookings.edu/techstream/when-are-readers-likely-to-believe-a-fact-check/

[29] Twitter was experimenting with a feature that asked readers to actually read an article before retweeting it but the results were not yet known when this endnote was included. See Rhiannon Williams. "Twitter prompts users to actually read articles before they retweet them". INews. [online 7Jul20> https://inews.co.uk/news/technology/twitter-retweet-prompt-read-articles-fake-news-trial-443411

[30] James Surowiecki. *Wisdom of the Crowds*. Random House LLC. [online 11Jul20> https://amzn.to/3iVrwwo

[31] "Understanding Dressing Percentage of Slaughter Cattle". Government of Alberta. [online 13Jul20> https://www.alberta.ca/understanding-dressing-percentage-of-slaughter-cattle.aspx

[32] Francis Galton. "Vox Populi". *Nature*. No 1949, V75, pp405-406

[33] It is also possible, of course, that the *experts* rightly guessed the weight whereas the *novices* guessed high and low of the actual weight in roughly equal measure such that the novice estimates canceled out and the expert estimates generated the accurate median value.

[34] Jan Lorenz, Heiko Rauhut, Frank Schweitzer, Dirk Helbing. "How social influence can undermine the wisdom of crowd effect" *PNAS* May 31, 2011 108 (22) 9020-9025; https://doi.org/10.1073/pnas.1008636108

[35] Philip Ball. "'Wisdom of the crowd': The myths and realities". BBC, Future. [online 13Jul20> https://www.bbc.com/future/article/20140708-when-crowd-wisdom-goes-wrong

[36] Geoffrey W. Sutton. Review of *The Wisdom of Crowds* by James Surowiecki. Anchor Books, 2005. *Journal of Psychology and Christianity*. 2008 pp.372-373

[37] Francis Galton. "Vox Populi". *Nature*. No 1949, V75, pp405-406

[38] Kenneth F. Wallis. "Revisiting Francis Galton's Forecasting Competition". *Statistical Science* 2014, Vol. 29, No. 3, 420–424 DOI: 10.1214/14-STS468

Endnotes

[39] Richards Heuer and Randolph Pherson. *Structured Analytic Techniques for Intelligence Analysis*. CQ Press.

[40] Charlan Jeanne Nemeth, Joanie B. Connell, John D. Rogers, Keith Brown. "Improving Decision Making by Means of Dissent". *Journal of Applied Social Psychology. 2001*, 31, 1, pp. 48-58. [online 7Mar20> http://charlannemeth.com/wp-content/uploads/2017/03/DA1.pdf

[41] Note that Dr. Nemeth refers to *playing* devil's advocate which frames devil's advocacy as an inauthentic and less effective form of dissent, setting it apart from dissenters who truly believe in their position. Dr. Nemeth acknowledges, however, that devil's advocacy offers benefits when compared to the absence of any challenge – a situation that may be common in the business setting due to groupthink, fear of retribution, etc. Further, it's not clear to me how the authenticity of dissent is reliability determined inside or outside of the research laboratory setting. I agree that authentic dissent is important and suggest that a *true* Devil's Advocate **is** an authentic dissenter. I wholeheartedly recommend that you read Dr. Nemeth's book, *In Defense of Troublemakers*, for her more comprehensive views.

[42] Renata Silva de Carvalho Chinelato, Maria Cristina Ferreira, Felipe Valentini, Ralph Van den Bosch. "Construct validity evidence for the individual Authenticity Measure a Work in Brazilian samples". *Journal of Work and Organizational Psychology.* [online 26Apr20> http://dx.doi.org/10.1016/j.rpto.2015.03

[43] Michael I. Krauss. "On Lawyers Defending Views They Don't Believe In". *Forbes*. March 11, 2014 [online 25Apr 20> https://www.forbes.com/sites/michaelkrauss/2014/03/11/on-lawyers-defending-views-they-dont-believe-in/#60c67c6e2b32

[44] "In truth, the defense lawyer almost never really knows whether the defendant is guilty of a charged crime…defense lawyers often do not ask their clients if they committed the crime. Instead, the lawyer uses the facts to put on the best defense possible and leaves the question of guilt to the judge or jury." Janet Portman, JD. "Representing a Client the Lawyer Thinks Is Guilty". Nolo. [online 15Jul20> https://www.nolo.com/legal-encyclopedia/representing-client-whom-the-lawyer-thinks-is-guilty.html

[45] The original Devil's Advocacy relied upon lawyers from at least the time of Pope Alexander III (1159-1181). Kenneth L. Woodward. *Making Saints: How the Catholic Church Determines Who Becomes A Saint, Who Doesn't, and Why*. Touchstone (April 26, 2016)

[46] Devil's Advocates can certainly seek out the opinion of those who have expertise the advocate lacks. Devil's Advocates can also encourage those experts who hold the majority view to rigorously challenge their own position, revealing any risks and uncertainty that they should have considered in arriving at their judgments and conclusions. It is vital, of course, that Devil's Advocates recognize when they have insufficient subject matter understanding to offer a useful counter position and to either not start a Devil's Advocacy effort or to disengage from an effort that has been initiated.

[47] Sydney Finkelstein. "Don't Be Blinded by Your Own Expertise". Harvard Business Review. May–June 2019 Issue [online 24Jun20> https://hbr.org/2019/05/dont-be-blinded-by-your-own-expertise

⁴⁸ Elisabeth Braw. "Want to Avoid the Next Pandemic? Hire a Devil's Advocate". *Foreign Policy*. [online 20May20> https://foreignpolicy.com/2020/05/06/want-to-avoid-the-next-pandemic-hire-a-devils-advocate/

⁴⁹ Charlan Nemeth. *In Defense of Troublemakers: The Power of Dissent in Life and Business*. Basic Books. p181

⁵⁰ Fred C. Lunenburg. "Devil's Advocacy and Dialectical Inquiry: Antidotes to Groupthink." *International journal of Scholarly Academic Intellectual Diversity*. Volume 14, Number 1, 2012

⁵¹Steinar Brandslet. "How to get good at disagreeing." *Norwegian SciTech News*. [online 29Jul20> https://norwegianscitechnews.com/2020/07/how-to-get-good-at-disagreeing/

⁵² Jake Herway. "How to Create a Culture of Psychological Safety". Gallup Workplace. [online 11Aug20> https://www.gallup.com/workplace/236198/create-culture-psychological-safety.aspx

⁵³ Rand Fishkin. *Lost and Founder: A Painfully Honest Field Guide to the Startup World*. Penguin. [online 11Aug20> https://www.amazon.com/Lost-Founder-Painfully-Honest-Startup-ebook/dp/B074DGYVD5/

⁵⁴ Cynic. Merriam-Webster Dictionary. [online 21Apr20> https://www.merriam-webster.com/dictionary/cynic

⁵⁵ Olga Oksman. "Conspiracy craze: why 12 million Americans believe alien lizards rule us". The Guardian. [online 23Jun20> https://www.theguardian.com/lifeandstyle/2016/apr/07/conspiracy-theory-paranoia-aliens-illuminati-beyonce-vaccines-cliven-bundy-jfk

⁵⁶ Skeptic. Merriam-Webster Dictionary. [online 21Apr20> https://www.merriam-webster.com/dictionary/skeptic

⁵⁷ Paul Kurtz. *Exuberant Skepticism*. "The New Skepticism, A Statement of Principles". Prometheus Books. 2010 Chapter 17

⁵⁸ AU Section 316, "Consideration of Fraud in a Financial Statement Audit". SAS No. 99; SAS No. 113. P1719

⁵⁹ Hernan Murdock. "The Three Key Elements of Professional Scepticism". *MIS Training Institute*. [online 13May20> https://www.misti.co.uk/internal-audit-insights/the-three-key-elements-of-professional-scepticism

⁶⁰ Jonathan H. Grenier. "Encouraging Professional Skepticism in the Industry Specialization Era: A Dual-Process Model and an Experimental Test". Department of Accountancy. Miami University

⁶¹ Dharmesh Shah. "Skeptics vs. Cynics: Know Which Are Toxic?" LinkedIn, May 6, 2013 [online 21Apr20> https://www.linkedin.com/pulse/20130506120216-658789-skeptics-vs-cynics-know-which-are-toxic/

⁶² Joseph E. Uscinski. *Conspiracy Theories and the People Who Believe Them*. Oxford University Press. [online 26Jun20> https://www.amazon.com/gp/product/B07HCJCGHT

⁶³ John M. Grohol, Psy.D. "Fighting Cognitive Dissonance & The Lies We Tell Ourselves". 8 July 2018 [online 25Apr20> https://psychcentral.com/blog/fighting-cognitive-dissonance-the-lies-we-tell-ourselves/

[64] World Economic Forum [online 19Apr19> https://www.weforum.org/
[65] "The Future of Jobs Report 2018". *World Economic Forum* [online 19Apr19> https://www.weforum.org/reports/the-future-of-jobs-report-2018
[66] The idea of learning organizations referred to in the Forum Report is not new and has been popularized by others like Peter Senge in his book, *The Fifth Discipline,* which was originally published in 1990.
[67] Shvetank Shah, Andrew Horne, Jaime Capellá. "Good Data Won't Guarantee Good Decisions". *Harbard Business Review*, April 2012 [online 19 Apr 19> https://hbr.org/2012/04/good-data-wont-guarantee-good-decisions
[68] Dan Lovallo, Olivier Sibony. "The case for behavioral strategy". *McKinsey Quarterly* [online 20Apr19> https://www.mckinsey.com/business-functions/strategy-and-corporate-finance/our-insights/the-case-for-behavioral-strategy
[69] "The Global Learner Survey, 2019". Pearson, The Harris Poll [online 19Mar20> https://www.pearson.com/content/dam/global-store/global/resources/Pearson_Global_Learner_Survey_2019.pdf
[70] Annette LaPrade, Janet Mertens, Tanya Moore, Amy Wright. "The enterprise guide to closing the skills gap: Strategies for building and maintaining a skilled workforce". *IBM Institute for Business Value.* 2019
[71] An example of a "life decision" is using a condom to avoid contracting a sexually transmitted disease, or managing expenses to avoid bankruptcy
[72] H.A. Butler, C. Pentoney, M.P. Bongc. "Predicting real-world outcomes: Critical thinking ability is a better predictor of life decisions than intelligence". *Thinking Skills and Creativity, V25*, Sep2017
[73] Nancy Chick, CFT. "Metacognition". Center for Teaching, Vanderbilt University. [online 26May20> https://cft.vanderbilt.edu/guides-sub-pages/metacognition/
[74] "What are Metacognitive Skills" Talent Education [online 26May20> http://www.talenteducation.eu/toolkitforteachers/metacognicalskills/what-are-metacognitive-skills/
[75] Van Gelder, T. (2005). "Teaching Critical Thinking: Some Lessons from Cognitive Science". *College Teaching*, 53(1), 41-46.
[76] Donna Kienzler, Frances M. Smith. "What Our Students Have Taught Us About Critical Thinking". *Journal of Family and Consumer Sciences Education*, Vol. 21, No. 2, Fall/Winter, 2003
[77] Peter Senge. *The Fifth Discipline: The Art & Practice of The Learning Organization.* Random House. 2010
[78] Thomson Atomic Model. Encyclopaedia Britannica. [online 16Apr20> https://www.britannica.com/science/Thomson-atomic-model
[79] Charlie Wood. "What Is String Theory?" *Space* [online 16Apr20> https://www.space.com/17594-string-theory.html
[80] William G. Gale, Hilary Gelfond, Jason Fichtner. "How Will Retirement Saving Change by 2050: Prospects for the Millennial Generation". *The Brookings Institution* [online 25May19> https://www.brookings.edu/wp-content/uploads/2019/03/How-Will-Retirement-Saving-Change-by-2050.docx.pdf

[81] Emmie Martin. "Here's how many Americans have nothing saved for retirement". *CNBC* [online 12Dec19> https://www.cnbc.com/2019/06/27/how-many-americans-have-nothing-saved-for-retirement.html

[82] Alfred Korzybski. *Encyclopaedia Britannica* [online 11Apr20> https://www.britannica.com/science/general-semantics

[83] George E. P. Box. *Informs* [online 11Apr20> https://www.informs.org/Explore/History-of-O.R.-Excellence/Biographical-Profiles/Box-George-E.-P

[84] The Institute of General Semantics [online 22Apr2019> https://www.generalsemantics.org/the-general-semantics-learning-center/alfred-korzybski/

[85] Process. Merriam-Webster [online 5Feb20> https://www.merriam-webster.com/dictionary/process

[86] for a concise but informative discussion about groupthink, see to: Em Griffin, , Andrew Ledbetter, Glenn Sparks. *A First Look at Communication Theory* (pp. 235 - 246). New York: McGrawHill.

[87] Groupthink. [online 8May20> https://www.merriam-webster.com/dictionary/groupthink

[88] Lucy Burns. "The rise and fall of the five stages of grief". BBC News [online 4Jul20> https://www.bbc.com/news/stories-53267505

[89] Note that the Kübler-Ross model does offer the benefit of a roadmap to help therapists patients understand the emotions that they are experiencing. Any model, however, begins to limit understanding and options when adopted as a rigid and immutable orthodoxy.

[90] Equifinality in developmental psychology is expressed when the individual genetics, family dynamics and environments of different people can lead to the same kind of behavior. An example of equifinality would be when a girl who is raised in a wealthy and stable family and a boy raised in an impoverished and dysfunctional family both exhibit a shared condition like chronic depression. An example of multifinality may be a case of twin girls who are raised in the same household and only one girl develops an eating disorder.

[91] Varun Aggarwal. *Apple's Biggest Failures*. LiveMint. [online 4Jun20> https://www.livemint.com/Leisure/b69npRlXSKUdtF1DV6KFpM/Apples-biggests-failures.html

[92] Kapsali, Maria. "Equifinality in Project Management Exploring Causal Complexity in Projects". *Systems Research and Behavioral Science*. 30. 2-14. 10.1002/sres.2128.

[93] Sihvonen, A., & Pajunen, K. "Causal complexity of new product development processes: a mechanismbased approach". *Innovation: Management, Policy and Practice, 21(2)*, 253-273. https://doi.org/10.1080/14479338.2018.1513333

[94] Walter J. Boyne. "The Checklist". *Airforce Magazine*, July 29, 2013 [online 11Feb20> https://www.airforcemag.com/article/0813checklist/

[95] "WHO Surgical Safety Checklist". *World Health Organization* [online 11Feb20> https://www.who.int/patientsafety/safesurgery/checklist/en/

[96] A free introductory course on Six Sigma is offered by Master of Project Academy [online 27Mar20> https://masterofproject.com/courses/145916/lectures/11913035

[97] "Define, measure, analyze, improve, and control (DMAIC) is a data-driven quality strategy used to improve processes. The letters in the acronym represent the five phases that make up the process, including the tools to use to complete those phases." The Define, Measure, Analyze, Improve, Control (DMAIC) Process. American Society for Quality. [online 2May20> https://asq.org/quality-resources/dmaic

[98] Heidi Wiesenfelder. "Dealing with a Bad DMAIC Project". *Bright Hub Project Management* [online 25Mar20> https://www.brighthubpm.com/six-sigma/70254-what-is-a-bad-six-sigma-project/

[99] Best practice. Merriam-Webster [online 5Feb20> https://www.merriam-webster.com/dictionary/best%20practice

[100] Structured processes like PRINCE-2 provide for "tailoring", essentially the option to utilize only those parts of the process that managers deem appropriate for the project at hand. My experience has been that managers quickly turn to tailoring to expedite project completion, bypassing what could be important steps, particularly when the project is behind schedule and the manager is under withering pressure from the C-Suite. Occasionally, someone in the C-Suite mandates tailoring against the opinion of project managers - who are still held responsible should failure occur due to an ill-tailored decision from above.

[101] Abbie Griffin. "Metrics for Measuring Product Development Cycle Time". *J. Prod Innov Manag, 1993*;10:112-125

[102] "Best Practices in Education". *SERC*. [online 1Apr20> http://www.bestpracticeswiki.net/view/SERC-Best_Practices_In_Education

[103] Trailblazing. Merriam-Webster Dictionary [online 3Mar20> https://www.merriam-webster.com/dictionary/trailblazing

[104] Steve Blank, Pete Newell. "What Your Innovation Process Should Look Like". *Harvard Business Review*, September 11, 2017 [online 7Feb20> https://hbr.org/2017/09/what-your-innovation-process-should-look-like

[105] Steve Blank. "McKinsey's Three Horizons Model Defined Innovation for Years. Here's Why It No Longer Applies". *Harvard Business Review*, February 01, 2019 [online 8Feb20> https://hbr.org/2019/02/mckinseys-three-horizons-model-defined-innovation-for-years-heres-why-it-no-longer-applies

[106] Canon. Merriam-Webster Dictionary [online 7Feb20> https://www.merriam-webster.com/dictionary/canon

[107] Determinism. Merriam-Webster [online 11Apr20> https://www.merriam-webster.com/dictionary/determinism

[108] Objective metrics and the determination of a sufficient number of instances is, of course, difficult to ascertain. Consequently, the threshold parameters are likely unknown and threshold is a model concept rather than a formulaic expression.

[109] Kapsali, Maria. "Equifinality in Project Management Exploring Causal Complexity in Projects". *Systems Research and Behavioral Science*. 30. 2-14. 10.1002/sres.2128.

[110] Philip E. Tetlock, Dan Gardner. Superforecasting: The Art and Science of Prediction. P92. Random House. [online 2Jun20> https://www.amazon.com/dp/B00RKO6MS8

[111] "Stacy Matrix". Praxis [online 12June20> https://www.praxisframework.org/en/library/stacey-matrix

[112] David J. Snowden, Mary E. Boone. "A Leader's Framework for Decision Making". Harvard Business Review, November 2007

[113] "WHOW matrix". Praxis. [online 1Jun20> https://www.praxisframework.org/en/library/whow-matrix

[114] "Who Is Epictetus? From Slave to World's Most Sought After Philosopher." *Daily Stoic.* [online 28Apr20> https://dailystoic.com/epictetus/

[115] Baltzly, Dirk, "Stoicism", *The Stanford Encyclopedia of Philosophy* (Spring 2019 Edition), Edward N. Zalta (ed.), URL = <https://plato.stanford.edu/archives/spr2019/entries/stoicism/>.

[116] Robert Taibbi. "What Stoics Can Teach Us About Mental Health". *Psychology Today.* [online 30Apr20> https://www.psychologytoday.com/us/blog/fixing-families/201910/what-stoics-can-teach-us-about-mental-health

[117] Ben Martin, Psy.D. "In-Depth: Cognitive Behavioral Therapy". *Psych Central.* [online 2May20> https://psychcentral.com/lib/in-depth-cognitive-behavioral-therapy/

[118] "Dual Process Theory". *American Psychological Association* [online 2Apr20> https://dictionary.apa.org/dual-process-theory

[119] Bertram Gawronski, Laura A. Creighton. "Dual Process Theories". D. E. Carlston (Ed.). (2013). *The Oxford handbook of social cognition* (pp. 282-312). New York, NY: Oxford University Press.

[120] Daniel Kahneman. *Thinking, Fast and Slow.* Penguin https://www.amazon.com/dp/B00555X8OA

[121] Daniel Kahneman. "Of 2 Minds: How Fast and Slow Thinking Shape Perception and Choice [Excerpt]". *Scientific American* [online 2Apr20> https://www.scientificamerican.com/article/kahneman-excerpt-thinking-fast-and-slow/

[122] Epstein S. "Integration of the cognitive and the psychodynamic unconscious". *Am J Psychol. 1994*; 49:709–24.

[123] Heuristics. Psychology Today [online 3Apr20> https://www.psychologytoday.com/us/basics/heuristics

[124] Jill G Klein. "Five pitfalls in decisions about diagnosis and prescribing". *BMJ. 2005 Apr 2;* 330(7494): 781–783 [online 3Apr20> https://www.ncbi.nlm.nih.gov/pmc/articles/PMC555888/

[125] "Diagnostic Errors". Patient Safety Network. [online 22Jun20> https://psnet.ahrq.gov/primer/diagnostic-errors

[126] Melissa Bateson, Daniel Nettle, Gilbert Roberts. "Cues of being watched enhance cooperation in a real-world setting". *Biol. Lett. (2006) 2*, 412–414 [online 13May19> https://www.staff.ncl.ac.uk/melissa.bateson/Bateson_etal_2006.pdf

[127] Shu Wen Tay, Paul Ryan, C Anthony Ryan. "Systems 1 and 2 thinking processes and cognitive reflection testing in medical students". *CMEJ 2016, 7(2)*: e97-e103

[128] Shane Frederick. "Cognitive Reflection and Decision Making". *Journal of Economic Perspectives, Volume 19, Number 4*, Fall 2005, pp 25–42

[129] The CRT is known to many because of its use and references on social media, consequently, subjects who are familiar with the CRT should not be included in studies that use this survey tool. Validated variations of the original CRT may also be used.

[130] John Brockman (editor). *Thinking: The New Science of Decision-Making, Problem-Solving, and Prediction*. Harper Perennial. p391.

[131] System. English Oxford Dictionary [online 3May19> https://en.oxforddictionaries.com/definition/system

[132] Foundation for Critical Thinking [online 16May19> http://www.criticalthinking.org/pages/critical-thinking-where-to-begin/796

[133] Argument. Oxford Dictionary [online 22Apr19> https://en.oxforddictionaries.com/definition/argument

[134] conclusions may form the basis of additional premises that support additional conclusions

[135] "Validity and Soundness". *Internet Encyclopedia of Philosophy* [online 21Feb20> https://www.iep.utm.edu/val-snd/

[136] "Deductive and Inductive Arguments". *Internet Encyclopedia of Philosophy* [online 21Feb20> https://www.iep.utm.edu/ded-ind/

[137] Christopher Crockett. "What is retrograde motion?" *Astronomy Essentials*. [online 7Aug20> https://earthsky.org/space/what-is-retrograde-motion

[138] Alvaro Castillo-Carniglia, Rose M.C. Kagawa. "California's comprehensive background check and misdemeanor violence prohibition policies and firearm mortality". *Annals of Epidemiology, V30*, February 2019, Pages 50-56 [online 12Mar20> https://www.sciencedirect.com/science/article/abs/pii/S1047279718306161

[139] Webster D, Crifasi CK, Vernick JS. "Effects of the repeal of Missouri's handgun purchaser licensing law on homicides". [published correction appears in J Urban Health. 2014 Jun;91(3):598-601]. *J Urban Health*. 2014;91(2):293–302 [online 12Mar20> https://pubmed.ncbi.nlm.nih.gov/24604521-effects-of-the-repeal-of-missouris-handgun-purchaser-licensing-law-on-homicides

[140] Bias. Merriam-Webster Dictionary [online 25Apr19> https://www.merriam-webster.com/dictionary/bias

[141] Fallacy. Merriam-Webster Dictionary [online 25Apr19> https://www.merriam-webster.com/dictionary/fallacy

[142] David McRaney. *You Are Not So Smart*. Penguin Group (USA) LLC [online 25Apr19> https://read.amazon.com/kp/embed?asin=B0052RE5MU

[143] You Are Not So Smart website [online 30May19> https://youarenotsosmart.com/

[144] Bradley Dowden. "Fallacies". *Internet Encyclopedia of Philosophy* [online 16Mar20> https://www.iep.utm.edu/fallacy/

[145] Yvonne Raley. "Character Attacks: How to Properly Apply the Ad Hominem". *Scientific American*, June 1, 2008 [online 27Apr19> https://www.scientificamerican.com/article/character-attack/

[146] Barnes RM, Johnston HM, MacKenzie N, Tobin SJ, Taglang CM. "The effect of ad hominem attacks on the evaluation of claims promoted by scientists". *PLoS ONE* 13(1) (2018)

¹⁴⁷ Dilemma. Merriam-Webster Dictionary [online 26Apr19> https://www.merriam-webster.com/dictionary/dilemma
¹⁴⁸ Dichotomy. Merriam-Webster Dictionary [online 26Apr19> https://www.merriam-webster.com/dictionary/dichotomy
¹⁴⁹ Jacinta Bowler. "The COVID-19 Virus May Have Been in Humans for Years, Study Suggests". *ScienceAlert*. [online 4May20> https://www.sciencealert.com/the-new-coronavirus-could-have-been-percolating-innocently-in-humans-for-years
¹⁵⁰ Wet markets have been described as similar to farmers' markets in the US but with a mixture of processed foods and live animals, some of which are brought in from the wild and which can transmit virus to their handlers and market customers; see: Dina Fine Maron. "'Wet markets' likely launched the coronavirus. Here's what you need to know". *National Geographic* [online 20Apr20> https://www.nationalgeographic.com/animals/2020/04/coronavirus-linked-to-chinese-wet-markets/
¹⁵¹ Julia Musto. "Gordon Chang: China and WHO acted maliciously, tried to deceive the world". *Fox News* [online 20Apr20> https://www.foxnews.com/media/gordon-chang-china-world-health-organization-coronavirus-deceit
¹⁵² Amy Mitchell, Jeffrey Gottfried, Michael Barthel, Nami Sumida. "Distinguishing Between Factual and Opinion Statements in the News". *Pew Research Center* [online 20Apr20> https://www.journalism.org/2018/06/18/distinguishing-between-factual-and-opinion-statements-in-the-news/
¹⁵³ Dan Lovallo, Olivier Sibony. "The case for behavioral strategy". *McKinsey Quarterly, March 2010* [online 31May19> https://www.mckinsey.com/business-functions/strategy-and-corporate-finance/our-insights/the-case-for-behavioral-strategy
¹⁵⁴ Cottingley Village History Society [online 5Mar20> https://history.cottingleyconnect.org.uk/index.html
¹⁵⁵ Arthur Conan Doyle. *The Coming of the Fairies*. [online 5Mar20> https://www.amazon.com/Coming-Fairies-Annotated-Arthur-Conan-ebook/dp/B085F1TB2W
¹⁵⁶ Cooper, Joe. "Cottingley: At Last the Truth". *The Unexplained, No. 117*, pp. 2338-40, 1982 [online 5Mar20> https://www.lockhaven.edu/~dsimanek/cooper.htm
¹⁵⁷ David McRaney. "The Backfire Effect". *You Are Not So Smart* [online 3Mar20> https://youarenotsosmart.com/2011/06/10/the-backfire-effect/
¹⁵⁸ Wood, T., Porter, E. "The Elusive Backfire Effect: Mass Attitudes' Steadfast Factual Adherence". *Polit Behav 41*, 135–163 (2019) [online 3Mar20> https://doi.org/10.1007/s11109-018-9443-y
¹⁵⁹ Matt Nurse. "The winding story of the backfire effect". *Communication Science* [online 3Mar20> https://www.communicationscience.org.au/2019/06/29/the-story-of-the-backfire-effect/
¹⁶⁰ James Chen. "Suvivorship Bias". *Investopedia* [online 3Mar20> https://www.investopedia.com/terms/s/survivorshipbias.asp
¹⁶¹ J.B. Maverick. "What is the average annual return for the S&P 500?" *Investopedia* [online 2Mar20> https://www.investopedia.com/ask/answers/042415/what-average-annual-return-sp-500.asp

[162] Dave Ramsey "Return on Investment; the 12% Reality". [online 31May19> https://www.daveramsey.com/blog/the-12-reality

[163] "DJIA 101: How Does the Dow Jones Work?" *Investopedia* [online 31May19> https://www.investopedia.com/investing/what-moves-the-djia/

[164] "4 famous companies that were dropped from the Dow". *Investopedia* [online 31May19> https://www.investopedia.com/articles/investing/113015/4-famous-companies-dropped-dow-jones.asp

[165] David Roos. "Here Are Warning Signs Investors Missed Before the 1929 Crash". *History* [online 31May19> https://www.history.com/news/1929-stock-market-crash-warning-signs

[166] John Gramlich. "5 facts about crime in the U.S." *Pew Research Center*, January 3, 2019 [online 26Apr19> https://www.pewresearch.org/fact-tank/2019/01/03/5-facts-about-crime-in-the-u-s/

[167] Matt Ford. "What Caused the Great Crime Decline in the U.S.?" *The Atlantic*, April 15, 2016 [online 30Apr19> https://www.theatlantic.com/politics/archive/2016/04/what-caused-the-crime-decline/477408/

[168] Halo. Encyclopaedia Britannica. [online 20Apr20> https://www.britannica.com/art/halo-art

[169] Thorndike, E.L. (1920). "A constant error in psychological ratings". *Journal of Applied Psychology, 4(1),* 25–29. https://doi.org/10.1037/h0071663

[170] Phil Rosenzwig. *The Halo Effect*. Simon and Schuster [online 29Apr19> https://smile.amazon.com/Halo-Effect-Business-Delusions-Managers-ebook/dp/B000NY128M

[171] Post hoc: "made or happening only after an event, not planned or decided before it happens" Cambridge Dictionary. [online 19May20> https://dictionary.cambridge.org/dictionary/english/post-hoc

[172] James Chen. "Hindsight Bias". *Investopedia* [online 3Mar20> https://www.investopedia.com/terms/h/hindsight-bias.asp

[173] Tversky, Amos; Kahneman, Daniel. "The Framing of decisions and the psychology of choice". *Science. 211 (4481)*: 453–58. [online 30Apr19> http://www.stat.columbia.edu/~gelman/surveys.course/TverskyKahneman1981.pdf

[174] Sam Mattera. "3 Steve Ballmer Quotes That Explain Why Microsoft's Mobile Effort Failed". *Motley Fool*, Oct 12, 2013 [online 26June19> https://www.fool.com/investing/general/2013/10/12/3-steve-ballmer-quotes-that-explain-why-microsofts.aspx

[175] Laura Woods. "Warren Buffett's failures: 15 investing mistakes he regrets". *CNBC MakIt*, Dec 15, 2017 [online 25June19> https://www.cnbc.com/2017/12/15/warren-buffetts-failures-15-investing-mistakes-he-regrets.html

[176] Cap Allon. "The List — Scientists who Publicly Disagree with the Current Consensus on Climate Change". *Electroverse* [online 16Mar20> https://electroverse.net/the-list-scientists-who-publicly-disagree-with-the-current-consensus-on-climate-change/

[177] Becky Little. "When Cigarette Companies Used Doctors to Push Smoking". *History* [online 16Mar20> https://www.history.com/news/cigarette-ads-doctors-smoking-endorsement

[178] Stanford University Research into the Impact of Tobacco Advertising [online 30Apr19> http://tobacco.stanford.edu/tobacco_main/index.php

[179] History of the Surgeon General's Reports on Smoking and Health. CDC [online 16Mar20> https://www.cdc.gov/tobacco/data_statistics/sgr/history/index.htm

[180] Bragg MA, Miller AN, Elizee J, et al. Popular Music Celebrity Endorsements in Food and Nonalcoholic Beverage Marketing. Pediatrics. 2016;138(1):e20153977

[181] Marc Pauly. "Conspiracy Theories". *The Internet Encyclopedia of Philosophy*, ISSN 2161-0002, [online 14Mar20> https://www.iep.utm.edu/conspira/

[182] Soroush Vosoughi, Deb Roy, Sinan Aral. "The spread of true and false news online". *Science*, 09 Mar 2018: Vol. 359, Issue 6380, pp. 1146-1151[online 3Mar20> https://science.sciencemag.org/content/359/6380/1146

[183] Justin Kruger, David Dunning. "Unskilled and Unaware of It: How Difficulties in Recognizing One's Own Incompetence Lead to Inflated Self-Assessments". *Journal of Personality and Social Psychology, 1999, Vol. 77*, No. 6.] 121-1134

[184] Sanchez C, Dunning D. "Overconfidence among beginners: Is a little learning a dangerous thing?" *J Pers Soc Psychol. 2018 Jan;114(1)*:10-28

[185] Brian Resnick. "An expert on human blind spots gives advice on how to think". *Vox*, Jan 31, 2019 [online 30Apr19> https://www.vox.com/science-and-health/2019/1/31/18200497/dunning-kruger-effect-explained-trump

[186] David Dunning. "We Are All Confident Idiots". *Pacific Standard*. 14 June 2017 [online 26Apr20> https://psmag.com/social-justice/confident-idiots-92793

[187] Epictetus. *The Enchiridion*. [online 26Apr20> http://classics.mit.edu/Epictetus/epicench.html

[188] Nassim Nicholas Taleb. *The Black Swan*. Random House [online 12Mar20> https://www.amazon.com/Black-Swan-Second-Improbable-Incerto-ebook/dp/B00139XTG4/

[189] Andrew Bloomenthal. "Bell Curve Definition". *Investopedia* [online 6Mar20> https://www.investopedia.com/terms/b/bell-curve.asp

[190] "Standard Deviation Formulas". *Math is Fun* [online 10Mar20> https://www.mathsisfun.com/data/standard-deviation-formulas.html

[191] Adam Hayes. "Tail Risk". *Investopedia* [online 10Mar20> https://www.investopedia.com/terms/t/tailrisk.asp

[192] Trevir Nath. "Fat Tail Risk: What It Means and Why You Should Be Aware of It". *Nasdaq* [online10Mar20> https://www.nasdaq.com/articles/fat-tail-risk-what-it-means-and-why-you-should-be-aware-it-2015-11-02

[193] Brian J. Bloch. "Black Swan Events and Investment". *Investopedia* [online 3Mar20> https://www.investopedia.com/articles/trading/11/black-swan-events-investing.asp

[194] Nassim Nicholas Taleb. "The Corona Crisis is Not a Black Swan". *Bloomberg* [online 5Apr20> https://www.youtube.com/watch?v=Tb2pXXUSzmI

[195] Dave Mosher. "A thermonuclear bomb slammed into a North Carolina farm in 1961 — and part of it is still missing". *Business Insider* [online 20Apr20> https://www.businessinsider.com/nuclear-bomb-accident-goldsboro-nc-swamp-2017-5

Endnotes

[196] Danijela Maras, Martine F. Flament, et.al. "Screen time is associated with depression and anxiety in Canadian youth". *Preventive Medicine 73 (2015)* 133–138

[197] Jade Wu, PhD. "Does Social Media Cause Depression? It's Complicated". *Quick and Dirty Tips* [online 31Mar20> https://www.quickanddirtytips.com/health-fitness/social-media-depression

[198] Stephanie Denning. "How Kahneman Won the Nobel Prize". *Forbes* [online 7Apr20> https://www.forbes.com/sites/stephaniedenning/2016/12/28/the-undoing-project-how-to-judge-a-book-by-its-cover/#95709c51372f

[199] Daniel Kahneman. *Thinking, Fast and Slow*. Farrar, Straus, and Giroux. p194 https://www.amazon.com/Thinking-Fast-Slow-Daniel-Kahneman-ebook

[200] A. Pluchino, A. E. Biondoy, A. Rapisardaz. "Talent vs Luck: the role of randomness in success and failure". *Advances in Complex Systems Vol. 21*, No. 03n04, 1850014 (2018) [online 20May19> https://arxiv.org/abs/1802.07068

[201] "The Matthew Effect". *American Psychological Association* [online 20Mar20> https://dictionary.apa.org/matthew-effect

[202] "Story of Three Servants". *Contemporary English Bible*. Matthew 25:29 [online 20May19> https://cev.bible/

[203] "The 25 Best Inventions of 2017". *Time* [online 16Mar20> https://time.com/5023212/best-inventions-of-2017/

[204] Doug Bouton. "How I Got Here". *LinkedIn* [online 20May19> http://bit.ly/2HsILUQ

[205] Nate Silver. *The Signal and the Noise* (preface). Penguin Books [online 7Mar20> https://www.amazon.com/Signal-Noise-Many-Predictions-Fail-but/dp/0143125087

[206] Amy Feldman. "Away Luggage Hits $1.4B Valuation After $100M Fundraise". *Forbes* [online 11Mar20> https://www.forbes.com/sites/amyfeldman/2019/05/14/at-a-valuation-as-high-as-145b-valuation/#2a16ec7c33d7

[207] Jen Rubio. "How I Built This with Guy Raz". March 18, 2019 [online17June19> https://www.npr.org/2019/03/08/701651787/away-jen-rubio

[208] "MacKenzie Bezos pledges to give half her $36 billion fortune to charity". *The Washington Post* [online 29May19> https://www.washingtonpost.com/business/2019/05/28/mackenzie-bezos-pledges-give-half-her-fortune-charity/

[209] World Series of Poker (WSOP) [online 11Mar20> https://www.wsop.com/

[210] Annie Duke. *Thinking in Bets*. p.19 [online 11Mar20> https://www.amazon.com/dp/B074DG9LQF

[211] Annie Duke. *Thinking in Bets*. p.29 [online 11Mar20> https://www.amazon.com/dp/B074DG9LQF

[212] Frank H. Knight, PhD. *Risk, Uncertainty and Profit*. Houghton Mifflin Company. Chapter VIII, p232, 1921

[213] "How to Shoot Dice". WikiHow [online 9Apr20> https://www.wikihow.com/Shoot-Dice

[214] In a casino setting, the dice player may be presented with several dice and then chooses two of the die to toss

[215] "Conditional Probability". Math is Fun. [online 9May20> https://www.mathsisfun.com/data/probability-events-conditional.html
[216] Adam Barone. "Conditional Probability". *Investopedia*. [online 9May20> https://www.investopedia.com/terms/c/conditional_probability.asp
[217] Richard Hoshino. "Probability of Winning at Craps". Department of Mathematics & Statistics. Dalhousie University [online 9May20> https://bit.ly/2yGSKo9
[218] Eric Weisstein. "Craps". *Wolfram Research* [online 9May20> https://mathworld.wolfram.com/Craps.html
[219] The Red Green Show [online 17Mar20> https://tvtropes.org/pmwiki/pmwiki.php/Characters/TheRedGreenShow
[220] Julia Franz. "A 'David and Goliath' Story for Personal Computers". *Science Friday* [online 5Mar20> https://www.sciencefriday.com/segments/a-david-and-goliath-story-for-personal-computers/
[221] "Laffer Curve Napkin". *National Museum of American History* [online 5Mar20>
[222] "Laffer Curve". *Investopedia* [online 31Mar20> https://www.investopedia.com/terms/l/laffercurve.asp
[223] James Chen. "Line of Best Fit". *Investopedia* [online 5Mar20> https://www.investopedia.com/terms/l/line-of-best-fit.asp
[224] "How to conduct a failure modes and effects analysis (FMEA)". Siemens Product Lifecycle Management Software Inc, 2016 [online 1May19> http://bit.ly/2Td7ZKG
[225] Dai, W., Cheung, W.M., Tang, X.Q., Maropoulos, P.M. "Decision-Making in Product Quality Based on Failure Knowledge". *Int. J. Product Lifecycle Management, Vol. 5*, No. 2-4, pp.143-163 (2011)
[226] Karl Tate. "The Space Shuttle Challenger Disaster: What Happened? (Infographic)". *Space.com* [online 20Feb 20> https://www.space.com/31732-space-shuttle-challenger-disaster-explained-infographic.html
[227] Richard A. Clarke, R.P. Eddy. *Warnings: Finding Cassandras to Stop Catastrophe.* pp.39, 40 [online 30Mar20> https://www.amazon.com/dp/B01MDTF63G
[228] Kouroush Jenab, Sam Khoury, Samuel Rodriguez. "Effective FMEA Analysis or Not?!" *Strategic Management Quarterly, June 2015, Vol. 3*, No. 2, pp. 25-36 [online 31Mar20> http://dx.doi.org/10.15640/smq.v3n2a2
[229] "Foundations of Fuzzy Logic". *Mathworks* [online 31Mar20> https://www.mathworks.com/help/fuzzy/foundations-of-fuzzy-logic.html
[230] Belu Nadia, Rachieru Nicoleta, Anghel Daniel Constantin. "Fuzzy Failure Mode and Effect Analysis Application to Improve Laser Cutting Process". *Advanced Materials Research Vol. 1036* (2014) pp 280-285 [online 31Mar20> https://www.researchgate.net/publication/266508911_Fuzzy_Failure_Mode_and_Effect_Analysis_Application_to_Improve_Laser_Cutting_Process
[231] I'm including this weighted method example from the search and rescue community in which I served as a former member (New Jersey Search and Rescue)
[232] Peter Moore. "The birth of the weather forecast". Peter Moore. BBC News [online 14Apr20> https://www.bbc.com/news/magazine-32483678

ENDNOTES

[233] "What is the Meaning of PoP". *National Weather Service* [online 1May19> https://www.weather.gov/ffc/pop?

[234] "How Reliable Are Weather Forecasts?" *SciJinks.* [online 2May20> https://scijinks.gov/forecast-reliability/

[235] Noriaki Kano et.al. "Attractive Quality and Must-Be Quality". *Journal of the Japanese Society for Quality Control 14(2)*, 147-156, 1984-04-15

[236] "Charts of Annual Inflation Rate in the United States". *StatBureau* [online 10May19> https://www.statbureau.org/en/united-states/inflation-charts-yearly

[237] "Present Value of an Annuity". *Investopedia* [online 2Apr20> https://www.investopedia.com/terms/p/present-value-annuity.asp

[238] John F. Magee. "Decision Trees for Decision Making". *Harvard Business Review* [online 7Jan20> https://hbr.org/1964/07/decision-trees-for-decision-making

[239] The Systems Thinker website [online 15Dec19> https://thesystemsthinker.com/

[240] The Thinking Tools Studio website [online 14Apr20> https://thinkingtoolsstudio.org/

[241] Steve Hartman. "Businessman who surprised students with free tuition says it's his responsibility". *CBS News*, February 7, 2020 [online 11Feb20> https://www.cbsnews.com/news/free-college-tuition-scott-high-school-pete-kadens-toledo-ohio-students-responsibility/

[242] Stocks are quantities of elements at a given point in time (e.g. dollars, units) and flows are the changes in stocks over time (e.g. dollars/quarter, units/year). Stock and flow models emulate mathematical functions of integration and differentiation.

[243] "Financial Modeling for Beginners". *Corporate Finance Institute* [online5May19> https://corporatefinanceinstitute.com/resources/knowledge/modeling/financial-modeling-for-beginners/

[244] Dogan Ibrahim. "Using the excel spreadsheet in teaching science subjects". *Procedia - Social and Behavioral Sciences Volume 1, Issue 1, 2009*, Pages 309-312 [online 5May19> https://www.sciencedirect.com/science/article/pii/S1877042809000603

[245] Software simulation tools offer a variety of built-in functions from basic arithmetic, to statistical functions, to programmatic logic - all are very handy for advanced simulation requirements.

[246] Simulator 3D (positions of the planets). [online 16May20> http://www.astronoo.com/en/articles/positions-of-the-planets.html

[247] Kyle A. Pearson. "Predicting planets from orbital perturbations using deep learning". *TensorFlow Blog* [online 16May20> https://blog.tensorflow.org/2019/07/predicting-planets-from-orbital-deep-learning.html

[248] "Exploratory Modelling and Analysis (EMA) Workbench". TUDelft. [online 19May20> http://simulation.tbm.tudelft.nl/ema-workbench/contents.html

[249] Halim, Ronald A.; Kwakkel, Jan; Tavasszy, Lorant. "A scenario discovery study of the impact of uncertainties in the global container transport system on European ports". *Futures: the journal of policy, planning and futures studies*. DOI 10.1016/j.futures.2015.09.004

[250] Steven W. Popper. "Robust decision making and scenario discovery in the absence

of formal models". *Futures Foresight Sci.* 2019;1:e22. https://doi.org/10.1002/ffo2.22

[251] Frode Heldal, Endre Sjøvold, Kenneth Stålsett. "Shared cognition in intercultural teams: collaborating without understanding each other". *Team Performance Management: An International Journal.* Vol. 26 No. 3/4, 2020 pp. 211-226 DOI 10.1108/TPM-06-2019-0051

[252] Jennifer Senior. "In Conversation: Antonin Scalia". New York Magazine. 2013 [online 10Apr20> https://nymag.com/news/features/antonin-scalia-2013-10/

[253] "FM 6-0 Commander and Staff Organization and Operations". *Department of the Army.* May 2014 [online 21Apr20> http://www.milsci.ucsb.edu/sites/secure.lsit.ucsb.edu.mili.d7/files/sitefiles/fm6_0.pdf

[254] Consent decision-making is also known as "formal consensus", but I avoid using that term to clearly differentiate between consent and unanimous consensus approaches.

[255] "Sociocracy, A brief history" [online 25May19> https://sociocracy30.org/a-brief-history/

[256] Ricardo Semler. *Maverick: The Success Story Behind the World's Most Unusual Workplace.* Grand Central Publishing [online 25May19> https://amzn.to/2M9jQdA

[257] Note that many may associate the word "exploit" with its secondary meaning, "to make use of (a situation) in a way considered unfair or underhanded". Exploit is used here by its primary meaning, "to make full use of and derive benefit from (a resource)" - nothing unfair or underhanded is proposed.

[258] Amy Gallo. "How to Disagree with Someone More Powerful than You". *Harvard Business Review.* [online 11May20> https://hbr.org/2016/03/how-to-disagree-with-someone-more-powerful-than-you

[259] "What Is Net Promoter?" Satmetrix Systems, Inc. [online 11May19> https://www.netpromoter.com/know/

[260] Not to be confused with Mary Teresa Bojaxhiu, also known as Saint Teresa of Calcutta

[261] Image of Monsignor Verde [online 8Mar20> http://ekladata.com/Rh1LhSSyQTAIamz7JufNF3pj9lY.jpg

[262] Image of Sister Thérèse [online 8Mar20> https://i1.wp.com/bibledude.life/wp-content/uploads/st-theresa-of-lisieux.jpg

[263] Therese de Lisieux (Author), John Clarke (Translator). *The Story of a Soul.* I C S Publications [online 1Feb20> https://amzn.to/2Ojq753

[264] "Indulgences". *Catechism of the Catholic Church.* The Holy See, [online 3Mar20> http://www.vatican.va/archive/ENG0015/_P4G.HTM

[265] The Basilica [online 10Feb20> https://www.therese-de-lisieux.catholique.fr/en/lisieux-3/the-basilica/

[266] Jonathan Wright. "How to become a Doctor of the Church". *Catholic Herald.* 21 February 2019 [online 11Feb20> https://catholicherald.co.uk/magazine/how-to-become-a-doctor-of-the-church/

[267] Between 1609 and 1618, mathematician Johannes Kepler stated his three laws of planetary motion which captured the observed motions of the planets, including their

elliptical paths around the sun. In 1687, Isaac Newton published his laws of motion and universal gravitation which helped explain and expand upon Kepler's laws, increasing astronomers' understanding of how planets and other bodies can influence each other's motion. Astronomers were able to apply these laws of planetary motion to accurately predict the motion of planets in the solar system, and to help resolve odd motion when planets seemed to ignore the laws.

[268] Reportedly, Neptune had been observed early on by Galileo and others who followed. These observations, however, were misunderstood to be of a distant star rather than a planet in our solar system. Consequently, those earlier observers are not credited with "discovering" Neptune; see : Geoff Gaherty. "Cosmic Quest: Who Really Discovered Neptune?" *Space.com*, 28 August 2014 [online 28Feb20> https://www.space.com/26972-neptune-planet-discovery-skywatching.html

[269] "Precession of Mercury's orbit". Physics Channel. [online 7Aug 20> https://www.youtube.com/watch?v=NXlg3nTqSnk

[270] "Discovering Planet Vulcan". *ScienceFriday* [online 1Mar20> https://www.sciencefriday.com/articles/discovering-planet-vulcan/

[271] A simple demonstration of this concept is a ball placed atop a stretched fabric sheet. The ball deforms the sheet into a "cup" that bends around the surface of the ball, representing how space-time bends around heavenly bodies. If you place a smaller ball onto the edge of the sheet, then it naturally rolls toward the cupped depression in the sheet near the original, larger ball; see: Gravity Visualized (video). Dan Burns. [online 11Mar20> https://youtu.be/MTY1Kje0yLg

[272] Thomas Levenson. *The Hunt for Vulcan*. Random House, 2015, https://www.amazon.com/o/ASIN/0812998987

[273] Peter Sims. "Five of Steve Jobs's Biggest Mistakes". *Harvard Business Review, January 21, 2013* [online 26Apr19> https://hbr.org/2013/01/five-of-steve-jobss-biggest-mi

[274] Zameena Mejia. "Steve Jobs almost prevented the Apple iPhone from being invented". *CNBC Make It*, [online 26Apr19> https://www.cnbc.com/2017/09/12/why-steve-jobs-almost-prevented-the-apple-iphone-from-being-invented.html

[275] Rick Tetzeli. "Steve Jobs, The Movie: 11 Things That Aren't True About the Apple Cofounder". *Fast Company*, 10/09/15 [online 30Apr19> https://www.fastcompany.com/3052092/steve-jobs-the-movie-11-things-that-arent-true-about-the-apple-co-founder

[276] J.D. Simkins. "Green plastic Army women set features working dogs and handlers, Rosie the Riveter." Military Times. [online 29Jul20> https://www.militarytimes.com/off-duty/military-culture/2020/03/05/green-plastic-army-women-set-features-working-dogs-and-handlers-rosie-the-riveter/

[277] Ross H.M. Hatley, Dirk von Hollen, Dennis Sandell, and Lois Slator. "In Vitro Characterization of the OptiChamber Diamond Valved Holding Chamber." *Journal of Aerosol Medicine and Pulmonary Drug Delivery*. Aug 2014.S-24-S-36 http://doi.org/10.1089/jamp.2013.1067

[278] "What is Sigma and Why is it Six Sigma?" Six Sigma Institute. [online 29Jul20> https://www.sixsigma-institute.org/What_Is_Sigma_And_Why_Is_It_Six_Sigma.php

[279] Keith M. Bower. "What Is Design of Experiments (DOE)?" *American Society for Quality*. [online29Jul20> https://asq.org/quality-resources/design-of-experiments

[280] Yugue, R. T. & Maximiano, A. C. A. (2012). "Project Complexity and Management Processes". *Paper presented at PMI® Research and Education Conference, Limerick, Munster, Ireland*. Newtown Square, PA: Project Management Institute.

[281] Abdolreza Babamahmoodi, Hamidreza Goodarzynejad. "Project Management of Randomized Clinical Trials: A Narrative Review". *International journal of the Iranian Red Crescent Society*. August 2015 17(8) DOI: 10.5812/ircmj.11602

www.ingramcontent.com/pod-product-compliance
Lightning Source LLC
Chambersburg PA
CBHW071355210526
45465CB00001B/101